The Nation Writ Small

SUSAN Z. ANDRADE

The Nation Writ Small

African Fictions and Feminisms, 1958–1988

Duke University Press   DURHAM AND LONDON   2011

© 2011 Duke University Press
All rights reserved
Printed in the United States of America
on acid-free paper ∞
Designed by C. H. Westmoreland
Typeset in Arno Pro by Keystone Typesetting, Inc.
Library of Congress Cataloging-in-Publication Data
appear on the last printed page of this book.

Contents

Acknowledgments

Books are rarely written without financial support, as Virginia Woolf has crisply pointed out. I thank The University of Michigan for a fellowship, the University of Pittsburgh for two summer Hewlett grants, and, in particular, Mbye Cham and the Rockefeller Foundation for a year's leave which afforded me time to read and rethink this project. Money is not everything. The intellectual beginnings of this book stem from dialogue with Greg Diamond, in years of discussions about the interrelation between culture and politics, fact and fiction. His example and encouragement allowed me to take the leap into the graduate study of comparative literature with the belief that I could indeed make a living at it. At the University of Pittsburgh, Jim Knapp, Marianne Novy, Phil Smith, Steve Carr, and especially, Dave Bartholomae, helped me negotiate institutional hurdles; I am grateful to them for their support. As directors of women's studies, Kathy Blee and Jean Ferguson Carr welcomed me and encouraged my interdisciplinary teaching. For a brief but very important moment in my life, in the two years before they left for Chicago, Iris Marion Young and David Alexander fed me dinners and, especially, their conversation; I was sorely in need of both. The writing that emerged from those conversations about African women's rebellions and the relation of public protest to literary writing and the Habermasian public sphere has since been published elsewhere, but was originally imagined as part of this book's conclusion. Before her untimely death, Iris saw some of that work.

For discussions both convivial and pointed, at conferences, in corridors, in cafés, and by e-mail, for inviting me to share and test my work publicly, I thank Koffi Anyinefa, Jane Bryce, Bella Brodzki, Odile Cazenave, Brenda Cooper, Eleni Coundouriotis, Hester Eisenstein, Ken Harrow, Isabel Hofmeyr, Judy Miller, Tony O'Brien, Chikwenye Ogunyemi, Teju Olaniyan, Sarah Nuttall, Reinhard Sander, and Barbara Webb. Years ago, Madhu Dubey argued vigorously with me about gender, genre, cultural nationalism, and Marxism; the critical edge of those conversations has left their mark on these chapters. Odile was and remains my best source for the latest in literary developments in francophone writing, for which I am grateful. David Shumway generously invited me to organize with him a year's worth of speakers on Realism for the Carnegie Mellon University Humanities Center in 2008–2009; I doubt he knows how much good that did. It allowed me to recover a project I had put aside, and it provided me pleasurable and serious conversation with him, our speakers, and the group who met over the year. In different spheres of my life and from different parts of the country, Eileen Julien and Janet Skupien have been unwavering in their encouragement even through their very difficult times. Abiola Irele scrutinized the introduction, shared his erudition, and saved me from some gaffes. Years earlier, Richard Bjornson, then the new editor of *Research in African Literatures*, encouraged me to submit my first essay to the journal; it turned into the germ of chapter 1 and made an impact in African literary history, especially feminist studies. I remain grateful for his confidence and know how much was lost when we lost him. Through their own writing, Julie Hakim Azzam, Susan Hallstead, Aarti Madan, Tiffany Magnolia, Raji Vallury, and Brenda Whitney have taught me about relations between literature and politics.

Some of my friends took their pens to my paper, and I am delighted to thank them for their bracing comments on individual chapters. Deidre Lynch vigorously edited an earlier draft of chapter 1. Uzo

Esonwanne's essay on Mariama Bâ provoked my thinking about liberalism and the public sphere, and his initial argument with chapter 2 sharpened my thinking. Conversations in Dakar with Ken Harrow about Senegalese politics and his own essay on *Xala* encouraged me to broaden my interpretive scope. Charlie Sugnet's essay on *Nervous Conditions* and his later comments on the section of chapter 3 about Tsitsi Dangarembga stimulated me; however, I needed the prodding of Elizabeth Ann (aka Beth) Willey to complete the work. Patricia Alden gave me helpful editorial comments on the section about Nuruddin Farah, and Charlie insisted that first and foremost I see Farah as a critic of all nationalism. I finally took his advice. Reading Anne Donadey's book on Assia Djebar and Leila Sebbar meant that I began my thinking about Djebar's fiction at a more complex level than I might have otherwise. Anne carefully read an early draft of chapter 4, and her comments helped me find my own reading of the relation between two novels. Thanks to Ken Wissoker for his confidence in the project, and to Mark Mastromarino for his help in turning the manuscript into a book.

Jonathan Arac began his presence in my mind's life as an enigma and became a complexity. Overcoming the initial awkwardness has taken us both time, and that itself has taught me about the inexorable force of the dialectic. Through our conversations, I have learned yet more about the ways intellectual history informs literary history, as well as that the imagination is not always constrained by history. Over the years, I have come to better appreciate his generosity in reading and in talking, and I hope to know and love it and him yet more.

My love of reading can be traced directly to my father especially since he bought me my first books. As a girl in Dar es Salaam, Tanzania, I was proud of my own small shelf, which stood next to his several shelves of American novels and magazines. When my father died a few years ago and I delivered his eulogy, I confronted the fact that fully one third of his life had been determined by his blindness. In the spirit of narratives known and remembered though not always retold, I dedicate this book to his memory, as well as to my mother.

Introduction

Readers of novels continue to experience and interpret the public and private realms of human life as separate, despite the fact that feminism and Marxism have taught us that they are linked. By focusing on the interconnected nature—indeed, the interpenetration—of the private and public spheres of life (in this case, the domestic and national spheres), I redefine the terms of conversation about politics and gender in Africa. I focus on how collectivity is understood and how novels represent the individual's relation to the collective. For the first generation of postcolonial African novelists, who published between 1958 and 1988, the most obvious manifestation of political commitment took the form of anticolonial resistance and agitation for national sovereignty. Thematizing colonialism in public terms is not the only way to tell a political tale, however. I argue that reading allegorically allows one to elucidate new meanings in the domestic sphere of life and in intimate relations between people. The domestic, where women historically have set their novels, offers as sharp an analytic perspective on collectivity and national politics as does the arena of public political action. As readers of African literature, we must learn to read this realm more carefully.

The novel has a complex relation to Africa and cultural national-ism, first, because unlike poetry and drama, it is the genre commonly believed to have originated outside the continent and therefore to have become African only as part of the colonial enterprise. Second, although the novelistic tradition in indigenous languages such as Kiswahili, Wolof, Yoruba, and Xhosa has mushroomed in the twen-tieth century, the African literature that is most significant to the world is written in European languages.[1] Moreover, at least one so-ciologist of literature has claimed of Nigeria, for example, that the production of African novels in English far outpaces that of novels in Igbo or Yoruba. "When Nigerians write novels," says Wendy Griswold (2000, 31), "they normally do so in English."

As the story goes, novel writing in both francophone and anglo-phone Africa emerged on the world literary scene in the 1950s and '60s as part of the cultural renaissance that accompanied decoloniza-tion. Négritude, which flowered in the 1940s and '50s and came out of francophone West Africa and the Antilles, was the first literary move-ment made thus visible, though its primary genre was poetry.[2] West African literature, francophone and anglophone, from Senegal, Cam-eroon, Nigeria, and Ghana was the first literary expression of pan-continental African nationalism. Although East African novelistic production was not as great as that of West Africa, the region soon produced international writers such as Ngugi wa Thiong'o, and it nourished several important literary journals such as *Transition* and *Penpoint*, the first of which originated in Uganda, became continent-ally important, and ultimately moved to Ghana. Moreover, Kiswahili, more than its West African counterparts, flourished as a regional literary language, and it has been claimed to be a pan-continental language that speaks more for and to the continent than any other indigenous language.

There was a lag in time between state decolonization and black enfranchisement in southern Africa, in some cases a prolonged lag filled with varying degrees of armed struggle. Because of this dé-calage, and especially because of the more heterogeneous population —in part, white settler populations—southern African literature de-veloped differently from that of West Africa and East Africa. Full citizenship rights came late to Zimbabweans (1981) and even later to

South Africans (1994). The 1970s and especially the 1980s were both politically active and literarily rich.[3] Northern African writing, in rough terms, is either Maghrebi, in which French cultural influences are strong, and writers, especially those of the independence period and earlier, expressed themselves primarily in French, or in Arabo-African, for writers came from nations such as Libya, Sudan, and Egypt, whose literary language has always been Arabic.

Appropriating the language and narrative form of the colonizers, African novelists as diverse as Camara Laye, Chinua Achebe, Ferdi-nand Oyono, Mongo Beti, Ousmane Sembène, Kateb Yacine, Ngugi wa Thiong'o, and Alex La Guma imagined communities, invented traditions, and wrote themselves into History and Literature. The novel in Africa answered back to colonial silencing and helped to consolidate disparate religious, ethnic, racial, and class differences into a single national identity. In telling this story, I nevertheless aim to challenge its simplicity and note some lacunae that make the received narrative inaccurate in some important ways. I do not—indeed, cannot—offer a complete history of the continental novel. Nevertheless, my working historical model insists first and foremost on Africa as more than a cluster of countries south of the Sahara and sees Africa as a continent inhabited by people of different ethnicities, religious practices, languages, hues, and racial phenotypes. Objecting vehemently to the racially based separation of sub-Saharan from North African literature, the Cameroonian curator and novelist Si-mon Njami calls the will to divide the two a historical revisionism whose refusal to seek links between various cultures or peoples itself represents a colonial neurosis:

> En effet, dans la plupart des esprits, l'Afrique se limiterait à l'ensem-ble des pays situés au sud du Sahara. Au nord commencerait une autre région, un autre monde presque. Cette forme de révision-nisme, qui voudrait opposer la fraction "éthiopienne" à la fraction "méditerranéenne" d'un continent sur lequel le désert s'ouvre comme une interminable parenthèse, est pathologique, car elle pré-tend nier les influences multiples qui, depuis le Moyen Age, ont été nourries par les échanges entre les grands métropoles sahéliennes et leurs voisines du Maghreb. Elle prétend nier l'importance de la réli-

4 *Introduction*

gion musulmane à travers 'Afrique noire' et ce, bien avant l'arrivée des "découvreurs" européens, à la négritude avérée des premiers Égyptiens. En un mot, elle prétend nier la communauté d'histoire qui mêle les destins de nations ayant toute été colonisées par les même puissances et les luttes de libération qui en découlèrent. Comme si l'Europe qui se construit sous nos yeux ne présentait pas des contradictions tout aussi criantes. Il est des cercles encore plus larges d'ont celui d'autres continents qui, avec l'Afrique, on constitué le cortège de ce que Frantz Fanon baptisa "les damnés de la terre." (Njami 2005, 15–16)

Most people think of Africa as being limited to a group of countries south of the Sahara, with the region that starts in the north as almost another world. This kind of revisionism, eager to set the "Ethiopian" against the "Mediterranean" fraction of a continent across which the desert opens up like an interminable parenthesis, is pathological, for it seeks to negate the multiple influences fueled by exchanges between the large Sahelian cities and their North African neighbors since the Middle Ages. It contradicts the importance of Islam throughout sub-Saharan Africa, already present well before the European "discoverers" set foot there. In short, it seeks to negate the common history that united the destinies of nations colonised by the same powers and their ensuing struggles for liberation. As though Europe being built before our eyes did not present equally glaring contradictions. Wider circles exist too, including the ones encompassing other continents which, along with Africa, have formed a procession of what Frantz Fanon called "the wretched of the earth." (Njami 2006, 113–14)

Njami's words introduced the extraordinary "Africa Re-Mix," one of the largest, most elaborate, geographically inclusive, and media-inclusive exhibitions of contemporary African art ever mounted. Within the genre of exhibition, Njami's choices are difficult to criticize. His wide-ranging choice of forms (photography, sculpture, video, painting, and mixed media), artists (male and female), and races (white, Asian, Arab, and black), as well as his showcasing of uncommonly seen media and inclusion of frequently neglected artists, particularly those from lusophone Africa, made "Africa Re-Mix" a practice of what he preached in the introduction to the catalogue, which, in its insistence on diversity as political strategy, speaks to the very first principle of an African literary history I outline here. Africa is represented in its continental diversity, not in simple racial, regional, or linguistic terms—though, to be sure, all of those terms and definitions help shape Africa and its many literatures.[4] In some ways, the continentalist mode of African literature I propose, which claims that geography and proximity ought to be reassessed and revalued as models of cultural affiliation and political solidarity, works against Pan-Africanism, since the latter form of cultural nationalism employs a racial principle of organization, linking blacks in the diaspora to those of the continent but, in turn, categorically excludes Africans of Arab, European, and South Asian origin. Njami's choice of plastic artists illustrates a broad non-racialism. His citation of Frantz Fanon suggests his own wish to straddle a line between the activist-philosopher's evocation of Pan-Africanism, on the one hand, while embracing Fanon's non-racial humanism, on the other. By referencing Fanon—*The Wretched of the Earth* (1968), in particular—Njami signals something that most of the later chapters of this book elaborate: that Fanon's most famous and most important book has exerted a powerful inspirational influence on African novelistic writing. I will refer to this point again in the chapters that follow.

Second, in the period I examine, the category of gender does not exist; it can neither be comprehended apart from colonialism, nor is it legible apart from the cultural nationalism that arose in response to colonialism. Many of the works in the first big wave of novels written by men celebrated nationalism as a response to the colonial enterprise or explored it for its limits in effecting social transformation. However, one would scarcely realize from reading early novels written by women that nationalist struggles were then being waged in African minds and on African land. Early female writers' representation of politics rarely involved explicitly nationalist or syndicalist themes. Partly for this reason, writing by women has been considered apolitical—which means concerned only with domestic issues—and certainly not part of the national narrative. Even inquiring about female writers' relation to politics has been difficult within African literary studies because of a scholarly environment that historically has been inhospitable to feminism, rejecting it as a European import. Critics are far less openly dismissive now than they were fifteen or twenty years ago, but their history of dismissal has left a defensive critical legacy: feminist readers of African literature have tended to celebrate writing by women simply because they give voice to feminine subjectivity.[5] My study grows out of a larger question: at a time when novels written by men were understood to be deeply involved in the project of anticolonial nationalism, why were novels written by women understood to be apolitical? In sketching a broad literary history, I attempt some answers. After briefly outlining a context for why feminists have not rigorously scrutinized women's writing in public political terms, I turn my attention to how such a scrutiny might take shape.

It was not only women's novels that were marginalized in nationalism's schemes for regulating the field of African writing and distributing cultural capital within it. Novels published by men as late as the 1930s, but before anticolonial sentiment reached its height in western and southern Africa, were also excluded from the consolidating canon of African novels. Critical attention by and large has focused on a narrow conception of resistance, and literary criticism has not yet fully acknowledged that African independence struggles did not gain momentum until after the Second World War. Not until after that set of global wars was settled did a francophone black cultural nationalism make itself heard, which is precisely what happened in the case of Négritude. One of Négritude's tenets involved the claim to moral superiority over whites precisely because Africans did not engage in the forms of warfare and civilian slaughter that became visible after the war.

With a few exceptions, novelists who published before Négritude have been obscured by mid-twentieth-century genealogies constructed by both readers and critics, or if they have been noted, their importance has diminished, which Alain Ricard ably illustrates in *The Languages and Literatures of Africa* (2004). This fate befell Amos Tutuola, whose writing did not conform to the resistance model of cultural nationalism. Attention to these early novels highlights the stakes for Africans of both genders entering an emerging public sphere of novelistic writing. Moreover, African literary criticism, which defined itself as a field in the 1960s, has tended to read and represent itself instrumentally rather than for an aesthetic sensibility, and anticolonial nationalism has shaped that political thrust.

Well before the publication of *Things Fall Apart* (Achebe 1958), *L'enfant noir* (Laye 1953), or *Une vie de boy* (Oyono 1958), several writers from different parts of the continent published variously successful long narratives with anticolonial content. Yet until the 1980s, when europhone African literature began to be incorporated more fully into the body of world literature, many of these writers had not been acknowledged as part of African literary history by critics and scholars. One of the most remarkable of these lacunae is Sol Plaatje's *Mhudi* (1930), one of the earliest anglophone African novels. Its title is now fairly well known, but it remains rarely taught outside specialized courses in southern African studies, and until very recently, it was not much written about, despite Plaatje's importance as a co-founder of what became the African National Congress. A still earlier novel is *Ethiopia Unbound* (1911) by the Sierra Leonean Joseph Caseley-Hayford.[6] The Senegalese writer Ousmane Socé published *Karim: Roman sénégalais* in 1935 (translated into English in 1938) and the Nigerian Daniel Fagunwa published his first novel, *Ogboju ode ninu igbo irunmale*, in Yoruba a few years later (translated by Wole Soyinka as *The Forest of a Thousand Daemons* [Fagunwa 1968]).[7] None of these early authors, not even Plaatje, appears in Gerald Moore's canon-shaping work of literary criticism, *Seven African Writers* (1962), or in his subsequently revised and expanded version, *Twelve African Writers* (1980).

Négritude, the first major black cultural nationalist literary movement, exerted a powerful influence on African belles-lettres of the 1940s and '50s, although poetry was its important genre. As a literary movement, Négritude is understood to have been assimilated into French literary culture through the publication of the enormously successful *Anthologie de la nouvelle poésie nègre et malgache de langue française* (1948), edited by Léopold Sédar Senghor and prefaced by Jean-Paul Sartre's essay "Orphée Noir." The book's translation into English meant that anglophone Africans, particularly Nigerians and Ghanaians, could be energized by its aesthetic and political spirit.[8] By the 1950s, the novel had displaced poetry as the dominant genre even in francophone Africa. Although Laye, Oyono, and Mongo Beti were embraced early on for their aesthetic sensibility, as well as for their politics, critics did not link their work to earlier literary forays. I know of no scholarship, for example, that places any of the three writers in relation to Socé's *Karim*, a novel that explores the theme of assimilation. And with the notable exception of Abiola Irele, I know of no scholarship that juxtaposes *Karim* to Cheikh Hamidou Kane's lyrical and much admired novel *L'aventure ambiguë* (1962), which also explores assimilation through the protagonist's struggle between religious tradition and faith, on the one hand, and his experience of cultural change within the secular world, on the other.

Only now are critics of African literature beginning to elaborate the connections between these earlier authors and the traditions that emerged shortly after independence. By the 1980s, Fagunwa had become known to those not fluent in Yoruba, and *The Forest of a Thousand Daemons* is now read in English translation alongside works by Tutuola, Soyinka, and Ben Okri.[9] Fagunwa published *Forest* in 1938; Tutuola, the celebrated *The Palm-Wine Drinkard* in 1952; and Cyprian Ekwensi, *People of the City* in 1954. Nevertheless, it is Achebe's *Things Fall Apart* that became the single novel read by those who knew nothing about African literature; it also became the novel that scholars of African literature returned to again and again. C. L. Innes bestowed upon Achebe the honorific "father" of African fiction, and Simon Gikandi elaborated her claim that *Things Fall Apart* performs a certain literary work that makes it the first African novel. Gikandi says that Achebe imagines a collective vision from within a colonial prism and writes a strong narrative of the colonial drama that also projects itself into a future of national independence.

Achebe is immensely important to African literature as the author of several major novels and books of criticism—and, perhaps more important, for his founding editorship of the Heinemann African Writers Series. Nevertheless, to my knowledge, *Things Fall Apart* has not formally influenced any other novel—indeed, any other work of literature—as has, for example, *The Palm-Wine Drinkard*.[10] Tutuola's relation to a consolidating West African canon has been clearly established through genealogical readings, first, and most important, by Achebe himself in an essay delivered at the University of Ibadan.[11] Later, and perhaps more famously, this was expressed by Irele, and some twenty-five years yet later, it was elaborated on by Ato Quayson, who linked Tutuola to the more recent writing of Ben Okri. In this respect, *Things Fall Apart* is unlike *Efuru* (1963), and Achebe unlike Flora Nwapa, the first female Nigerian novelist. Nwapa's influence on Buchi Emecheta is explicitly thematized by Emecheta in what remains the younger writer's most famous novel, *The Joys of Motherhood* (1979). The relations between the two may seem obvious today, but they were not in 1990 when I first published an essay outlining the influence Nwapa had on Emecheta.[12]

It has become increasingly clear—within the europhone tradition, at least—that the novels that have become important are those that were read as, and thus performed the function of, national narratives. However, not all political novels were visibly nationalist in their anticolonialism; not all, therefore, were easily recuperated for a national(ist) tradition. Tutuola serves as one example, illustrating an indigenous West African magical realism before the popularity of the Latin American Boom.[13] Despite, or perhaps because of, his writing of non-realist prose, Tutuola has only recently secured a place in the pantheon of midcentury African writers. As the drive to read literature on behalf of an orthodox nationalism abated somewhat, and the wish to read against realism understood as transparent markedly increased, Tutuola's literary stock has soared since the 1980s, and anti-mimeticist writing, such as that by Okri, Yvonne Vera, Sony Labou Tansi, Dambudzo Marechera, and others, have captured the attention of the current generation of literary scholars of Africa.[14]

By 1980, shortly before the publication of Moore's restatement of the field in *Twelve African Writers*, a volume of criticism that, unsurprisingly, does not include any female authors, critics of African literature had established a nationalist aesthetic around anticolonial resistance. They had little imaginative space for female writers who were less interested in decolonization and national sovereignty than in "feminine questions." As time passed and gender became increasingly better received as a political category, female African writers were reviewed and written about more and, by the mid-1980s, were increasingly added to course syllabi and reading lists.[15] New entrants to the public space shaped by orthodox nationalism, early female novelists such as Nwapa and Grace Ogot had been invisible as writers, and they continued to be illegible as political writers. The regulative mechanism of this aesthetic has become more visible recently, and by attending to the public–private divide that frequently has shaped our understanding of women's writing, I hope we may begin to read for the complex, hesitant, and often ambivalent mix of political and cultural expression in which the first female novelists composed their first works. A reading structured along the axis of micro-politics and macro-politics makes visible a greater conversation between male and female writers wherein they address concerns raised by each other, regardless of gender.[16]

Amílcar Cabral and Mariama Bâ speak in very different, and differently helpful, ways to the questions I have raised. I quote from both and discuss their value for the sort of literary study I propose. In "Identity and Dignity in the Context of the National Liberation Struggle" (1973), Cabral, a revolutionary Marxist intellectual from Guinea-Bissau, takes a radically teleological approach to imperialism, claiming that despite its violence, imperialism ultimately benefited those who underwent it. Cabral gave this talk in English to the historically black student population of Lincoln University near Oxford, Pennsylvania, despite the fact that English was his second language (possibly his third) after Portuguese:

> It is not to defend imperialist domination to recognize that it gave new nations to the world, the dimensions of which it reduced and that it revealed new stages of development in human sciences in spite of or because of the prejudices, the discrimination and the crimes which it occasioned, it contributed to a deeper knowledge of humanity as a moving whole, as a unity in the complex diversity of the characteristics of development. (Cabral 1973, 58)

Cabral said in 1970 what we in the early twenty-first century all know: that imperialism brought many of the world's inhabitants closer and made them known to one another; that imperialism was produced by and, in turn, reproduced a form of internationalism and knowledge production; in effect, that imperialism originated what we now call global capitalism or globalization. The most prominent connection between imperialism and early capitalism in Africa is the Atlantic slave trade, a mass movement of people that changed the landscapes, cultures, and economies of most of the world. The slave trade did not lead to the immediate colonial conquest of Africa, although it was made possible by and, in turn, exacerbated internecine African warring. Slavery and local warfare together were responsible for the destruction of human life and waste of incalculable human potential.

Trade in slaves allowed Britain, France, Spain, and the Netherlands to compete with—and, in the case of Britain and France, to surpass—Portugal in establishing toeholds on the continent. Africa was not formally carved up and its spoils were not divided between European colonial powers until the late period of imperialism, at the Berlin Conference of 1885. While formal colonialism does not have a long historical presence in Africa, as it did in much of South and Southeast Asia or Latin America, the transatlantic, transnational practice of African slavery, begun in the sixteenth century, sharpened and entrenched racial hierarchies and contributed to Britain's and France's newly asserted sense of themselves as imperial powers. Trade in human flesh bound racial difference to the consolidation of commodity relations. Cabral's language resembles that of the youthful Marx, who in 1848 sweepingly condensed description and prescription into a single statement and attributed to the bourgeois villain of his tale greater agency than he did the proletarian protagonist. Marx "grasps the long-range dynamics at work behind and beyond what he actually sees, so that if one sentence of the *Manifesto* gives us the capitalism of 1848 [as established by the creative and dynamic bourgeoisie] the very next one gives us an image of what was yet to be," says Aijaz Ahmad (1999, 39) in his introduction to a special anniversary Indian edition of *The Communist Manifesto*. Marx's logic, some of which we hear echoed in Cabral, is that the economic and technological expansion of capitalism ultimately advances all of humanity, albeit at a far greater cost to some. For Cabral, imperialism appears as historically necessary as capitalism is for Marx. It ushers in a new stage of the life process, "reveals new stages of human understanding," seems to be an inherent part of the modern world and therefore, one of the stages humanity passes through to arrive at a non-racialized socialist world. I suggest that, although the novel is no more indigenous to Africa, as part of the imperialist enterprise it, too, constitutes part of the larger global contribution to a "deeper knowledge of humanity as a moving whole."

Bâ, one of the most important francophone female writers and certainly the most famous female Senegalese writer, focuses on similar concerns differently. In one of the very few interviews she gave during her short life, Bâ spoke as a woman and a Muslim about the vexed relation of modern educated women to Islam. Her perspective was also teleological. Unlike Cabral, who spoke on behalf of African socialism, her primary commitment was to the individual African woman, particularly the woman who wants to develop her abilities fully. Bâ was much concerned with the relation between the gifted woman and her more ordinary compatriots:

> In all cultures, the woman who formulates her own claims or who protests against her situation is given the cold shoulder. If the woman who expresses herself orally is already labeled in a special way, the women who dare fix their thoughts for eternity are criticized all the more. Thus women are still hardly represented among African writers. And yet they have so much to say and write about. . . . The woman writer in Africa has a special task, she has to present the position of women in Africa in all its aspects. There is still so much injustice. . . . We no longer accept the nostalgic praise to the African Mother, who, in his anxiety, man confuses with Mother Africa. (quoted in Schipper 1987, 36)[17]

Individual advancement is incompatible with culturally approved feminine behavior, noted Bâ unhappily, signaling an issue of increasing importance to the "New Woman" of independent Africa. Her statement stands as an early and direct riposte to the deeply gendered iconography of decolonizing nationalism, and, in particular, that of "Femme noire," an early and famous poem by her compatriot and fellow author Léopold Senghor. More important, Bâ recognized and named the topic of women's representational burden—one that has come to haunt African and, indeed, Third World or Global South feminist discourse as a whole. As a progressive African woman, Bâ was called on to stand for as well as to write about all African women ("the position of women in Africa in all its aspects"), thereby invoking both aspects of what has been meant by the word "representation." Judith Butler neatly sums up the difference between the two notions of representation I invoke. The first meaning is that of political function, wherein it "seeks to extend visibility and legitimacy to women as political subjects"; the second, that of its linguistic function, wherein language "is said either to reveal or to distort what is assumed to be true about the category of women" (Butler 1990, 1). The tension between representation as a legal-political phenomenon and representation as a semiotic phenomenon undergirds Bâ's comments, as well as those of other female authors.[18]

I have juxtaposed Cabral and Bâ to establish a conversation between decolonizing nationalism and gender politics as they bear on African literary history. The different tendencies, interests, and agendas Bâ and Cabral bring to this project are echoed in the work of Florence Stratton and Olakunle George, two contemporary scholars of African literature who are concerned with acknowledging literary genealogies and the politics of representation. In general terms, Stratton and George elaborate and extend a set of thoughts that the earlier intellectuals explored in the 1960s and 1970s: the relation of nationalism to Marxism; the longstanding idea that African cultures are best apprehended as in a state of perpetual tension between tradition and modernity, a tension that dominates modern self-understanding; the place of education, that instrument of self-advancement and form of alienation from the collective; and, perhaps most important, the relation of the public and private spheres to each other, and particularly to gender. Here Stratton and George each stand for diverging opinions on the question of representing Africa and things African. Both benefit from a reading through the term "reflectionism." Stratton's practice of thematic reading on behalf of feminism leaves little room for attention to form, nuance, or contradiction. George's reaction to the tendency to read African literature as unmediated drives him to emphasize mediation in the artistic interpretation of literature and to diminish attention to sheer content.

The rise of the anglophone novel to which Stratton devotes most of her attention in her pathbreaking *Contemporary African Literature and the Politics of Gender* (1994) was significantly shaped by missionary activity, such as that of the Church of Scotland, which dedicated itself to the education of young men above young women. The church's educational agenda put men in "the world" and women in "the home"; it did this despite the fact that, historically in most of Africa, women successfully and appropriately worked in public.[19] The consequences of missionaries' good intentions and local patriarchy have meant more limited access to higher education for women. Stratton is aware of the relation of extra-literary factors such as who writes and what each writes about. Nevertheless, her reading method is primarily normative. Through a set of intertextual readings Stratton concludes that a strongly and simply configured *topos* of gender runs through the literature of decolonization written by men. Women are celebrated or victimized, adored or abused; they are Mother Africa, an essential figure of nurturance, or they stand as prostitutes, figures who traffic in their own bodies and thus represent one of the nightmares of modernity. Stratton's insight, broadly configured in metaphorical terms, has captured an important psychodynamic of male-identified cultural nationalism: its need for an idealized mother, as well as its fear of a self-commodifying female figure run amok in modernity.[20] These figures arise from men's projection of their own sense of anxiety or degradation, and, as I extend and elaborate on Stratton's scholarship, I reveal an underside to the celebration of masculine agency. Unfortunately, Stratton also seems to assume that there is a single, correct way to represent women; that literature does—or should—accurately reflect the lives of African men and women; and that the measure of a work therefore lies in the truthfulness of its representation. Accuracy is an unspoken standard that she brings to bear against male writers, and, as one might expect, all of them fail in some way. Stratton's critique of Achebe's depiction of women in *Things Fall Apart* is one example. Although she claims that the priestess, Chielo, is part of Achebe's depiction of the "great depth and value and beauty of African cultures," Stratton interprets the witch's abduction of Ezinma as Achebe's intimation that "women are incapable of exercising power responsibly" (Stratton 1994, 31). The question of accurate representation is posed of few, if any, of the female writers. Moreover, Stratton's book is uninterested in the formal properties that constitute a text's literariness, for to take up that perspective seriously would mean acknowledging that literature is a cultural product, an act of representation with mediation at its heart.

Telling the story of a prostitute, one might argue, could produce a sympathetic rather than an alienated response in the reader about a woman in the sex–gender system, depending on the manner in which the story is told.[21] By focusing on vexed figurations of the feminine, Stratton's work clears conceptual space in which we may take up the consequences of women's engagement with modernity. For example, the figure of Mother Africa, which Bâ rejects so resoundingly, Stratton turns into a measuring stick by which to examine the gendered anxieties that accompany cultural nationalism's commitment to modernity. Extending the types of questions Stratton poses, I extrapolate to historical authors the complexities of beginning to publish—itself an act that ended the tradition of women's literary and publishing silence. I do this by examining the representation of women in literature by women, an examination that constitutes the bulk of this book. Olakunle George engages both cultural nationalism and the question of African representation itself. Postcolonial theory, he argues, does not adequately speak to the colonized and the African subject. In fact, some strands of postcolonial theory "stand in the way of productive dialogue with a discursive tradition like African letters" and as such is, according to post-structuralism's own logic, "self-contradictory" (George 2003, 188). Anglo-American critical theory, especially when read in historical relation to cultural nationalism, illustrates that nativists (George's term for cultural nationalists) were not opposed to modernity and in favor of a simple or monolithic Tradition; rather, they participated in the formation of their own modernity. George makes a persuasive argument through interpretation of the artistic work of Fagunwa and Soyinka that Africans have already named themselves in relation to the rest of the modern world.

George seeks to address critical conceptual limits through these readings, some of which bear on the manner in which representation is perceived. The strength of his argument lies in its theoretical claims, which are substantiated through readings of mid- to late-twentieth-century Nigerian literature. As George traces the idea, reflectionism is inadequate, which puts him on the other side of the looking glass from Stratton. Criticizing reflectionism, he calls it "one of the most resilient tendencies" in modern attitudes to literary depictions of the world. For him reflectionism "assume[s that it is] . . . a representation of reality in language that can (or should) strive to approximate that reality without 'inaccuracies' or 'distortions' " (George 2003, 188–89).[22] While he refuses to ignore the real-world politics that give rise to the desires for what reflection seeks to address, George is too committed to exposing the gap between the social and the representative to engage the relation of the aesthetic to the cognitive, which realism also involves.

George does once speak to reflectionism in a manner that makes it more than mere weak literary criticism, and in that one moment he suggests it might have analytic value. In discussing Achebe's concept of art, he juxtaposes reflection to what he calls an "art for art's sake" approach to literature. In so doing, he proposes a complex reading of Achebe's writing: "What Achebe demonstrates here is at once an acceptance of a modern Western apprehension of the role of literature in society, and a rejection of part of it. Achebe reveals a traditional (reflectionist) attitude to literary representation even as he rejects another traditional (aestheticist, 'art-for-art's-sake') view" (George 2003, 86). Reflectionism remains both an important and a vexed question.

Within literary critical discourse in general, the charge of reflectionism, part of the larger conversation about realism, often forms part of a critique of doctrinaire Marxism. In this context, it is treated as a crude optic that assumes an unmediated relation between the work of art and the world it represents. This critique is often made against the work of Georg Lukács, the Hungarian philosopher and most important Marxist advocate of literary realism. Whether or not one believes it is fair to call Lukács a reflectionist, George does not deploy the term "reflection" as systematically as Lukács does. He shows no hostility towards Lukács himself. Moreover, he seems to mean something simpler in his renunciation of the term: that African literature does not or cannot perform sociology or anthropology and that American students who believe they might fully know Africa by reading African literature are deluding themselves.

To elaborate the question of reflection that haunts criticism of the African novel, I turn to the ways by which one might use or understand the more richly complex term "mimesis." The American Heritage Dictionary defines "mimesis" as "the imitation, or representation, of aspects of the sensible world, especially human actions, in literature and art." At the first level of analysis, mimesis consists of the simple imitation or mirroring of the thing itself; this definition does not account for mediation or difference between world and art, between object depicted and the thing itself. At a second level, however, mimesis consists of an act of representation rather than reflection, a position that acknowledges the mediation that always inserts itself between art and object and thereby allows for mediation. This is the definition that Aristotle puts forth in *Poetics*. Because it is not formulated around the standard of accuracy, mimesis as representation differs from mimesis as imitation. Mimesis as representation understands that all art, all symbolization, produces a gap between sign and object. Remaining at the second level of analysis, one might examine each art work for similarity or difference from the object it seeks to depict; this approach understands the representation to be a thing in itself and not a mere distortion.

There is yet another, third, level by which one might understand representation, one that moves still further away from the question of accuracy. Here we perceive mimesis as the art of giving form, or the very process of representation itself. Through this understanding of mimesis, we can give serious thought to the manner or type of representation that, in novels, we would call genres, figuration, or modes of narration. In so doing, we encounter the means by which a work of art impresses itself as realist or antirealist. Finally, the representation of a thing in the world produces some form of change in the world itself. Once something has been represented in words or visual images, the world has been altered or transformed, for now the object represented exists alongside the representation, the object, and some form of itself that is also not itself.

In figure 1, a photograph taken in 1960 by Marilyn Silverstone, a young Lagosian boy looks at himself in a funhouse mirror, called "magic mirrors." The action takes place during the celebrations that accompanied Nigerian independence. The image of the boy in the mirror is elongated and obviously distorted. Although we see him reflected in the mirror, the shape and size of his reflected face is very different from the back of the head as captured by the camera alone, which presumably is the viewing eye. The mirror also shows us two boys, only one of whom can be seen just through the camera's eye. The photograph's angle captures in the same mirror the reflection of an older, uniformed male standing behind the two boys. The distortion does not hide his uniform—a hat, khaki shorts, and light-colored shoes. Though older than the boys, he is not a full adult but a teenager, presumably a uniformed Boy Scout and, if so, an example of Robert Baden-Powell's colonial legacy to the continent.[23] This young man appears to be carrying a long instrument, not a gun but probably a stick. Without the mirror, the Scout is not visible at all; he exists for the viewer only in the mirror's reflection, though in the mirror he looms larger than anyone else. Presumably, at the moment the photo was taken he stood directly behind the boys and out of view of the camera. The second boy, like the teenage Scout, is visible only in the mirror. The image in the funhouse mirror does indeed represent a reality: that of the boy himself, as well as that of his companion and the Boy Scout. And last, though certainly not least, it represents the potential for eros. The boy most visible to the camera clutches an armload of books and papers that we see more clearly through the reflected distortion of the mirror. One of the books is a paperback that, on closer inspection, reveals a blonde woman of European origin on the front cover.[24]

The relation of the mirror to the viewer's perspective allows for the glass to represent more than is available to the naked eye alone, which in this instance is the camera's eye. The angle at which the viewer sees the youngster suggests that there is knowledge in the representation that is not a mere duplication. My discussion here of interpretive practices makes the mirror a metaphor for the work of art, and, conversely, it makes the camera a "neutral" stand-in for the naked human eye. This interpretation heightens the perspective of the mirror's reflection. It stands for Art and for Art's relation to reality. The mirror can cast more light on a given situation than can the angle of the camera alone. A reading of the photo along these lines for African literature on the eve of independence might see in the boy an allegory of the youthful nation eager to exert itself under its own power. Pursuing the allegory, the contorted face, the hat (and the possible weapon) of the Scout in uniform would suggest the strongmen yet to come to power. The image as a whole does not merely duplicate the

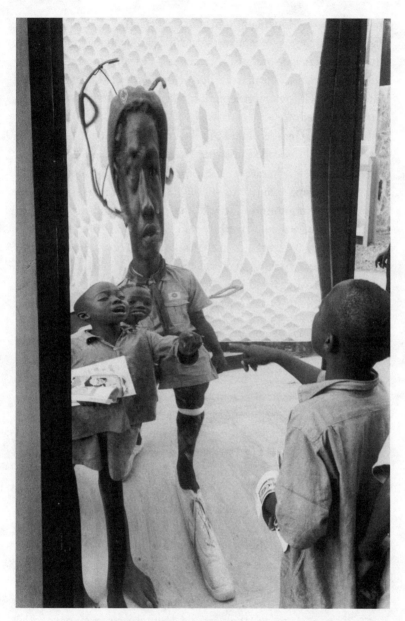

Young Nigerian boys in Lagos amusing themselves
in "magic mirrors" at a fair during independence celebrations.
Photograph by Marilyn Silverstone, BW *Photographe, Magnum Photos.*

image of the boy looking at himself, a perspective the camera alone offers. The image shows us an African (or Nigerian) present and future in one image, and it thus serves as an excellent example of the value of the wish to speak to reality—along with the belief that there is no reality without representation, even though representation is always mediated.

Stratton and George differently illustrate the limits of polemic or culturally blind one-sidedness that I seek to move beyond. Stratton expects a work of literature to mirror accurately and on behalf of African feminism. Against her wholly thematic readings, I assert the importance of attention to form, to the value of literature's ability to lie on behalf of a greater truth. Against George's more subtle antireflectionism, I assert substance or attention to content, the claim that much literary writing makes to the real.

According to Lukács, art becomes most powerful when it represents the momentous historical forces at work at a particular time. The importance and value of great art lies in its representation of the important causes and turning points in history, in making visible the means by which human beings make their history. I take from Lukács the notion that the novel, like other literary genres, comes about and exists to solve a social problem. Exploring a literary text for its less obvious meanings and resolution of contradictions gives the reader insight into a historically specific social problematic.[25]

To avoid redundancy, from now on I will assume that the reader is aware that African narrative prose and African authors are the primary subjects of this book. I no longer qualify each text or tendency with the adjective "African." When comparing things European, Latin American, or Asian to things African, however, I will, of course, be as precise as needed.

Male novelists have customarily told their tales in allegories of colonial resistance or national consolidation—or have been understood to do so—and like their female counterparts, they have often used the family as sign of the body politic. These national allegories have either unselfconsciously put themselves forward or have been interpreted as allegorical in the narrow sense, wherein the literal meaning becomes subsumed into the figural. The literal or less important entity, such as woman, child, or family, thereby necessarily stands as part of the larger, national one. Occasionally, as with Laye's *L'enfant noir*, this allegory functions as straightforward idealization. In *Things Fall Apart*, where the family is not quite so romanticized, the local with all its troubles disappears into the larger and more important national.[26] Female writers, themselves excluded from the hierarchies of national politics and historically perceived as unable to engage nationalist and feminist politics simultaneously, have often deployed one fiction to expose another. To invert a cliché, in the narratives of many African female writers, the family becomes the nation writ small.

The tendency of female novelists to tell domestic stories historically has gone hand in hand with nationalism's confirmation of a separate "domestic sphere." As a result of the dominance of nationalist reading paradigms, readers have not been alert to either the literal or the allegorical relations between private and public spheres and forms of power in their fiction. There are good reasons that we can expect to find precisely these relations in these novels. As I have suggested, Marxism and feminism alike have emphasized the continuities and interchanges between public and private life: that domestic labor is part of the labor of a collectivity, for instance; that women's taking it on makes possible a certain kind of public participation for the men who are freed of it; and that patriarchal authority within a family can under-pin a form of patriarchal authority practiced in the public sphere, or, alternatively, that it might serve as compensation for the public disen-franchisement of a group of men. If one comes to these novels by women with this understanding of the necessary implication of the domestic in the public, and with a knowledge of the highly allegorical texts that dominated the literary scene into and out of which these women wrote, then one may better perceive how domestic life functions both literally and allegorically in relation to nationalism.

History and theory written from the perspective and in the interest of the formerly colonized or developing world has a complex relation to the intellectual material of the First World of the colonizers, from which it takes some of its intellectual tools and against which it also struggles. In the introduction to *Recasting Women*, a groundbreaking collection of essays on feminist historiography in India, Kumkum

Sangari and Sudesh Vaid make clear the intellectual and political stakes of their work:

> Overarching theoretical formulations are helpful and necessary to undertake any work but they need constant testing and overhauling by historically and materially specific studies of patriarchal practice, social regulation and cultural production. . . . We are not making a plea for theoretical eclecticism or 'pluralism' but for flexibility within a field which is still being defined. (Sangari and Vaid 1990, 3)

Sangari and Vaid object not to theory as such but to a level of abstraction or generalization that loses sight of the fact that the data and paradigms under discussion do not have a longstanding scholarly tradition of debate and therefore are vulnerable to misreading. My intent, similarly, is to test and overhaul a broadly outlined literary history and theory against specific textual analyses of europhone African literature, a field similarly in the process of establishing itself. It may appear contradictory, even counterproductive, to assert theoretical flexibility, on the one hand, and discuss a notion of allegoresis, or reading strategies shaped in dialogue with the work of Fredric Jameson, on the other. In the next few pages, I illustrate the historical, political, and *literary* value of such a reading. Allegory is like all other figures of speech in that it refers simultaneously to two meanings for the same set of literary features. M. H. Abrams (1981, 4) defines "allegory" succinctly as a form in which "the agents and action are contrived to make coherent sense on the 'literal,' or primary level of signification, and also to signify a second, correlated order of agents, concepts and events." Tzvetan Todorov declares that "for some [scholars of allegory] the first meaning must disappear, while others require that the two be present together." Aligning himself with the camp wherein the vehicle disappears into the tenor, Todorov insists that the allegorical meaning not be the result of an interpretive act but inherent in the text: "this double meaning is indicated in the work in an *explicit* fashion; it does not proceed from the reader's interpretation (whether arbitrary or not)." Talal Asad (1986) offers another perspective by stating that "allegories are secured . . . by *teaching* people to read in certain ways."[27] Allegorical reading is culturally and historically bound. James Clifford suggests that there is no way to separate the essential from the allegorical. I suspect that most of us would claim that allegories are neither intrinsic nor natural but learned, and that our ability to perceive them has much to do with systems of education and literacy. They are legible according to how readers have learned to make sense of them. There is good reason to imagine that the context of African nationalism and the reception tradition of allegory in men's novels together create an interpretive opening for the reading of nationalist allegory in the women's novels. What follows via my extended discussion of two different works by Fredric Jameson is an argument for developing a political literacy about works to which we have hitherto been blind.

Jameson's "Third World Literature in the Era of Multinational Capitalism" (1986) is one of the more important and controversial essays on the topic of decolonization and literature to have been published in the past three decades. His sweeping interpretive paradigm for reading the artistic writing produced in formerly colonized countries provoked a scandal when first published, and rightfully so. As several critics have pointed out, for all its erudition and insight, the essay contains many wrongheaded assumptions, the most objectionable being that narratives from the Third World always contain within them a national allegory. However one might object to some of Jameson's assertions, the fact remains that more than twenty years after its publication the essay reveals itself to have been prescient in its understanding of the field of "postcolonial studies," which was just beginning to make its mark in the American academy. An outpouring of the study of these literatures has taken place in the intervening years, much of it focused precisely on the national allegory Jameson outlined and celebrated in 1986. We might understand this critical reception in two ways. One would be to agree that nationalism does in fact play a significant role in the imaginative literature of decolonization. The second is that scholars of this literature have themselves been limited in their ability to perceive other metaphors of collectivity or political organization and so have overly relied on a nationalism–individualism binary. Both readings are useful here, as I illustrate.

Jameson's essay is valuable for several reasons. First, and most important, it sympathetically represents the historical investment in nationalism as part and parcel of the decolonizing enterprise. From the "foundational fictions" of pre-independence Latin America to the fictions of disillusionment and its subgenre of novels of dictatorship in Africa and Latin America, the category of the national has proved to be a rich one for the literature of decolonization. Jameson's work is valuable also because here and elsewhere he seeks to theorize realism as something more than an outmoded aesthetic phase before modernism became aware of the market.[28] His project of cognitive mapping suggests a renewal in the First World of the project of realism.[29] And realism, after all, is the narrative mode in which (europhone) artistic texts from Africa, Asia, and Latin America continue to be most frequently written. Nevertheless, so preoccupied is he with discovering a way out of the seduction and paralysis of postmodernism that Jameson is willing to homogenize what he calls the Third World, making the entity into a single, coherent ground from which to resist the First World. His idealization runs the risk of reducing the Third World to a monolith rather than recognize it as a cluster of sites of resistance and co-optation. Worse yet, he fails to understand its literature as ambivalent, conservative, or, indeed, mediated in any way.

The novels I examine in *The Nation Writ Small* are particularly well suited to the dialogue with Jameson because, on the one hand, as literature from the African continent, they form a subset of the body of texts used to make the original theoretical assertions in "Third World Literature." (Recall that Sembène figures prominently in Jameson's essay.)[30] They ultimately uphold his claim that the category of the nation underpins many—though I say, not all—artistic texts from the Third World. On the other hand, most are written by women, and all help me articulate a feminist politics of reading. Capitalist culture imposes a radical split between public and private, politics and poetics. Jameson suggests that in the Third World, the relations of those spheres to each other function in a manner "wholly different" from those in the West or First World; moreover, he continues, though not repaired, the breach is fictionally reconciled in the Third World. This claim is the basis for his controversial assertions that Third World novels are inherently allegorical and that the allegory is always national. The claim leads him to the polemical though untenable assertion that for the Third World—though apparently for no one else—the national allegory functions as a passage between the two spheres:

All third-world texts are necessarily, I want to argue, allegorical, and in a very specific way: they are to be read as what I will call *national allegories,* even when, or perhaps I should say, particularly when their forms develop out of predominantly western machineries of representation, such as the novel. Let me try to state this in a grossly oversimplified way: one of the determinants of capitalist culture, that is, the culture of the western realist and modernist novel, is a radical split between the private and the public, between the poetic and the political, between what we have come to think of as the domain of sexuality and the unconscious and that of the public world of classes.... Our numerous theoretical attempts to overcome this great split only reconfirm its existence and its shaping power over our individual and collective lives.... I will argue that, although we may retain for convenience and for analysis such categories as the subjective and the public or political, the relations between them are wholly different in third-world culture. Third-world texts, even those which are seemingly private and invested with a properly libidinal dynamic—necessarily project a political dimension in the form of national allegory: *the story of the private individual destiny is always an allegory of the embattled situation of the public third-world culture and society.* (Jameson 1986, 69)

First, there is much here to explore at the level of the political. This polemical passage contains much of what is central to the problem, as well as the value, of Jameson's enterprise. Critics have responded to him by pointing out that it illustrates Jameson's representation of the Third World as wholly other than the First World and as marked by belatedness. They are correct to do so, since that is what the quotation rather baldly expresses. I submit, however, that the impulse behind this rhetorical move is one of wrongheaded idealization and willful blindness rather than intended indignity. Exploring the hows and whys of idealization proves far more productive in understanding Jameson's value, as well as his limits, as a fellow traveler. It also constitutes the first step in establishing a national allegory sympathetic to feminism in Africa.

Jameson is willing to romanticize the Third World, representing it as a unitary critical perspective, even as a possible site from which to cognize and act on resistance. His preoccupation with a way out of the seduction of postmodernism arises from the hopeful assumption that the cultural condition of postmodernism exists only in the First World. Because it is combined with his powerful hope that the industrially underdeveloped world has not (yet) experienced postmodernism, Jameson's assumption requires that the Third World be conceptually removed from its historical relation to capitalism. The essay must therefore shuttle between two positions: either the Third World never experienced the violent schism of public from private, or having experienced it, it was afterward able to suture those realms by virtue of its experience with decolonization. (Jameson appears to believe in the force or value of decolonization as suture, a gesture of great idealism on his part. Those who have objected to his essay see it as placing the Third World in the realm outside of history.) It may be of interest to note that Jameson considered the Third World essay a "pendant," or a supplement, to his work on postmodernism. In economic and political terms, Jameson recognizes that the Third World has been penetrated by capitalism. However, he does not seem to acknowledge capitalist penetration at the level of culture or structures of feeling.

Second, in literary terms, Jameson saves the personal for the political by reading the private (or personal) as a necessary and exclusive allegory of the public, by focusing on the libidinal or private realm of Third World fiction in literary terms. In so doing, he repeats in formal terms the same gesture made by many theorists of allegory: making the first meaning (or signifier) disappear in favor of the second meaning (or signified). This allegorical mode of reading is too simple and ahistorical, closer to Todorov than to Asad. Jameson's claim that the relation between private and public spheres is differently configured in the various nations and cultures subjugated under imperialism may well be true. Partha Chatterjee's discussion in *The Nation and Its Fragments* (1993) of how gender serves as the fulcrum conjoining and keeping separate the binaries of colonizer–colonized and tradition–modernity in nineteenth-century Bengal might even serve Jameson as an example. However, because of his desire for an uncontaminated space of resistance, the libidinal that Jameson describes can *only* serve as a vehicle of illumination, in other words, metaphor of the public ("*the story of the private individual destiny is always an allegory of the embattled situation of the public third-world culture and society"*). It can therefore never narrate a politics of its own.

Ahmad, Jameson's first, harshest, and still most instructive critic on this particular essay, objects to what he considers Jameson's enshrining of nationalism, which, Ahmad correctly points out, is only one among many political or cultural formations in the wake of decolonization. Jameson, he complains, ignores other, frequently more progressive social practices or movements in his rush to celebrate the national imaginary. Moreover, Ahmad perceptively notes a gesture Jameson makes in his reading of aesthetic forms within political terms, a gesture made only in relation to the Third World, so invested is he in a utopian space not saturated by the market relations of modernism and postmodernism and, therefore, so uncomplicated does he believe Third World literature to be. Ahmad is insightful about Jameson's flaws, and I often take my cue from him. His particular commitment to internationalism and to a global Marxism, however, blinds him to the value of Jameson's contribution to the developing literary histories of formerly colonized zones, including that of Africa. I begin with what Ahmad forgets: that nationalism did, and in some cases still does, haunt the imagination of writers from Africa, Asia, and Latin America and therefore offers one way, and an important way, to thematize literary history.[31]

One such example of a literary history with a central place for allegory might be found in *Foundational Fictions* (1991), in which Doris Sommer argues that reading historically for the national allegory in nineteenth-century and early-twentieth-century Latin American novels makes visible the resolution through marriage of the competing interests of white creoles, blacks, native Indians, and mestizos, those different populations who had to be represented collectively as the nations of Venezuela, Colombia, Argentina, and others.

Political tensions between races and classes are translated into the love plot; competition is displaced into eroticism. For Sommer, romance refers to both theme (courtly love) and genre (prose narrative about heroic characters). At the level of theme, Romance results in sanctioned reproduction, and at the level of form, it proleptically gives rise to the Boom—in other words, to magical realism, the particular form of the novel for which Latin American became famous. Sommer's historically particular attention allows us to notice that novels from Africa and Latin America are often so explicitly national-allegorical as to bear as title the name of a woman who stands as the figure of the nation. Just a few of the many Latin American examples include *Amalia* (1815), by José Marmol of Argentina; the extremely popular novel *María* (1867), by Jorge Isaacs of Colombia; and *Doña Barbara* (1929), by Romulo Gallegos, who later became president of Venezuela. All are foundational fictions to which Sommer gives significant attention and, when read together, help prove her thesis about literary problem solving. *Aura*, by Carlos Fuentes of Mexico, published in 1962, during the Boom's heyday, self-consciously plays on the allegory of fecund or barren woman as nation. The most famous North African novel that openly make of its eponymous female character a woman as allegory of the nation is *Nedjma* (1956), by Kateb Yacine of Algeria. Although *Bones* (1988), by Chenjerai Hove of Zimbabwe, does not bear the name of a female character, its title refers to the remains of its maternal heroine, Marita, a sacrificial mother of the nation. *Qui se souvient de la mer* (1962), by Mohammed Dib of Algeria, puns on the relation between mother and land and, here, land's synechdochal relation to ocean. And *The Home and the World* (1915), by Rabindranath Tagore of India, thematically binds the nationalist struggle to the emergence of the "New Woman" of Bengal. Feminine first names often serve as titles for these novels; more important, the female main characters are usually thinly individuated and saturated with symbolic value.[32]

As far as African novels are concerned, Jameson's paradigm is not entirely unproductive, for it seems ideally suited to elucidating the texts of Marxists whose notion of History is untroubled by the dialectics of public and private, such as that of the later narrative fiction of the Kenyan Ngugi wa Thiong'o. Ngugi's vaunted representation of women, particularly in *Petals of Blood* (1977) and *Devil on the Cross* (1980) come to mind. Though sexually used or abused, his female characters rarely articulate their suffering on a personal or subjective level. The grief they experience is not so much their own—that is, individualized—as it is collective; it points to a bigger story of violence. Simultaneous exploration of a gendered or sexual violence with the relation of that violence to that perpetuated by the state, whether native or colonial, simply does not appear in Ngugi's literary formulations. Similarly, the allegorical form Jameson proposes for the Third World requires that the allegory be inherent in the text and not produced as an interpretive act. This strict one-to-one correspondence between tenor and vehicle allows his presumed audience of parochial American readers no room to learn the various forms of legibility or meaning-making a text produces, or, more importantly, that a text produces in dialogue with its reader. By contrast, there is room for mediation, if not for interpretation, in Jameson's formulation of the national allegory as it appears in the work of the British modernist writer, Wyndham Lewis.[33]

Recognizing the literary and historical importance of nationalism does not mean that I here make a plea for its inherently progressive nature as both Jameson and Ahmad might think from their different vantage points, nor even would I claim that nationalism is the most progressive form of social movement that arose out of decolonization.[34] Rather, I seek to outline a literary history of gender and decolonization. Because decolonization took place under the sign of the nation and used gender—and, in some cases, ethnicity—as particular markers of cohesion and difference, we must pay particular attention to how the moment of national sovereignty offered the possibility for transformation of various social relations, as well as the literary effects of the success or failure of these relations.

The value of Jameson's work for my purposes therefore lies far more in the symptomatic reading practices that a full engagement with his notion of the dialectic involves than in unearthing buried or invisible national allegories. A corrective reading of "Third World Literature in the Era of Multinational Capitalism," therefore, illustrates the value of some of Jameson's concerns as they bear on those central to a progressive feminist politics of decolonization. African women's literary history might seem like an ideal tool of interpretation since novels from this part of the world are the ones Jameson uses to make his argument. These earlier novels by women give the literary lie to Jameson's desire for the Third World to rescue the First World politically, because they do not represent nationalism as such.

Only three major female novelists from the period I review express themselves in terms that are unambivalently anticolonial and nationalist while simultaneously rendering full female protagonists. They are Buchi Emecheta of Nigeria, Assia Djebar of Algeria, and Nawal El Sadaawi of Egypt. Emecheta and Djebar figure prominently in my project. A fourth, Ama Ata Aidoo of Ghana, who did notably depict a fully developed female character engaged with cultural nationalism also represented the story as taking place outside Africa, almost entirely in Germany, which I discuss briefly later. In short, it is rare to find female characters who function as more than flimsy metaphors of the nation, either beloved mothers or prostitutes with hearts of gold. And with regard to Emecheta and Djebar, I believe they have achieved the uncommon synthesis of nationalism and feminism in narrative by virtue of their membership in literary communities, a point to which I will return.

Two novels by female writers would seem to contradict my rough model here; both explicitly depict female characters in direct relation to the nation or state. The first, *L'ex-père de la nation*, (1987) by Aminata Sow Fall of Senegal laments betrayed hopes under the neo-colonial state. Sow Fall is a contemporary of the more famous Bâ and for many years has been a writer of pointed social criticism.[35] The second, *Cross of Gold* (1981), by Lauretta Ngcobo of South Africa, celebrates black nationalism as it squares off against the apartheid state. The protagonists of both, however, are men (the national president in Sow Fall's novel and the freedom fighter whose mother dies for him in Ngcobo's), and in both cases the moral force of the novel lies in the realm of national politics. Nationalism or national politics takes precedence over or usurps women's subjectivity, which supports my contention about the discursive limits of women's individuality and national collectivity in works written by women. My interest is in tracing the complex mechanisms (representational, as well, perhaps, as psychological) of the coming into being of a fully formed female character by a female author. At some level, therefore, I seek to juxtapose a form of feminine coming into being in the world (a narrative mode exemplified by the genre of the Bildungsroman) against and within the national narrative.

One of the most idiosyncratic of early female writers, and therefore one whose writing I read with special pleasure, is the Ghanaian Ama Ata Aidoo, who does openly tackle the thorny question of familial issues, female subjectivity, and public politics.[36] Aidoo's vigorous Pan-Africanism in *Our Sister Killjoy* (1977), combined with the assertive personality of its protagonist, Sissie, would appear to slip out of the nationalist injunctions I have been naming. But when one considers the novel's setting—Germany and England, not Ghana—it becomes clear that leaving the site of nationalist orthodoxy and focus has some bearing on the author's ability to withstand its silencing powers. Few other novels by women at this time deploy Aidoo's narrative strategy of exodus. It is also worth noting that Emecheta began writing only after she moved to London, away from the site of nationalist orthodoxy.

The very first black African women to publish novels, the Nigerian Flora Nwapa and the Kenyan Grace Ogot, appear silent in the face of national politics. Nwapa's *Efuru* and Ogot's *The Promised Land* (both published in 1966) are marked by a parochial tone and insular, rural settings. The female protagonists of this novelistic vanguard are themselves not unconventional. Both Nyapol and the eponymous Efuru are models of feminine decorum and propriety, wrapping themselves in mantles of traditional moral authority. Both novelists narrate stories set in a rural sphere seemingly untouched by Western modernity. I emphasize "seemingly." The fact that Efuru is much more of an individualist and ends up alone (which is to say, without a man) by choice after the disappointments of two husbands and childless (not by choice), but rich and well respected, especially by her female peers, has made her a character easily recuperated for feminism.

Later writers—in particular, two who have become part of the consolidating tradition of europhone writers—exemplify far greater self-confidence in depicting assertive or proto-feminist female characters within a political context more sympathetic to nationalism than do Ogot or Nwapa. We see this particularly in the cases of Bâ and Tsitsi Dangarembga. Bâ, whose first novel, *Une si longue lettre* (1979), allegorizes public politics in privately political terms, names the story of national disillusionment as a romantic failure. Dangarembga's first novel, *Nervous Conditions* (1988), narrates the struggle for self-determination of two teenage girls and yet never risks trivializing their youthful problems or making either girl a simple icon of national subjectivity. These departures from generic convention (representing a female character more complex than Wanja in Ngugi's *Petals of Blood* or the eponymous Nedjma in Kateb Yacine's novel) account for why, despite its great popularity, *Nervous Conditions* is only now perceived to function as a national allegory.[37] The novel tells a simultaneous, if obscured, tale of public politics that, as the Fanonian and Sartrian title suggests, is also a nationalist one. As one might expect, it rewrites Fanon, whose work either elides gender or, when engaging it, frequently echoes conservative aspects of decolonizing nationalism.

The focus of my argument and my commitment to a range of novels and regions does not allow me to fully develop an influence study that traces in detail changes in representational mechanisms that followed the first female authors' representation of female characters. Nevertheless, I venture some generalizations about the first twenty years of women's writing. Many of the very first novelists, such as Nwapa, Ogot, and Sow Fall, depict female characters who seem to be "flat" rather than psychologically complex. Of these particular novelists, not even Sow Fall, the youngest and, at the time of my writing, the only one still alive, has yet published a novel with significant depth of characterization. Nwapa's novels and especially those by Ogot and Sow Fall are plot driven rather than character driven and are frequently explicitly moralistic. Sow Fall's brilliant *La grève des bàttu* (1979), to which I devote some attention in chapter 2, illustrates how satire expresses two opposing states of feeling by locating converging perspectives in twists of plot rather than in character ambivalence. These characters belong to the tradition of fable, rather than demonstrating the nuance or "roundedness" we associate with those who populate the nineteenth-century and twentieth-century European novel.[38]

What, then, encouraged writers to move from the "flat" characterizations of Nwapa, Ogot, and Sow Fall to the rounder characters of Aidoo, Bâ, Dangarembga, and the South African–born writer Bessie Head, for whom ambivalence is part and parcel of character development? What is the relationship between literary history or periodization and characterization? I submit that what we call character depth is in some manner bound to social change: represented in literature or as the social condition of possibility that the author encounters and resolves. Psychological complexity is more fully represented (and representable) as characters enter a literary field with some sense of historical continuity—that is, when the author does not feel herself to be "the first" speaker or writer. African women's writing has proliferated since 1988, the year *Nervous Conditions* was published, and authorial voices have become more assured and explicit in rendering female characters and national contexts. I mention in passing *Triompf* (1999), by Marlene Van Niekerk of South Africa, which won the Noma Award for Publishing in Africa in 1995; *David's Story* (2001), by Zoë Wicomb of South Africa; and *Half of a Yellow Sun* (2006), by Chimananda Adichie of Nigeria, as illustrations of the most compelling writing.[39]

Complexity of characters evolves as authors explore juxtaposing individuals against one another rather than setting all-important character relations between an individual and the colonial state or another immense institution. In the cases of all of the female writers, though in different ways, conflict comes about through family relations. I suggest that in general, the representational form of the family differs between works by women and feminist men, on the one hand, and by most men, on the other.[40]

As the primary institution by which domestic collectivity is organized and represented, the family is often understood to be naturally given, biologically determined, and eternal in its duration. As an idealized institution imbued with unique social and moral force, its symbolic power exceeds its historical boundaries—that is, family is felt on the part of its members to have always existed in the way they know and feel it. The fact that family formations have changed dramatically from century to century and look very different from culture to culture appears to have little bearing on the fact that family is experienced by its members as natural, timeless, and universal. The same is true of the nation. Nation and family are units of social collectivity and fictions of symbolic totality, each provoking from its members sentiments of affiliation and nostalgic yearning. Moreover, when read in relation to each other, family and nation roughly correspond to the public and private spheres, the private and familial pertaining to the domain of women and the public and national to that of men.

If in their fiction men have represented the family through nostalgia-colored glasses—and I argue that indeed they have—women are far more likely to have depicted the institution as both a product and an instrument of social power. For men, family might serve as an organic mode by which the social hierarchy of national politics is sanctioned. Women, themselves excluded from the hierarchies of public politics, might well, along with their male feminist allies, deploy one fiction to expose another. So when the family becomes the primary site of social engagement, as it frequently does in women's writing, relations between family members are neither organic nor transparent. Instead, family relations commonly depict the consolidation and dispersal of social power. Novels written by men evolve out of their understanding of the economic and legal underpinnings of cultural acts, which bear directly on their representation of national phenomena. Novels written by women converge around the sphere of the familial as the orchestrating unit that looms over and plays out national dramas.

Women writers' representations of family relations often expose the consolidation and dispersal of social power. One example can be found in Emecheta's *The Joys of Motherhood*, in which Nnu Ego's husband, Nnaife, is impressed into the British Army from his place of work and sent to Burma to fight in the Second World War. So abrupt is the conscription that he cannot notify his family. Nnu Ego is informed later by his friend Ubani, whose counsel is, "There is nothing we can do. The British own us, just like God does, and just like God they are free to take any of us when they wish" (Emecheta 1979, 148). Later in the novel, Nnu Ego utters a very similar locution to a British magistrate who settles a domestic fight. She speaks in Nnaife's defense, unwittingly sending him to prison by explaining his role as patriarch: "Nnaife is the head of our family. He owns me, just like God in the sky owns us. So even though I pay the [school] fees, yet he owns me. So in other words he pays" (Emecheta 1979, 217). Through the explicit comparison of the marital relation to that of the colonial relation, the novel likens Nnu Ego's subordinate position in the family to the subordination (or "ownership") of the Nigerians by the British. Moreover, *The Joys of Motherhood* does not merely metaphorize one form of domination in terms of another. By illustrating the overlapping public and private realms and narrating them simultaneously, it comments on domination within the family and within the colony and points to how colonial and patriarchal relations structure not only the public realm of politics, war, and employment, but also the private one of food procurement and children's education. It suggests that colonial relations saturate all aspects of daily life and illustrates that the private realm is not immune to the violence of colonialism.

The allegorical model Emecheta offers is a relatively complex one, and extending Emecheta, I suggest that it is practiced by many female writers. In the example above, the novel's political meaning does not reside exclusively in either tenor or vehicle but in a conversation between the two, and it is this dialectic that informs or explains the forces that drive Nnu Ego and her relations with the world around her. Such a reading strategy has far more in common with the allegorical reading practice advocated by Jameson's magnum opus, *The Political Unconscious*, than it does the determinative model of "Third World Literature in the Era of Multinational Capitalism." Historically, part of the problem with reading novels written by women in genealogical terms has inhered in the sheer intelligibility of certain political practices. Jameson's reading model in "Third World Literature in the Era of Multinational Capitalism," which so usefully illuminates the work of many of their literary brothers, leaves the feminine works obscure. To make relations more visible, I take my lead from the passage quoted from *The Joys of Motherhood* in which the public and private are obviously interpenetrated, and the domestic and national realms are inseparable from each other. As readers, we make it possible to read the realms of intimate domestic life as not merely micro-political or insignificant but as interlocked with the macro-political, as that on which it depends.

In the early phases of novel writing, male authors probably did render public politics more directly than did their female counterparts. Certainly, they were more likely to represent an explicit relation between character and nation, whether through the use of obviously allegorical figures or by recounting stories that made strikes, group actions, or other obviously public political activity central to their plots. Their readers expected these writers to address politics through their aesthetic writing. Whether the writers intended to represent the nation (or some other form of collectivity), their works were read as national allegories—though rarely were they perceived as allegorical in the narrowest senses. The interpretive paradigms applied to novels by men were flexible enough to incorporate a diversity of texts and ways to understand the question of politics.[41]

Second, in contrast to the ways men were read, the interpretive model for novels written by women historically has been narrow in scope, a claim I elaborate further in the four chapters that follow. Women have not often represented explicitly national-allegorical feminine figures. (Again, it is the *reception* of their novels that has been particularly limited, a practice I hope to change.) Telling domestic tales at a time that anticolonial nationalism was expected to be a necessarily and exclusively public phenomenon has resulted in the political invisibility of fiction written by women. Readers who hope to understand the relation of women to politics face the task of developing new forms of literacy, new means of understanding these novels' mode of political representation. While the earliest female novelists commonly did "what was expected" of them, such as conform to or enact the discourse of tradition that conferred moral authority, on another level they also broke new ground: they entered the public sphere of the literary marketplace. Part of my book's intervention is to illuminate the relation of writing practices to political activity with a select group of authors from around the continent. These are practices to which we largely have been blind.

Finally, the fullest analysis of African novelistic production lies in interpretational flexibility—in this instance, noting differences produced in the writing over time. When used as a critical lens through which to read African women's novelistic writing of the period I have discussed, Jameson's schema illustrates at least three things, which make sense as one makes one's way into his model via his dialectical reading. First, as I have pointed out, women's novels expose a critical blindness on the part of Jameson's "Third World Literature in the Era of Multinational Capitalism," because on the face of it, these novels by women from the Global South do not immediately demonstrate a national allegory, as Jameson insists all such novels do. Many seem to be parochially domestic tales. Second, the novels help illustrate Jameson's critical insight at the level of interpretation. Any reader who takes seriously his methodology in *The Political Unconscious* believes that allegorical readings of the nation—or, indeed, any other collective entity—can be made visible through an act of reading and that such a reading might even allow for a more historically rich textual understanding than discovering a pre-existing figure on the page. Finally, and most important for my purposes, Jameson's model offers an interpretive possibility. By pointing to how the public–private divide, itself a necessary fiction instantiated and reified by capitalism, is essential to the understanding of contemporary human relations, he names a way by which one may place these African women's novels in dialogic relation with the men's. Since Jameson has never accorded feminism more than a rhetorical nod in his own writing, this is a salutary move. Gayatri Spivak offers a differently configured Marxist statement that is deeply informed by feminism: "For if the fabric of the so-called public sector is woven of the so-called private," a statement that rings true to the basic tenets of Marxism, then "the definition of the private is marked by a public potential, since it is the weave, or texture, of public activity. . . . The deconstruction of the opposition between the private and public is implicit in all, and explicit in some, feminist activity" (Spivak 1987, 103).[42] Spivak's formulation makes it possible to see within one sphere the possibilities of the other, one that recognizes both the practice of the divide and the day-to-day practice of obscuring a more complete understanding of social and political relations.

Jameson's move effectively occludes relations of power within the private sphere of the literary text. Unable to narrate a politics of its own, the personal in the Third World functions only through the national allegory in a synechdochal relation with the public sphere. However, in *The Political Unconscious*, which is probably still his most influential work on literary studies, Jameson deploys a much richer form of allegory, one better suited to advancing a complex Marxist reading strategy. Borrowing from Northrop Frye, who in turn borrows from the medieval exegetical tradition, Jameson establishes an allegorical model whose richness derives precisely from the reader's having to traverse it dialectically. Three of the four exegetical levels generate the next as a new or further level of meaning, illustrating that when he reads classical Greek or nineteenth-century and twentieth-century European literature, Jameson perceives allegory to be an impoverished—and impoverishing—figure when it insists on a one-to-one relation between interpretation and text. In explaining how medieval allegorists appropriated a pagan model saturated with inappropriate belief systems, he seeks to outline a system of literary interpretation that acknowledges, rather than contains, the contradictions: "The originality of the new allegorical system may be judged by its insistence on preserving the literality of the original texts: it is not here a matter of dissolving them into a mere symbolism, as a rationalistic Hellenism did when, confronted with the archaic and polytheistic letter of the Homerian epic, it rewrote the latter in terms of the struggle of the physical elements with one another, or the battle of vices and virtues." More explicit:

> Allegory is here the opening up of the text to multiple meanings, to successive rewritings and overwritings which are generated as so many levels and as so many supplementary interpretations. So the interpretation of a particular Old Testament passage in terms of the life of Christ—a familiar, even hackneyed, illustration is the rewriting of the bondage of the people of Israel in Egypt as the descent of Christ into hell after his death on the cross—comes less as a technique for closing the text off and for repressing aleatory or aberrant readings and senses, than as a mechanism for preparing such a text for further ideological investment, if we take the term ideology here in Althusser's sense as a representational structure which allows the individual subject to conceive or imagine his or her lived relationship to transpersonal realities such as the social structure or the collective logic of History. (Jameson 1981, 29–30)

This form of allegorical interpretation, which explicitly calls on the tension between the literal (here, allegorical, moral, and anagogical) and various levels of figural is, like the novels by African women to which I have referred, characterized by a productive interchange between different levels.[43]

For feminists, the family reasserts itself continually, interfering with the normative reader's desire or expectation that it give way to a "deeper meaning" or "higher truth" about national life. These fictions require that we perceive the simultaneous production of both literal and allegorical meaning: family does not disappear so that the glory or pathos of nation might be revealed. Instead, family retains its literalness, its banality, as well as its real material and social significance, thereby troubling the tendency of the national allegory to soar into the realm of the transcendent. The allegory produced under these circumstances is characterized by a quality of productive interchange between the figural and the literal.

Family rarely dissolves into a symbol; instead, it reasserts itself in literal terms and interferes with the normative expectation that it give rise to a "higher truth" about national life. The allegory produced is thereby characterized by a quality of interchange between the literal and the figural. The very title of Sow Fall's *L'ex-père de la nation*, for example, turns the naturalized nexus of family, gender, and nation into a single figure—by pointing to its undoing. Through an awkward syntax, Sow Fall's title and novel make visible the slippage between biology or parenting, on the one hand, and national politics, on the other, unstitching a metonymy that is rendered seamlessly in masculine nationalist iconography. It is precisely this quality of interchange instead of the understanding of allegory as a one-to-one correspondence between tenor and vehicle that Jameson does not imagine when writing about the Third World. In the chapters that follow, the dialogue between literal and figurative, domestic and national, is most sharply visible in allegorical readings of *Une si longue lettre* and *Nervous Conditions* and in the interconnected reading of *L'amour, la fantasia* and *Ombre sultane*.

Read in relation to "Third World Literature in the Era of Multinational Capitalism," the women's novels function as a deconstructive supplement to Jameson's argument. In tracing the maneuvers necessary to read this group of texts, I thereby also propose a corrective reading of Jameson's essay, which is fundamentally valuable to Africanists and those who study the Global South in general. Jameson fails to read complex interchange or tension in the Third World precisely because, at the literary level, he is unwilling to perceive this region as one that continues to be shaped by capitalism even after decolonization and, therefore, as over-determined instead of as simply determined. My appropriation of Jameson's national allegory therefore modifies some of his original claims. Novels written by women from the Global South often do have allegories within them, but they are usually subtle (or not immediately visible) and require an act of strong reading to discern them. Moreover, readers who employ allegorical reading strategies (regardless of whether the authors intended to write allegorically) will be more richly rewarded in their reading of the politics of African literature, whether the works are written by men or by women.

Chapter 1 investigates the making of an important nationalist genealogy and unearths a powerful feminine counter-discourse. Igboland was the region in Nigeria where anglophone literature was most actively produced. Flora Nwapa, the first published female novelist in Nigeria and an exemplar of feminine public political reticence in her writing, published her first novel at a time of great interest in nation building. Unlike the male Igbo authors of her generation Nwapa almost entirely ignores the world outside the village in which her protagonist lives, makes one reference to colonialism, and narrates public politics only in very private terms.[44] *Efuru* depicts a strong women's community; men's continual betrayal of the marriage contract is offset by a thriving domestic economy of monetary and social exchange. The novels' enumeration of the eponymous protagonist's traditional virtues (good wife, daughter-in-law, and successful businesswoman) symptomatizes Nwapa's hesitant first steps into the modern world of novelistic authorship. A mere thirteen years later, Buchi Emecheta wrote a novel with far more explicitly anticolonial and nationalist feminism. The open engagement of *The Joys of Motherhood* with the public social sphere, as well as with the private one, is predicated on its conscious self-understanding as a "literary daughter" to *Efuru*.

I read the relationship between the two novels using as a guiding metaphor the historical phenomenon of the Igbo Women's War of 1929. This anticolonial uprising (until the late 1980s, at least) had been written out of the Nigerian national narrative in much the same way that women's literary histories have been marginal to the national tradition.[45] The relation between Chinua Achebe and the Women's War itself is critically significant and points to a connection that is more than symbolic. *Things Fall Apart*, supposedly a "father text" of the contemporary anticolonial novel from Africa and ur-national narrative, can now be read as a direct, causal response to the flurry of anthropological writing that followed the British police response to the women's rebellion, suggesting that gendered anxieties have always lurked around canonical national narratives.[46]

Chapter 2 is also organized around a national-ethnic rubric, this time in francophone and Wolofized Senegal. Its thematic focus is post-independence betrayal, a premise that is the starting point for all three fictional texts and the theoretical-political essay from whose premises they depart: *Xala* (1973), by Ousmane Sembène; *Une si longue lettre* (1979), by Mariama Bâ; and *La grève des battú* (1979), by Aminata Sow Fall. Struggles for national self-determination have been corrupted into choices between various modes of consumption. The new state is driven by individual desire and self-gratification, for people and for things. The tone of the novellas is one of profound disillusionment; all of them take their cue, directly or indirectly, from Fanon's essay on the corruption of the national bourgeoisie. This is the first of two chapters that illustrates the depth and breadth of Fanon's importance to europhone African writers, male and female. All three narratives, and particularly *Xala*, owe an immense intellectual and inspirational debt to Fanon. I trace the relation between this constellation of novels and Fanon's unhappily prescient essay "The Pitfalls of National Consciousness," from *The Wretched of the Earth*. Beginning with *Une si longue lettre*, I read in reverse chronological order to explore the complex ties that bind this early female–feminist work to *Xala*, then I attend to the more straightforward linking of *Xala* to Fanon. In the process of rewriting Sembène's novella, Bâ promotes gender from the secondary to the primary level of analysis.

Une si longue lettre tells the tale of a romance gone wrong, a failed version of precisely the sort of relation Sommer charts in Latin America. Reconsidering this most canonical of novels by Africa women makes visible an intricate—and deeply ambivalent—relation between the novella itself and the polemical Marxist essay to which it is in some manner indebted. *La grève des battú*, published in the same year as *Une si longue lettre*, stands in every way as a "sister text" to it; it also stands in filial dialogue with *Xala*. The conceit of religious charity, specifically alms giving as a requirement of Islam, is turned into the grounds for a monetary, moral, and human economy and results in the beggars' walking off their job. Sow Fall's unsentimental and sharply humorous portrayal of neocolonialism takes up the other side of *Xala*'s Marxism and stands in sharp contrast to the sentimental feminism of *Une si longue lettre*. Moreover I find that being an early and even an important writer does not necessarily enable one to spawn a new writerly generation. With Bâ, it might mean instead that the author recasts stories by earlier writers in such a way as to make visible the assumptions of the older tale, thereby clearing the room for different and, in this case, feminine voices.

The concept of the Bildungsroman, that genre of individual development and, by extension, of conventionality and embourgeoisement, organizes chapter 3. The intertwining of subject formation with nation formation is examined through two very different novels from anglophone Africa of the 1980s: *Nervous Conditions* (1988), by Tsitsi Dangarembga, and *Maps* (1986), by Nuruddin Farah. Written at about the same time, both are novels of contemporary history. More important, both are explicitly feminist stories, invested in the plight of women of all sorts whether urban and educated or illiterate villagers, upwardly mobile or "traditional" and superstitious. Both novels recount the classic move of protagonist from country to city in search of education. The quintessential European and masculine hero of the Bildungsroman undertakes his quest alone; in both these African novels of development, however, the protagonist is doubled or mirrored.

The nation as such is never named in *Nervous Conditions* and must be found through an act of reading. Just as importantly—and inversely—the nation is expressly thematized in *Maps*, the subject of endless speculation only to be undone as a livable mode of social organization by the novel's end. *Nervous Conditions* tells the story of two cousins, intimate friends separated by class and ideology. The dialectic of the novel, however, predicates Tambu's path to education and self-knowledge on Nyasha's political astuteness, which in its extreme form turns into psychological instability. Tambu's sense of herself in the world as a raced, colonized, and class-formed subject, as well as as an ambitious girl, is formed in dialogue with Nyasha. The teleological impulse of the genre is both represented and made available for critique in this classically realist novel. Though Nyasha is better educated than Tambu and for much of the novel her mentor, Nyasha's sensitivity to injustice also makes her psychologically unstable and vulnerable. I read her as a Fanonian protagonist whose existential angst gives the novel its psycho-political dimension.

Chapter 4, which contains my last set of literary close readings, focuses on two novels by one of the most accomplished contemporary African writers, Assia Djebar. The novels' content and, in particular, their form strongly suggest that they be read as a pair, two halves of a whole, as a single Bildungsroman attempting to stretch its bounds. *L'amour, la fantasia* (1985a) and *Ombre sultane* (1987) share a structure of double-threaded narration. *L'amour* alternates between chapters on the public and the private: the domestic story of a girl growing up in Algeria in the 1930s is interspersed with the national conquest of Algeria by the French in 1830 and, later, the war of independence. In *Ombre sultane*, the alternation takes place between two characters, each chapter telling an interiorized tale of two women from the same time but different classes. The narrator, Isma, whose life resembles the growing girl of *L'amour*, is an educated, unveiled, and bourgeois woman. But it is Hajila—who comes from straitened circumstances and whose link to Isma is produced by Isma herself, both women having married the same man, though at different times—who drives the narrative action by secretly and rebelliously unveiling herself in public. Both novels use formal divisions to organize the narrative unfolding, ultimately suggesting toward the end, at the level of form and content, that the distinctions between public and private (domestic and national, even French and Arabic) ultimately cannot hold.

Both novels consist of three parts, the first two of which are sets of contrasting tales recounted in alternating sections. The third part consists of stories of women who are not otherwise part of the narrative action. In *Ombre sultane*, this choral section comes in part 3 and resembles the tale of *One Thousand and One Nights* that the original Scheherazade tells the sultan and her sister. In *L'amour*, the multi-voiced stories appear in part 2, turning into literature the oral-history tales of women who fought during the Algerian War of Independence. Each novel putatively tells the story of an individual entity (woman or nation) that is interrupted by sheer collectivity, the story of someone other than the Bildung protagonist. *Ombre sultane* offers the interiorized richness of Bildungsroman character subjectivity, while *L'amour* illustrates the outline of the development narrative: a girl who passes from childhood to marriage. Together they pose a challenge to the generic form, straining at its boundaries to tell another story.

1. The Joys of Daughterhood
Achebe, Nwapa, Emecheta

> People who had mothers like he had were lost if they did not know how to care for themselves. She looked at him in a sort of agony and thought: "Journeys into the soul are not for women with children, not all that dark heaving turmoil."—BESSIE HEAD, *A Question of Power*

I begin by tracing a particular narration of the African literary tradition, one that corresponds to and underlies the plotting of the anticolonial struggle. As I claimed earlier, most nationalist narratives written by men effaced female agency, featuring women primarily as items of exchange between men. Just as the historiographic tradition suppressed the feminine in its writing or telling of history, so, too, was literary historiography unable to comprehend women's novels that did not explicitly inscribe themselves within the nationalist drama. These invented traditions have been unable to assimilate either women's novels or those anticolonial uprisings by women that predated nationalism, because neither feminine discourse participated in the nationalist story as so named. The erasure of women as subjects is illuminated through examination of Chinua Achebe's

ultra-canonical first novel, *Things Fall Apart,* published in 1958. Reading this "father text" of African novels and its reception through the
critical lens of gender exposes some of the male anxieties manifested
in orthodox nationalism. I will juxtapose literary reading with the
Igbo Women's War of 1929—an indigenous women's uprising to
which *Things Fall Apart* has a complex and vexed relation—and with
two later novels written by women: Flora Nwapa's *Efuru* (1966) and
Buchi Emecheta's *The Joys of Motherhood* (1979). This reading illustrates nationalism's tendentious and gender-marked schemes for regulating the field of postcolonial African writing and for distributing
cultural capital within it. Achebe's fellow Igbo female writers, Nwapa
and Emecheta, must, according to orthodox understandings of African literary production, either plot themselves into a nationalist literary history whose outlines are masculinist or be consigned to the
heap of marginal writers. Emecheta does learn how to emplot herself
into this literary history; she embraces cultural nationalism while
continuing to make domestic politics of primary importance. I submit that her way of doing so is eased because of her awareness of
Nwapa as foremother. Nwapa's engagement with domestic politics
(to the exclusion of macro-politics) allows Emecheta to see what is
missing, encourages her to feel as if she is not the first to tackle these
topics. Her perspective as a second-generation writer and as a daughter allows her greater freedom of engagement and thus permits more
on the relation of macro-politics to micro-politics. (We will see something of this sort later, in the first novel by Mariama Bâ.)

Nwapa is the classic example of an early female writer who was too
timid to speak in the macro-political language of men. Unable to
change the nationalist story and patently lacking the confidence to
enter into dialogue with it, Nwapa, the first female Nigerian novelist,
appears to refuse engagement with nationalist politics altogether.
Efuru, her first novel, captures her imaginary resolution of a contradiction in the male-dominated ideology of the writers of her generation and employs a self-consciously feminine style and domestic subject matter to do so. Only with the subsequent publication of *The Joys
of Motherhood* by the more assertively feminist and openly nationalist
Emecheta, and with the advent of both another literary generation
and the outlines of a counter-discourse in African literary tradition,

does Nwapa's working out of the contradictions of nationalist ideology become visible. *The Joys of Motherhood* establishes an explicitly intertextual relationship with *Efuru* that acknowledges Nwapa's historical status and secures the earlier novel a place in literary history— indirectly exposing the older novelist's ambivalent representation of women's independence.[1]

Things Fall Apart, *Efuru*, and *The Joys of Motherhood* participate in the genealogy of an Igbo novelistic tradition, as well as of its putative "master" discourse, nationalism. The way that feminist anthropologists, historians, and now literary critics have reread the Igbo Women's War, rescuing it from semi-obscurity and re-inscribing it as an indigenous feminist instance of challenge to colonialism, serves as a metaphor for my reading of these two novels by women. If the act of writing is one of the most powerful ways by which women inscribe themselves into history, then the acts of female African writers inscribing themselves and re-inscribing their precursors into a literary history functions as a powerful response to Hegel's infamous dictum on the exclusion of Africans from history.[2] Moreover, when juxtaposed against the canonical *Things Fall Apart*, the popular rebellion of the Igbo Women's War invites an alternative reading of African literary historiography by pointing to the convergence of gendered and nationalist politics and by offering a productive tool with which to read both men's anxieties about gender and women's silence about nationalism.

Historians and anthropologists generally agree that the decentralized polities that constituted nineteenth-century and twentieth-century Igboland in Nigeria provided significant economic and social mobility to its people, particularly to its women. (In fact, social mobility is what allows Okonkwo to rise to the rank of a great man of the village, even though he began his adult life with no benefits from his father.) Igbo social institutions that helped protect women from patriarchal excesses were the *inyemedi* (wives of the clan) and the more influential *umuaada* (daughters of the clan) (Amadiume 1987; Van Allen 1976). Although most women could not own land, they could, and were expected to, make money by trading and could exert economic and political pressure if they prospered.

The Igbo Women's War of 1929 (Ogu Umunwanyi in Igbo) constitutes one such instance of feminine pressure. Archivally recorded by the British as the "Aba Riots," this uprising may be read as the violent culmination of traditional manifestations of Igbo women's power. The uprising was not the first, just the most violent. Other documented women's rebellions took place in Igboland in 1919 and 1925, according to Elizabeth Isichei (1976).[3] In her chapter on the Women's War, Judith Van Allen explains some of the mechanisms of precolonial Igbo women's power:

> To "sit on" or "make war on" a man involved gathering at his compound at a previously agreed upon time, dancing, singing scurrilous songs detailing the women's grievances against him (and often insulting him along the way by calling his manhood into question), banging on the hut with the pestles used for pounding yams, and in extreme cases, tearing up his hut (which usually meant pulling the roof off). This might be done to a man who particularly mistreated his wife, who violated the women's market rules, or who persistently let his cows eat the women's crops. (Van Allen 1976, 61)

This raucous and destructive behavior by women was usually directed at men who were perceived to threaten their personal or economic security.

Contrary to what its name might suggest, the British system of indirect rule under which these women lived did not retain traditional forms of government. The British established a system of native courts and designated Africans to serve on them. Called warrant chiefs, these men rarely held customary positions of respect, were ultimately beholden only to the British, and were, because of their linguistic abilities, powerful intermediaries between colonizer and the rest of the colonized. British reliance on these intermediaries was compounded by the fact that the British themselves rarely spoke the Igbo language. Under these conditions, the colonial judicial system soon became hopelessly corrupt.

With the onset of world economic depression in 1929, and with the steadily falling price of palm oil, a crucial resource in the women's economy, the political setting was complete. When the British indicated that they would extend direct taxation to the eastern provinces, meaning the taxation of adult individuals rather than just of men as heads of household, the women took collective action. In November and December 1929, tens of thousands of Igbo and Ibibio women from the Calabar and Owerri provinces "made war on" the warrant chiefs, as well as on the British overlords. They originally mobilized around the issue of the taxation of women, but their demands soon included abolition of the native courts (or the inclusion of women on them) and the return of all white men to their own country. Information and money for the uprising had been conveyed through the elaborate system of women's market networks.[4]

These uprisings were conducted in a manner consonant with women's traditional exercise of power in the village. Van Allen (1972, 175) describes the Women's War this way:

> Traditional dress, rituals and "weapons" for "sitting on" were used: the head wreathed with young ferns symbolized war, and sticks, bound with ferns or young palms, were used to invoke the powers of the female ancestors. The women's behavior also followed traditional patterns: much noise, stamping, preposterous threats and a general raucous atmosphere were all part of the institution of "sitting on" a man.

The war ended violently, however; approximately fifty women were killed, and another fifty were wounded by gunfire from the police and soldiers. According to Van Allen (1972, 174), "The lives taken were those of women only—no men, Igbo or British, were even seriously injured." Significantly, the women had not believed that they would be hurt, so culturally appropriate were their actions. Of the archival (mis)representations of the Women's War as the Aba Riots, a name that limits its scope and de-politicizes its feminist impetus, Van Allen (1972, 60–61) notes that the control of language means the control of history:

> The British "won," and they have imposed their terminology on history; only a very few scholars have recorded that the Igbo called this the "Women's War." And in most histories of Nigeria today one looks in vain for any mention that women were even involved. "Riots," the term used by the British, conveys a picture of uncontrolled irrational action, . . ."Aba Riots," in addition, neatly removes

women from the picture. What we are left with is "some riots at Aba"—not by women, not involving complex organization, and not involving thousands of women over most of southeastern Nigeria.

Rather than a devastating political reverse, the uprisings can be more accurately read as one of the many blows dealt the colonial state by the natives. The women succeeded in toppling the corrupt system of the warrant chiefs, though none of their other demands were met. As a result of their efforts, the British attempted to emulate the pre-colonial Igbo model through a new system of administration.

In the introduction, I pointed out that although other Africans had published novels before it, *Things Fall Apart* is not only the novel most commonly taught and written about in contemporary African literature, but it has been claimed for paternity. As C. L. Innes (1992, 19) puts it, Achebe "may be deemed the father of the African novel in English." Simon Gikandi elaborates this claim and even when challenged has continued to espouse it (1991, 2001). He anchors this filiative model in the suggestion that Achebe was unique in his ability to recognize the function of the novel both as a depiction of reality and as a vehicle of limitless possibility for constructing and representing a new national identity:

> Achebe's seminal status in the history of African literature lies precisely in his ability to have realized that the novel provided new ways of reorganizing African cultures, especially in the crucial juncture of transition from colonialism to national independence, and his fundamental belief that narrative can indeed propose an alternative world beyond the realities imprisoned in colonial and postcolonial relations of power.

Gikandi reads Achebe's contradictions as inherent in the anxieties of an early anticolonial nationalist, and, like Achebe, he accepts as unchallenged the idea that nationalism consolidates itself through gendered formations. In an earlier version of this chapter (1996), I interpreted mainstream literary nationalism—represented here by *Things Fall Apart*—and in particular, the character of Okonkwo—as an unmediated expression of masculine anxiety. My intent was to sketch the psychic landscape onto which women's novelistic writing emerged, so

as to make visible the obstacles writers had to surmount in getting to
publish. Filiation, which I attribute to Gikandi on Achebe, is commonly associated with male authors. It captures two different perspectives, both of which shape my understanding of the gendering of
African novelistic history. One involves beginnings, in this case that
which helps make visible literary traditions, male and female. The
other sense of filiation, family relations, refers to the intimate or domestic sphere which organizes much of women's writing and through
which it has been read. I claimed of the established terrain, where the
novel loomed large, that feminist readers have long noted that female
characters are generally absent from—and are silent when they do
appear in—this novel.[5] Okonkwo's mother, whose lineage gives the
novel's hero seven years of protection; his senior wife; and almost all of
his daughters are unnamed.[6] This was more than simple inattention to
women, for the absent presence of women was necessary to the construction of the novel's nationalist ideology. Igbo women's social organizations and their "war-making" are effaced in orthodox nationalist
history so that masculine anticolonial rebellion can avoid occupying a
subordinate, feminized role. Achebe's novel is structured by erasures
in a roughly analogous manner and attempts to avoid the representation of colonial relations in gendered terms by inscribing an excessively masculine Igbo man. Female characters are not represented in
any significant numbers; anticolonial nationalist subjectivity operates
in a gendered social space defined primarily by male bodies, namely,
Okonkwo; Unoka, his somewhat lazy father; and Nwoye, his gentle
son. I also claimed that Achebe's preoccupation with the implicitly
gendered pattern of colonial relations meant he could only imagine
male characters as negatively masculine (violent, impatient, proud,
driven to prove self-worth) such as Okonkwo, or negatively feminine
(passive, lazy, perhaps gentle) such as Unoka and Nwoye. Achebe, I
claimed, had no room for a celebratory representation of masculinity. I
was mistaken on the last point.[7]

The preoccupation with anxiety in reading and writing literary
history, especially in feminist studies, is, as Jennifer Fleissner (2002)
notes, itself marked as representing the author in ideological terms,
wherein the critic, removed from the maelstrom of history, is able to
select valuable aspects of what an author says against less valuable

aspects: "[T]his reduction of thought to 'culture'—indeed the nearly universal assumption that 'culture' is the overarching field in which we do our work—has tended to result in the understanding of literary works as the product not of any rational individual expression but rather of collective 'anxieties'" (50). Authorial choice and responsibility is diminished at the cost of producing a structure: forces determine writing. I suggest that Achebe chose his battles.

In an essay that predates the regular practice of gender-oriented scholarship in African literature, Harold Scheub (1970) names Okonkwo as a highly flawed character. Scheub draws attention to how Okonkwo's tendency toward violence and rigidity is juxtaposed against what later feminist critics might call the characteristics of judicious moderation belonging to his friend, Obierika. Above all, says Scheub, Obierika does not distort the communal ideal and that he might better stand as the novel's hero. In disagreeing with my earlier work, Abiola Irele says that the narrative arc of the novel illustrates that Okonkwo's "adoption of the manly ideal is excessive and even wrong-headed" (11). Though a great warrior like Okonkwo and, more important, someone Okonkwo respects, Obierika differs from his friend in at least three significant ways. He disapproves that Okonkwo strikes down the sacrifice-victim, Ikemefuna; in this respect, Obierika and the feminized Nwoye are linked. Obierika sympathetically represents the bond between the long-married old couple Ozoemena and Ndulue, a once-great warrior, telling Okonkwo that Ozoemena died immediately after her husband, explaining to an incredulous Okonkwo that Ndulue always wanted his wife's opinion on important matters (1996 [1958], 47–48). And Obierika is even critical of some violent religious customs of Umuofia, particularly the infanticide of twins.

Anticolonial struggles are frequently represented as a dichotomy; in what I outlined earlier, the colonial/European side is characterized as masculine, while the weak and disorderly native/African side is necessarily feminine. Achebe's dilemma is a difficult one: how to narrate the brutality of imperialism without relying on the model that inscribes African men as submissive or "feminine." One result is his hyper-masculine protagonist Okonkwo, a character who is frequently inflexible in his relations with others. In diametrical opposition, his son Nwoye, who Biodun Jeyifo points out has the most affinity for the "feminine" arts of storytelling, is also the one who "goes over to the colonizers and more or less embraces the colonialist ideology of the 'civilizing mission'" (Jeyifo 1993, 855).

Okonkwo's hyper-masculinity is contrasted in part against the relative moderation of Obierika and in part against the passivity of his own father and son, Unoka and Nwoye. They prefer the "womanish" activities of storytelling and playing the flute. Neither is particularly interested in the warlike exploits that move Okonkwo. It is generally recognized that one of Okonkwo's tragic flaws includes his drive to succeed and be powerful, a drive that is motivated by a fear of appearing weak and ineffective like his father. Thus, he works his way up the social and economic ladder, although his father left him nothing. The irony of Okonkwo's anxious reaction to his paternal inheritance is that the violent masculinity of his life path leads to a death that is just as shameful as that of the lazy Unoka. Neither man can be given a proper burial; instead, both father and son are cast into the Evil Forest. Obierika's gender-balance, then, makes of him a successful warrior, a provider for his family, yet reflective enough to criticize the group without breaking with it. Of course, he is less tormented and tragic—and therefore, far less interesting as a source of narrative action, especially for telling a tale of survival which contains within it a sense of past loss.

While, as I have noted, the historical reception of the Women's War might have significance as a metaphor for an Igbo women's literary tradition, the uprising has a more direct—and problematic—significance for an orthodox masculine nationalist genealogy. Although the war ended violently, its scope and radical potential nevertheless posed a sweeping challenge to British authority and might well have been etched in the memory of some of the Igbo still living during the period when Achebe wrote his first novel. Testifying to the link between colonial power and knowledge, the Igbo historian S. N. Nwabara declares that "the revolt was therefore a major factor that led the government to encourage the study of Ibo indigenous society" (Nwabara 1978, 201).[8] In fact, the anthropologist Sylvia Leith-Ross, who in the 1930s formed part of the British group sent to study Igbo culture in the service of the colonial state, indicates that she was particularly interested in "how much the Riots were still remembered and what shape they took," continuing that "as palm-oil dominates the economic-social situation, so do the Aba Riots still dominate the psychological situation" (Leith-Ross 1965 [1939], 174). Her book *African Women: A Study of the Ibo of Nigeria* is both proto-feminist and one of the early examples of the interrelation of colonial power and women's independence.

In a reading of the impact of Westernization on *Things Fall Apart*, Rhonda Cobham suggests that Achebe's own investment in a type of Victorian ideal of feminine decorum made it possible for him to elide not only the Women's War but also feminine Igbo institutional structures such as the *umuaada*, which helped give rise to it. Because in his nonfiction prose Achebe named Joseph Conrad and Joyce Cary as significant negative literary influences, much has been made about his response to the racism of turn-of-the-century English narrative prose. Extending Cobham's analysis, I suggest that the literary influence of the European novelists on *Things Fall Apart* is shared with that of the anthropological texts generated by Leith-Ross and others, which themselves constitute a discursive response on the part of the British state to the phenomenon of the Igbo Women's War. Achebe famously responded to Conrad's *The Heart of Darkness* in "An Image of Africa" (1978) and responded more directly to anthropological discourse in "Colonialist Criticism" (1975), an essay about a scathing and racist critique of *Things Fall Apart* by a British woman. There he indicated that he was well aware of the conflation of colonial anthropology and state hegemony, observing that the critic's literary style "recalls so faithfully the sedate prose of the district-officer-government-anthropologist of sixty or seventy years ago" (Achebe 1975, 5).

Nowhere is the response to colonial self-consolidation more trenchant than in Achebe's description of the district commissioner, whose projected book, *The Pacification of the Primitive Tribes of the Lower Niger*, reduces Okonkwo's tragic story to "a reasonable paragraph" (1996, 148). The novel's closure, then, in this way overtly sets itself against the discourse of Leith-Ross and other anthropologists. *Things Fall Apart* represents a history, subjectivity, and narrative voice that have been excluded from or misprized in imperial history. This male voice, however, speaks, even if unwittingly, over the silence of the raucous Igbo women who preceded it. Within this reframed literary history, the absence of a novelistic trace of either the Women's

War or even the women's organizations that facilitated it becomes glaring.

In returning to Fleissner's critique of the overuse of the figure of anxiety as a critical tool, I touch on Achebe's final novel. Having been taken to task for the gender politics in his fictional writing, Achebe has taken pains to depict female characters as active political agents. His last novel, *Anthills of the Savannah* (1987), has a female protagonist, Beatrice Okoh, and even includes references to the Women's War of 1929. (It also contains a scene of Beatrice making explicit reference to and aligning herself with Chielo, a priestess in *Things Fall Apart*.) In many ways, *Anthills* is a deeply utopian novel, but it is also rightly characterized by David Maugham-Brown (1991) as vague or ambivalent in its narration. I cannot say whether its weaknesses stem from a sort of narrative diffusion in rendering critically important characters such as Beatrice Okoh, on whom so much of the story depends, or whether it is the result of Achebe's own ambivalence about commitment to strong leadership (that which has failed in the past) along with the idea that the masses own the country. Whatever the source of the limits, this novel does not know how precisely to name for itself the great forces at work at a given historical moment. It cannot sharply delineate the social problem and so falls short of imagining a narrative resolution.[9]

The sociologist Ifi Amadiume, who comes from Achebe's hometown of Nnobi and did fieldwork there, points out, for example, how Achebe rewrites gendered behavior in transferring it from history to literature, always obscuring the "feminine." One example involves his making a local water goddess, the same divinity worshipped by and who gives license to Nwapa's Efuru, into a water god in *Things Fall Apart* (Achebe 1958 [1996], 121). By investigating the local history that Achebe used as a source for the novel, Amadiume illustrates other elisions of the feminine. In the course of representing the Umuofian response to the imported Christian religion that threatens to envelop the Africans, the novel first recounts the story of a fanatical Christian who kills a python—a sacred Igbo totem—then narrates the community's violent response to the incident. According to the village annals Amadiume consults, that particular historical event was very specifically gendered as feminine. It was the women who were affronted by the killing of the python, and their response was to "sit on" the man.[10] In *Things Fall Apart*, however, the transgression is answered by the entire village, the gender specificity neutralized, and no violence or strong action is deployed (110–14).

Despite its paradigmatic status as the first Nigerian women's novel and as one of the first African women's novels, relatively little critical attention has been paid to *Efuru*.[11] Early critics, most of them male, dismissed Nwapa's writing as trivial, useful only for understanding domestic village life. Conversely, defenders of Nwapa, most of them female or feminist, argued that it was precisely *because* she offers such a narrative of Igbo domesticity that she deserves her place in the African canon. My interest here lies less in the authenticity of Nwapa's representation of village life than in the tensions that the first novel written by a woman must confront when written in a colonial or neocolonial situation. Nwapa manipulates the language and narrative form of the colonizer while narrating the story of an "authentic" and independent female character against the backdrop of frequently pejorative representations of female characters by male authors.

Efuru tells the story of a woman notable for her noble birth, beauty, and poise, as well as for her remarkable skill in trading and making money. The eponymous protagonist is also distinguished for her inability to bear children. (Although she does in fact give birth to a daughter who dies in infancy, Efuru is consistently characterized as barren.) Moreover, each of the two men she marries lets her down at some crucial moment in her life, and it is the female village community that sustains her. Efuru's marriage to Adizua, with which the novel opens, is not initially sanctioned, so she helps her new husband earn the bride price that will satisfy her father and tradition. While she becomes increasingly successful at trading, then gives birth to their daughter, he spends increasingly less time at home, then disappears altogether. Shortly afterward, their daughter dies; Adizua does not return for the burial. Nor does he return later for the more important burial of Efuru's father. Later, Efuru takes up with and marries Gilbert, whose Igbo name is Eneberi. Although this marriage appears more promising and is accorded more space in the narrative, Gilbert also reveals himself to be an irresponsible husband by staying away from home, fathering a child without informing Efuru, and even believing unsubstantiated rumors about Efuru's adultery. For her part, Efuru devotes more time to worshiping the female goddess Uhamiri as she continues to prosper. Instead of celebrating her apotheosis, however, the novel ends ambivalently, juxtaposing her economic and social success against her failure at motherhood. *Efuru's* entry into the male-dominated body of African literature marks the beginning of an Igbo dialogue on gender in which Emecheta will later participate.

The text by a man that Nwapa appears most clearly to interrogate in *Efuru* is Cyprian Ekwensi's extremely popular *Jagua Nana*, a novel about a middle-aged prostitute published in 1961. Lloyd Brown called Jagua "one the most frequently discussed heroines of African fiction."[12] Ekwensi depicts a deracinated and narcissistic—if personable—woman whose economic independence derives from her physical desirability and her constant search for sexual gratification. Jagua the prostitute obviously fits one of the two recurring symbols of African literary femininity (the other being Mother Africa). Florence Stratton has pointed to the pervasiveness of this Janus-faced figure for African literature. In the introduction, I argued that these figures function dialectically. Bearing in mind that tradition and modernity are not fixed but contingently formed discourses, I suggest that Efuru is partly such a "traditional" heroine in reaction to the sordid modernity of Jagua Nana.

True to form, Jagua yearns for a conventional married life, despite her unorthodox success. She attempts to bribe Freddie, her young lover, to marry her by financing his college education abroad. Moreover, Jagua's economic independence is explicitly interwoven with her rejection of ethnic identity and embrace of the vices of urban living. She and Freddie "always used pidgin English, because living in Lagos City they did not want too many embarrassing reminders of clan or custom" (Ekwensi 1961, 5).[13] Efuru and Jagua both become quite wealthy, but there the similarity ends. Efuru remains in the village, acquiring economic and social success through the traditional—and morally sanctioned—method of trading. She is untainted by employment or location and thus is of commanding moral stature. And unlike Jagua, who uses her male partners for economic gain, Efuru is deserted by hers, though she accepts this abuse with dignity. In a comparative reading of *Efuru* and *Jagua Nana*, both of which address "the woman question," Uzoma Esonwanne addresses the dilemma of the "united front" stance adopted by cultural nationalists. "The problem was: how to articulate the specificity of women's oppression at precisely the moment when the dominant ideology eschewed internal critique? Those of us who grew up in Nigeria in the late '60s and '70s remember so well how this problem was resolved: Ekwensi's *Jagua* was the literary symptom of a pervasive attempt by men to displace this problem from the realm of the political economy dominated by men to that of an abstracted sexual probity of women themselves. Read against *Jagua*, then, *Efuru* emerges as a far more serious, but ultimately unsatisfactory, attempt through literary art to resolve this contradiction in the ideology of nationalism."[14]

With Efuru, Nwapa disclaims the "naughty" Jagua, thereby rejecting the prostitute side of the binary. Moreover, she subtly aligns her first heroine with the favored Mother Africa side, attributing to her the traditional virtues—except that of fecundity. Because it is a historical novel set in a rural rather than urban environment, and because it was published after *Things Fall Apart*, *Efuru* does conform to the "Achebe School." Unlike most of its male-authored counterparts, novels written by men of this group, *Efuru* does not openly address what Innes and Bernth Lindfors consider to be a defining characteristic of that school: "the conflict between old and new values in Iboland" (Innes and Lindefors 1978, 5–6). As I outlined in the introduction, the dialectic of tradition and modernity and its relation to either the new state or European colonialism is emblematic of nationalist discourse. But because nationalism is such a problematic terrain for women writers, neither it nor any of its avatars, such as the tradition–modernity opposition, is openly engaged in *Efuru*. The patriarchal narrative of nationalist literary history has ignored altogether the gendered logic by which it operates. Much less was it able to acknowledge differently emplotted women's narratives, as Jean Franco notes:

> Without the power to change the story or to enter into dialogue, [early women writers] have resorted to subterfuge, digression, disguise, or deathly interruption. [These situations are pre-feminist]

insofar as feminism presupposes that women are already partici-
pants in the public sphere of debate. This makes it all the more
important to trace the hidden connections and continuities, the
apparently isolated challenges and disruptions of the social narrative
which testify to a history of struggle and disruption, though not
necessarily of defeat. (Franco 1989, xxiii)

Franco exposes the gendered logic that undergirds much nationalism and perceptively points out that, although masculinism "invents"
traditions, this discourse nevertheless functions to circumscribe
much of women's literary response. By rereading *Efuru* as Nwapa's
initial and imaginary resolution of contradictions in the masculinist
nationalist ideology, we may thus put in perspective the ambivalent
response of her protagonist's subjectivity.

While Nwapa's primary object of implied critique is male-dominated nationalism, her novel also indirectly implicates Eurocentric
feminism. At the moment of *Efuru*'s publication, Europe and the
United States were witnessing the birth of the second wave of European feminism. Simone de Beauvoir's *The Second Sex*, originally published 1949, appeared in English translation in 1952, and Betty Frie-
dan's *The Feminine Mystique* appeared in 1963. That *Efuru*'s life
appears to have no contact with Europe, and certainly none with
European-style feminism, means that the narrative's prototype of
female power is Igbo—a notable statement in the face of a post–
Second World War feminism, which implied that the global liberation
of women would begin in the West. Indeed, as the example of the
Women's War of 1929 attests, Igbo culture contains sanctioned opportunities for women's gendered social expression, opportunities that
permitted critiques of men's power. Understanding this obviates locating Europe "as the primary referent in theory and praxis," to use a
phrase from Chandra Mohanty (1987, 52), and it illustrates a recent
historical example of just the localized feminist modes of analysis
Mohanty advocates.

Efuru operates in a feminine register depicting a world of domestic
activity where dialogue is privileged over action and where, in the
words of Carole Boyce Davies, "Men are shown to be intruders"
(Davies 1986b, 249). Cooking, fashion, proverbs, rumors, childrearing,

and marketing stratagems, the defining discourses of rural Igbo femininity, occupy the narrative's center stage. Elleke Boehmer celebrates Nwapa's expression of "a self-generating orality" and declares that she uses a Kristeva-like "choric language" to enable and empower, to evoke "the vocality of women's everyday experience" (Boehmer 1991 12, 16). Masculine tales of adventure and men's social space are relegated to the periphery of the novel. Men are portrayed as desirable and occasionally admirable but often as completely incomprehensible, as in the examples of the three unreliable husbands: Adizua, Adizua's father, and Gilbert.

A folktale Efuru tells some of the village children on a moonlit night serves as metaphor for the larger novel's investment in a women's community—and reveals its anger with men. The tale's only male character is the villain. The (unnamed) protagonist is "so beautiful that she was tired of being beautiful"; Nkwo, the youngest, is also very beautiful and "the kindest of them all" (Nwapa 1966, 106). When the protagonist is pursued for marriage by a maggot-eating blue spirit so strong that their mother cannot protect her, she turns for help to her sisters, whose names correspond to the four days of the Igbo week. Eke, Afo, and Orie refuse her, but Nkwo takes in both sister and her new husband, helping the girl negotiate around a dinner of maggots. At night, the two sisters trick the spirit, run out of the house while he is sleeping, and burn it and him down. At the tale's end, Efuru tells Gilbert (and the readers) that women spend Nkwo day buying and selling (Nwapa 1966, 116), then collecting their debts.[15]

Efuru recounts the tale directly before her upcoming marriage to her second husband and soon after she formally leaves the house of the first. Positioned liminally, the tale foreshadows the end of her marriage to Gilbert. It claims unambiguously that women's relationships with each other are the most secure and that these relationships, like the days set aside for them, are imbricated in an economy of exchange, particularly that of trading commodities. It is in trade (and thus through relations with each other) as much as in marriage and childbirth that women obtain power in Igbo society.

While the outer frame of narration offers a more subdued challenge to the institution of marriage, it nevertheless substantiates the embedded tale's claims about gender solidarity through its presentation of the friendship of Efuru and Ajanupu, and it binds the feminine exchange of gossip and advice with the (equally feminine) exchange of goods and money. Early in the novel, Ajanupu, a character who frequently advises Efuru on domestic matters, offers to collect some of Efuru's debts, since the younger woman is not as practiced at this feminine art. Ajanupu is intransigent with Efuru's debtor and when she returns home finds on her doorstep one of her own creditors, who, rather fittingly, is equally intransigent with her. Through this episode, the novel illustrates its circulation of the overlapping discourses of domestic economy and market economy.

It is at the novel's end, however, that the power of a feminine community is made manifest, and then only in response to masculine perfidy. Efuru's unknown illness is rumored to have resulted from adultery, although no sexual partner is ever named. Gilbert believes the rumors, and Ajanupu vigorously comes to Efuru's defense, questioning his judgment, education, and even his family history for believing such a scandalous thing of his wife. Angered, he slaps her so hard that she falls down. Her response evokes the traditional power of Igbo women: "She got up quickly for she was a strong woman, got hold of a mortar pestle and broke it on Gilbert's head. Blood filled Gilbert's eyes" (Nwapa 1966, 217). The pestle, an important domestic tool, is also the same instrument brandished by angry Igbo women when they "sit on" a man. In its position at the end of the novel's penultimate chapter, this incident underscores Efuru's move toward a woman's community, which culminates in the eventual worship of Uhamiri. Only with a great deal of ambivalence can the novel bring itself to represent an economically and socially powerful woman who is desirable to men *and* represent many of those men as lacking. Precisely because *Efuru* has no strong precursors in novels written by men (as Efuru, the character, herself had no strong female role models while growing up), Nwapa can only inscribe such a strong woman tragically, and the logic of the text, which so validates femininity, appears to lead Efuru to the quintessential marker of femininity: biological motherhood. Unlike Achebe's Okonkwo, whose tragic flaw is psychological, Efuru's "tragic flaw"—her barrenness—is utterly biological. Given the flexible construction of sex and gender in Igbo societies, this gender mark is ironic indeed.

Nwapa launches her feminist critique not at the institution of motherhood so much as at that of marriage (or of heterosexual relations in general); more accurately, it confronts all obstacles to women's strength and self-sufficiency. What the narrative represents as incomprehensible is why Efuru's two ex-husbands should spurn such an extraordinary, desirable, and accommodating woman. This unanswered—perhaps unanswerable—*psychological* question about marital relations is displaced into the *biological* problematic of childlessness. In fact, marriage as such is a narrative casualty, while childrearing is not. Not only are Efuru's two marriages failures; so is that of her first husband Adizua's parents. Few successful marriages are visible. Neither marital relations nor the presence of husbands impede Ajanupu or other significant characters from their trading, socializing, or childrearing. The novel's doubts about male–female relations are displaced onto their fundamental biological consequence, that of reproduction; this means, ironically, that biology does appear to determine destiny in the first Nigerian woman's novel. Because the text cannot bring itself to reject the normative discourse of marriage, it posits failed or absent versions of the married couple and inscribes its protagonist with the "tragic flaw" of barrenness, which removes her from marital circulation. Yet the novel also challenges marriage as women's only avenue to power by staging a confrontation between married life and participation in an independent female community (represented here by the different women of the village and culminating in Uhamiri worship) and it couples Efuru's failure within marriage (her infertility) with her exercise of another traditional, female-gendered virtue: making money.

Although *Efuru* moves toward a celebration of the protagonist's independence, economic success, and goodness, the novel displays a constant undercurrent of doubt, ending on a note of profound ambivalence about the ability of any woman without children to be completely happy. In the Bakhtinian sense, *Efuru*'s dialogism comprises the competing discourses of economic independence and maternal satisfaction, the latter of which, I have argued, is a result of displaced concern regarding male–female marital relations. Repeatedly the text offers advice on what a woman should do to conceive and how she should conduct herself during pregnancy, childbirth, and the upbringing of the child. In fact, Oladele Taiwo calls the narrative "almost a manual of mothercare" (Taiwo 1984, 54).[16] But motherhood is the one condition that the otherwise perfect Efuru cannot satisfy. Except for this defining trait, she conforms in every way to the ubiquitous Mother Africa figure, signifier of tradition, which so dominates the discursive landscape of cultural nationalism. Deploying tradition strategically, Nwapa creates a protagonist who conforms to certain aspects of tradition in the service of a modern literary subjectivity and genre.

The ambivalence over motherhood resonates most audibly in the novel's closing lines, which have been read by several critics, including Lloyd Brown (1981) and Maryse Condé (1972), as key to understanding the text. Although Uhamiri appears to have everything she needs, the narrative suggests that motherhood is necessary to completely fulfill her and, by extension, her disciple Efuru:

> Efuru slept soundly that night. She dreamt of the woman of the lake, her beauty, her long hair and her riches. She had lived for ages at the bottom of the lake. She was as old as the lake itself. She was happy, she was wealthy. She was beautiful. She gave women beauty and wealth but she had no child. She had never experienced the joy of motherhood. Why then did the women worship her? (Nwapa 1966, 221)

Although it was published only thirteen years after *Efuru*, Emecheta's *The Joys of Motherhood* emerged into an existing women's literary community and does not show the same hesitancy or ambivalence as the earlier novel.[17] While acknowledging her debt to *Efuru* through the similarity of the protagonists' stories, Emecheta revises and extends that novel and launches a biting critique of both indigenous patriarchy and colonialism.

Emecheta derived her title from the quoted paragraph from *Efuru*. More important is *The Joys of Motherhood*'s recognition of its precursor's ambivalence about the childless woman's possibilities for happiness. The later narrative gives *its* protagonist, Nnu Ego, Efuru's primary unfulfilled wish—many times over, to the point of misery. By (re)writing the phenomenon of Nnu Ego's "barrenness/fecundity" to coincide with her change of husbands, Emecheta interrogates Efuru's "tragic flaw" by shifting responsibility for conception to the man. This textual move is especially important in African literature, where motherhood is so frequently thematized and infertility routinely is assumed to be the "fault" of the woman. Moreover, Emecheta's very act of writing this novel draws attention to the ironic status of the "barren" *Efuru* as the "mother" text of (anglophone) African women's literature. In so doing, Emecheta deftly appropriates the male purview of the production of texts by conflating it with the female production of children—and comments on the exclusion or absence of women from the tradition of African letters. She also rescues Nwapa from domestic oblivion and reintroduces her as a political actor.

For much of their stories, the protagonists of *Efuru* and *The Joys of Motherhood* have similar personal and family histories. Both Efuru and Nnu Ego come from Igbo villages. Both are very attractive women, the cosseted only daughters of their fathers. The fathers, Nwashike Ogene and Nwokocha Agbadi, respectively, are wealthy warrior athletes, important men who are highly respected in the community. Each daughter is also her father's favorite, in part because she is the only child of his favorite woman. The determining narrative similarity appears to be that the mothers of both protagonists are dead when the narratives open, leaving their daughters with no strong female model on which to pattern their search for independence. Indeed, both daughters are particularly attached to their fathers. Having been educated primarily by conservative fathers, Efuru and Nnu Ego are deeply invested in attaining the respect that adherence to traditional feminine mores offers. Perhaps because of their privileged backgrounds, neither is particularly rebellious. Both marry twice; in each case, the first marriage is terminated because the husband rejects her. And for at least a short time, both are stigmatized by an inability to bear children. Finally, both are skilled market women who achieve some measure of economic independence through successful trading.

Emecheta's depiction of a female character who shares so much of Efuru's background must inevitably call attention to the difference between the two. Through the character of Nnu Ego, Emecheta interrogates Nwapa's idealistic portrayal of a woman's struggle and of Efuru as the perfect (Igbo) woman. Rachel Blau Du Plessis (1985, 84–85) suggests that celebrating a female character because she is exceptional only reinforces the norm of prescribed behavior for other women, setting "in motion not only conventional notions of womanhood but also conventional romantic notions of the genius, the person apart, who, because unique and gifted, could be released from social ties and expectations." Apparently adhering to this logic, Emecheta questions the ease of Efuru's success by presenting a much less exceptional female character. In contrast to the noble, talented, and indomitable Efuru, who overcomes her life's problems and eventually determines her own destiny, Nnu Ego is substantially weaker and pettier in her dealings with others. Also in contrast to Efuru, Nnu Ego leaves the village, and any protection it might offer, for Lagos. It is there that she experiences the brunt of indigenous patriarchy and the brutal effects of poverty under imperialism. Ultimately, she dies an ignoble death, alone.

Emecheta also responds to Nwapa's more guarded treatment of imperialism for Igbo people as she represents two less idealized feminine figures in *The Joys of Motherhood*. The first is Ona, a woman of the precolonial period; the second is her colonial daughter, Nnu Ego. The historical specificity of this later text indicates that Efuru's contemporary is not Nnu Ego but her mother, Ona. Emecheta thus comments both chronologically and tropologically on her predecessor's protagonist, for while the events of Efuru's life parallel Nnu Ego's, it is with Ona that Efuru shares a certain precolonial, culturally sanctioned independence in village life. *The Joys of Motherhood* affirms *Efuru*'s claim that precolonial Igbo women had more freedom than did their colonized descendants. Of the difference between the two generations, the later narrator says: "To regard a woman who is quiet and timid as desirable was something that came after his [Ona's lover Agbadi's] time, with Christianity and other changes" (Emecheta 1979, 10). However, acknowledging that Igbo women enjoyed far less freedom under colonialism does not blind Emecheta to their subjection under indigenous patriarchy. Ona's struggles with her lover, Agbadi, occasionally result in her public humiliation. Moreover, being a "male daughter" accords her status and permits her to contribute sons to her father's diminishing line but prevents her from marrying.

Reading *The Joys of Motherhood* from the perspective of *Efuru*, however, offers a different vantage point on the effects of European imperialism than if we read the text solely on its own terms. Although the later narrative vividly depicts the misery of colonialism, it represents it as an act committed *on* Africans and declines to comment on African complicity with or resistance to the phenomenon. While *The Joys of Motherhood* does not depict the precolonial period as paradisiacal, it barely examines colonial relations of power within the Igbo village hierarchy. In contrast, *Efuru* offers a perceptive, albeit narratively marginal, account of the events that preceded colonialism and aided in its acceleration; in so doing, it manages a subtle critique of the protagonist's family history. Efuru's family, which historically has had both stature and wealth, is secure in the village hierarchy: "Her family was not among the newly rich, the wealth had been in it for years" (Nwapa 1966, 19). Toward the end, however, the novel undermines that stature by revealing at her father's death the manner in which he obtained his riches:

> It was the death of a great man. No poor man could afford to fire seven rounds of a cannon in a day. . . . The cannons were owned by very distinguished families who themselves took part actively in slave dealing. . . . Now the shooting of the cannon did not only announce the death of a great man, but also announced that the great man's ancestors had dealings with the white men, who dealt in slaves. (Nwapa 1966, 200–201)

This narrative move puts into question some of the history from which Efuru's family derives its prestige. Moreover, the novel suggests that the construction of Igbo history—indeed, of Igbo patriarchy—is determined by the interests of the hegemony. Because of both Nwashike Ogene's stature and the chronological removal of their ancestors' histories, Nwosu and the fishermen do not connect the death of this great man with the cannon that celebrates his greatness. His role in the slave trade will probably slip through the cracks of communal memory; only his wealth and stature will be remembered. Thus, *Efuru* rejects the nostalgic approach to Ogwuta's past, pointing instead to traces of colonial violence evident in the structures of the current hierarchy. In the more active narrative style of *Things Fall Apart*, imperialism signifies a sudden cultural collision. By contrast, Nwapa intimates the gradual ways in which European violence permeated and transformed Igbo culture. In dialogue with this predecessor-novel, then, *Efuru* illustrates the complicity of some Africans with the European colonialist enterprise, the commoditization of Africans that developed from the slave trade, and the resulting colonial conquest of the continent.

Although the precolonial period is not idealized, *Efuru* is idealistic in its representation of a supportive women's community. Emecheta challenges this idealism by representing the great desire for—and continual frustration of—such a community. She also engages Nwapa's idyllic depiction of rural Igbo life by conjoining it to a depiction of urban life as it develops under the conditions of colonialism. For Nnu Ego, this lack of community partly results from the absence of other, older women. The cross-generational protection from men's power that Ajanupu, the sister of Efuru's mother-in-law, offers Nwapa's heroine is rewritten as the unsuccessful attempt of Nnu Ego's mother, Ona, to secure greater freedom for Nnu Ego than she had herself enjoyed. Ona's deathbed wish of Agbadi is "to allow [their daughter] to have a life of her own, a husband if she wants one" (Emecheta 1979, 28). Agbadi agrees, but soon arranges one marriage after another for their pliant daughter. Later, after she has moved to Lagos, Nnu Ego's friendship with Cordelia is cut short when Cordelia's husband finds work far away. Since Cordelia had helped Nnu Ego survive the loss of her first baby and had explained gender and racial power relations in Lagos, the loss of this friendship is especially felt. Nnu Ego's friendship with the Yoruba woman Iyawo, who at one point saves Nnu Ego and her son from starvation, is always tenuous because of the economic inequality of their situations.

It is through the character of Adaku, Nnu Ego's co-wife in Lagos, that *The Joys of Motherhood* most thoroughly explores the possibility of a neocolonial urban Igbo women's community; it is also through her that the text illustrates such a community's failure. The tension between the women is due partly to their competition for limited resources in the urban colonial context. The cramped single room in which the Owulum family lives in poverty contrasts with the clearly delineated women's living space that distinguishes the rural life described in *Efuru* and with the greater control that women in that context claim over their economic resources and their sexual activity.[18]

Through its depiction of the failed cooking strike mounted by the co-wives, *The Joys of Motherhood* challenges the patience with which Efuru waits for her husbands to behave responsibly. In an attempt to force Nnaife to give over all of his money to his hungry family instead of spending much of it on alcohol, Adaku instigates a cooking strike and convinces Nnu Ego to join her.[19] Within a village economy, men would have no recourse other than to capitulate or do their own cooking. In the city, however, Nnaife's male co-workers share their lunches with him, thus illustrating new and modem forms of brotherhood. The women's strike is soon abandoned.

The quiet acceptance and waiting characteristic of Efuru are proved ineffective in this new context, and *The Joys of Motherhood* suggests that in new contexts different modes of women's resistance have to be adopted. Adaku's departure from the Owulum family and her brief period of prostitution may be read as just such a strategy of resistance. By becoming a prostitute, Adaku is able to accumulate enough capital to begin a more prosperous cloth vending business and move out of the room, leaving little doubt that she is happier in her new living arrangement. Moreover, her new economic security represents a significant measure of success in the context of Igbo valorization of women as good traders, and it contrasts sharply with Nnu Ego's continued poverty. Through Adaku, *The Joys of Motherhood* responds to and subverts the authority of Jagua Nana, the "naughty" Igbo prostitute of Ekwensi's novel. Through his titillating representation of Jagua as a violator of traditional taboos, Ekwensi upholds the patriarchal discourse she is supposed to subvert. In contrast, Emecheta's text does not linger on the details of Adaku's prostitution. It depicts only her decision and the subsequent horror of the Ibuza community in Lagos.[20]

By emptying prostitution of glamour and foregrounding it as a variant of commodity exchange, the feminist narrative thus refigures the topos of the prostitute. Most important, unlike Jagua (or Efuru and Nnu Ego), Adaku is not interested in (re)marriage, choosing to live outside the boundaries of patriarchal protection: " 'I want to be a dignified single woman. I shall work to educate my daughters, though I shall not do so without male companionship.' She laughed again. 'They do have their uses' " (Emecheta 1979, 170–71).

The Joys of Motherhood interrogates Efuru's easy success and adherence to a certain tradition by separating passive acceptance of tradition from active pursuit of power and locating them in rival characters.[21] "Tradition" is represented by Nnu Ego (who bears the children Efuru desires); the more "modern" woman is represented by Adaku (who controls her destiny and matches Efuru's economic independence and her status as successful trader). This strategy permits Emecheta to privilege the latter over the former, thus valorizing Efuru's independence without undercutting her success, as does Efuru's creator, Nwapa. In this light, the final passages of *The Joys of Motherhood* constitute a response to the famous last paragraph of *Efuru*. If one of the most important moments of ideological negotiation in any work occurs in the choice of a resolution, then Nwapa's resolution of her novel deserves special consideration. The ambivalence characteristic of the later part of *Efuru* becomes so acute and the discourse of motherhood so elevated by the time one reads the concluding paragraph that the success of Uhamiri and, by extension, of Efuru is subverted. In response, Emecheta blatantly criticizes her precursor's privileging of motherhood through *her* last lines. The poignant depiction of Nnu Ego's death represents the final undermining of *Efuru*'s maternal discourse:

> After such wandering on one night, Nnu Ego lay down by the roadside, thinking that she had arrived home. She died quietly there, with no child to hold her hand and no friend to talk to her. She had never made many friends, so busy had she been building up her joys as a mother. . . .
>
> Stories afterwards, however, said that Nnu Ego was a wicked woman even in death because, however many people appealed to her to make women fertile, she never did. . . . Nnu Ego had it all, yet still did not answer prayers for children. (Emecheta 1979, 224)

By highlighting Nnu Ego's self-abnegation in favor of her children, *The Joys of Motherhood* responds to its precursor's last line ("Why then did the women worship her?"). It thereby signals a return to the discourse of economic independence that the childless Uhamiri represents in *Efuru*.

A closer look, however, reveals that Emecheta is invested most in critiquing women who passively accept oppressive institutional structures under the guise of adherence to "tradition." We see this in much of Nnu Ego's later life; the same adherence to "tradition" informs Efuru's self-doubt about marriage and motherhood. Moreover, *The Joys of Motherhood* claims that, while it might have been possible to be compliant during precolonial (and even colonial) times, imperialism and neocolonialism demand a vigorous and different response. Though passive to her husbands' indifferent treatment of her, Efuru is protected by the larger women's community. In *The Joys of Motherhood*, the lack of such a community—the result of the ravages of colonialism, modernization, and the constant uprooting the two engender—is named as a cause of Nnu Ego's suffering. What might appear to be "modern" in Adaku, such as her entrepreneurial spirit, independence, and stamina, are, in fact, traits intimately associated with the audacious (and "traditional") market women who rose up in the Women's War.

The division of Efuru's discourse into that of Nnu Ego and Adaku favors that of Adaku. By foregrounding the passivity and misery of Nnu Ego, the narrative suggests that Adaku's greater rebellion contributes to her greater happiness. Adaku's break with the conventions of Ibuza society, however, also brings about her exclusion from it and, ultimately, from the narrative itself. Although independent and well-to-do, she and her daughters nevertheless live apart from the community of Ibuza emigrants, which disapproves of her. Once she leaves the Owulum family, she virtually disappears from the narrative. The last times she appears are special occasions for Nnu Ego's children, and both times Adaku gives them expensive presents. Adaku's subsequent behavior suggests that, had Nnu Ego been willing, a friendship free from the strain of close quarters and food shortages might have developed between the two women. Despite her curiosity about Adaku's new lifestyle, Nnu Ego is too proud and worried about her standing within the community to maintain a friendship with her former co-wife. As a result of the break, no news of Adaku's personal life or business dealings is offered. It is as if the text cannot contain so radical a choice as becoming a prostitute. By consigning such rebellious acts to the margins, Emecheta articulates both their potential and their social consequences while preventing them from dominating the rest of the narrative.

The topos of rebellion links these two novels. Nwapa's creation of a heroine who is a financially and socially successful Igbo woman constitutes an act of rebellion against an Igbo literary tradition dominated by male writers and female absences. Yet this assertive depiction of Efuru marginalizes the day-to-day struggles that such a character must confront. Moreover, Efuru's desire to be traditional (to uphold the institution of motherhood) threatens to subvert the text's manifest assertion of women's independence. Thirteen years after *Efuru's* publication, Emecheta interrogates Nwapa's elision of indigenous patriarchy and the colonial oppression of Igbo women, an oppression that *Efuru's* insistence on the valorization of tradition reinforces. Despite the critique of *Efuru* by *The Joys of Motherhood*, the relation of the second text to the first is not a violent rewriting. Rather, their intertextual relation is one that ultimately emphasizes the affinities that marginalized women writing in a shared tradition must acknowledge. In its rebellion against the "mother text," *The Joys of Motherhood* writes the conservatism of its precursor into the text through Nnu Ego and its rebelliousness out of it through Adaku. The silencing of Adaku's radicalism need not be equated with absence, however. Instead, it can be read as eluding textual compromise. The nearly silent presence of Adaku, like that of the historical phenomenon of the Women's War, resists narrative closure and thereby marks a rebellious potential that has not yet run its course.

Although gender should constitute a primary category of analysis, it is (still) too often conceived of as a marginal and private discourse within African letters. Both African historiography and literary historiography have pretended to be gender-neutral when, in fact, their genealogies reveal an implicit ideology of gender. As a result, the "feminine" has been elided, and until now nationalism has lacked the means by which to integrate either the Igbo Women's War or the first Nigerian woman's novel into its narrative. The "real" Women's War, itself a historical link to *Things Fall Apart* and a metaphorical link between *Efuru* and *The Joys of Motherhood*, serves as a reminder to the male-dominated nationalist tradition of the rebellious potential of the feminine. Its eruption into history challenges conventional, patriarchal, and top-down historiographies. Emecheta's self-consciously intertextual dialogue with her predecessor, Nwapa, about the lives and representations of Igbo women similarly reclaims for African women their own rightful inscription into literary history.

2. The Loved and the Left

Sembène, Bâ, Sow Fall

The winner of the first Noma Award, the oldest and still the most important African book prize, *Une si longue lettre* (1979) caused something of a stir when it was first published.[1] It became, and remains today, one of the most (if not the most) frequently taught African novels by a woman in Europe, North America, and sub-Saharan Africa. It is one of the most discussed francophone novels by students at all levels of African literature, from master's theses and chapters in doctoral dissertations to refereed journal articles and chapters in anthologies. At one level, *Lettre* is important because of its great popularity. Its brevity, clarity, and moments of lyricism have made it one of the most commonly used texts in introductory French literature courses in the United States and England.[2] Christopher Miller (1990) makes a strong claim for it as a canonical novel. In translation, it has been a mainstay in secondary-level and tertiary-level anglophone African courses and syllabi. Early on, it was recognized as speaking a particularly powerful human truth. *Ngambika* (Davies and Graves 1986), the first collection of feminist criticism on African literature, is dedicated to Bâ and, indeed, the two essays therein that address francophone writing both focus on *Lettre*. Bâ's second novella, *Un chant écarlate* (1982), curiously enough, has not received the same level of scholarly engagement.[3] The outsize place that *Lettre* occupies in genealogies of francophone writing has meant that not until fairly recently did Nafissatou Diallo's *De Tilène au plateau* (1975) receive its due as the first autobiographical novel by a woman from Senegal.[4] For those who consider autobiographies too close to the genre of memoir to constitute "real" novels or fiction, the honor of being the first female novelist historically, if quietly, has gone to Aminata Sow Fall, also of Senegal, whose *Le Revenant* was published in 1976.

Although Bâ did not call herself a feminist, *Lettre* has nevertheless been embraced for an African feminist tradition. Feminism in African literature exists in diacritical relation to cultural nationalism. Because African feminist theory was strongly determined by the politics of independence movements, feminist literary criticism developed in diacritical relation to cultural nationalism. That is to say, although it has been in defensive engagement with cultural nationalism, African feminist literary criticism has always included within its self-understanding a strong component of the advocacy of cultural nationalism. *Lettre* has attained so much visibility that, until quite recently, one would have been hard pressed to name African women who had written novels in French before Bâ. Indeed, although he is well aware of the novels by both Diallo and Sow Fall, Miller (1990, 270) says of Bâ that "the explicitness of her position on writing and on women's issues as well, would appear to place her in the role of leader, and, posthumously, of prophet; she seems to speak and write as the founder of a tradition yet to come."[5]

For many, though not for Miller, the tradition–modernity binary has long stood as the sum total of the novel's statement: that of a "traditional woman," meaning a woman who refuses divorce, stoically accepting her diminished marital lot in life, in this instance narrating her story from within the space of a Muslim widow's confinement.[6] As a result, the thoroughly modern question of the novel's relation to a larger Senegalese literary history has not been much addressed. This is what Miller admirably wishes to do. I am in sympathy with his claim that Bâ is a foremother and her first work, a progenitor. He says of the novel that the "text [has] the aura of prophecy, as the harbinger of a general coming of women to writing (the production of a corpus) and perhaps even of a *canon* that is to come" (Miller 1990, 273–74). As of 2009, I know of no literary texts that *Lettre* has inspired, as either epigone or antagonistic interlocutor.[7] If, however, one were to read Bâ not as an authorial foremother or inaugurator but as a follower herself, a "daughter" or, perhaps, "sister," one might produce a richer set of family metaphors through which to understand the novel as it engages with Senegalese preoccupations of the 1970s, the decade that followed independence. I contend that Bâ writes herself as a woman and feminist into an already existing Senegalese novelistic tradition. Her entrance does indeed alter "the male corpus of francophone writing" as Miller (1990, 285) asserts, but the tradition that she alters and the alteration itself is most fully explicated by attention to what the novel engages, retains, amplifies, and discards. It is the act of alteration that allows the sharpest glimpses of Bâ's importance, which goes beyond her status as "first" and helps explain her continuing popularity. Through my reading of *Lettre* and its intertexts, I show how a national literature emerges, not magically or autochthonously, but dialogically and intertextually, sometimes polemically and sometimes ambivalently, out of a set of preoccupations, anxieties, conversations, and silences.

Like chapter 1, this chapter is constellated around a national-ethnic rubric—in this instance, the francophone Wolof of Dakar.[8] Ethnicity itself is less important than ethnic culture. The previous chapter, on Nigerian literary culture, traced a relation between the Igbo and the British, between male and female writers, between and among different female writers themselves, and through it all between the writing of alternative histories in relation to the vexed question of feminine beginnings. Here I propose an intertextual reading of three novellas and a film, and I pay particular attention to how each represents disillusionment in Senegal of the mid-to-late 1970s. *Lettre* is one of those novels. *La grève des bàttu*, Aminata Sow Fall's second novel, also published in 1979, is another. The third novel—and film—that shapes and inspires both Sow Fall and Bâ is Ousmane Sembène's *Xala* (1973), a novella he wrote out of the screenplay for his film in 1974 of the same name.

The bureaucrat's crucial advantages are his education and specialized training, which make his activities mysterious and un-
intelligible to many of the subjects, as well as his institutional
position as an officer of the state. . . . The people may not have
the means to understand just *how* they are being swindled, but it
must be said that they do (at least among the Wolof) realize that
they *are* swindled. The apparatus of Senegalese officialdom is lo-
cally seen at least in broad outline as a parasitic body.
—DONAL O'BRIEN, 1975

Donal O'Brien's acid critique of corruption in post-independence
Senegal might appear tangential to a discussion of early feminism and
gender politics in the Senegalese novel. My contention is that all of
the authors I examine—Bâ, Sembène, and Sow Fall—represent versions of his caustic depiction of the malaise that gripped Senegal in
the mid-1970s. All three novellas and the film depict the aftermath of
independence as a period of broken promises and failure, and all
contrast the current moment with the idealism, hope, and lost potential of the time of independence, a moment that is now squarely in
the past tense. All represent the postcolonial bourgeois character
who, to different degrees, resembles O'Brien's swindling bureaucrat,
unwilling or unable to live up to the responsibilities of his new position. Everywhere this character engages in "mysterious and unintelli-
gible" acts, and in the works by both Sembène and Sow Fall, he
clearly functions as a parasite on the national body. At the level of
basic type in the novellas and the film, the character who most visibly
stands for the national bourgeoisie is a middle-age man who acts
selfishly rather than on behalf of the collectivity, whether that be
nation or family; individual gain and self-aggrandizement win over
the more virtuous pre-independence behavior in favor of the group
he once espoused. All three novellas were produced fifteen to eighteen years after independence during a period in which Senegal was a
one-party state.

Senegal became independent in 1960 with a constitution that divided power between the president, Léopold Sédar Senghor, and the
prime minister, Mamadou Dia. In 1962, Dia staged an unsuccessful
coup d'état and was removed from office. In 1963, Senghor ushered in a
new constitution that greatly increased his presidential power. He

formed the Senegalese Socialist Party (UPS) in 1966, which he headed;
it became the state's only legal political party. Unsurprisingly, Senghor
was reelected in 1968 and 1973. Civil unrest accompanied this consolidation of power—for economic as well as political reasons. For some
years, the price of peanuts had fallen on the world market, and aid from
France had diminished. All of this was exacerbated by a Sahelian
drought of several years, which greatly increased the number of people
who left farms in northern Senegal for the cities, especially Dakar.
Senegal was also rocked by a series of strikes around this time, especially in 1968, 1971, and 1973. This is the background against which the
texts I examine came into existence.

The film *Xala* had been shown elsewhere before it was seen in
Senegal, where it was screened in 1975, although state censors required that it first undergo a dozen edits.[9] It was immensely successful and so was in a position to serve as a point of conversation,
perhaps provoking Sow Fall and Bâ to respond in their novels, both of
which were published in 1979. Bâ and Sow Fall retain in their fiction
the disillusionment with nationalism that is so visible in *Xala*, although both discard some aspects of Sembène's critique. Sow Fall
drops Sembène's use of explicit sexual topics, although she shares a
representation of popular uprising with him. At the level of plot, Sow
Fall makes a much more sympathetic claim for religion than does
Sembène. The case of Bâ is more complicated. Not only does her
work significantly diminish Sembène's pointed critique of class relations, but it also removes the sharp and biting humor of interclass
tensions. In refusing the satiric mode of the African fable, *Lettre*
produces—and develops—the register of novelistic sentiment, exploring the suffering and disillusionment of its protagonist, Ramatoulaye.[10] *Lettre* is structured around competing notions of love, framing
important questions in Ramatoulaye's life in terms of marriage, sexuality, and children. Thickening the description of the novel's world
allows me to illustrate its ideological limits, which produce generic
innovations that are more pronounced than in Sow Fall.

Unlike Miller, who opposes what he perceives to be a tendency
within African literary studies to celebrate nationalism blindly and
who has sought alternative modes of reading around themes of ethics
and ethnicity, I suggest that the stakes of *Lettre* are not fully visible
until one examines its interlocking structure of erotics and politics,

which throws into relief the relation of the novel to decolonization and, especially, to nationalism. By reading *Lettre* for a public political agenda bound up with the new nation-state, rather than simply celebrating its feminine voice, I affirm a genuinely new perspective on the relation of the middle-class intellectual, particularly the female intellectual, to the new nation. This novel written by a woman has been celebrated primarily as a personal and psychological statement, and I claim that reading for the figure of the nation in *Lettre* discloses an evident but relatively undiscussed engagement with macro-politics, which begins with the family but extends beyond it. When juxtaposed against two other texts of the same period, *Lettre*'s representation of what I have called erotics and politics (and might also be called family and nation) exposes its commitment to the sentimental and the individual and, in this case, makes clear its valuing of gender parity over class equality. Above all, in modifying the original fable, Bâ expands and elaborates on sentiments associated with the novel that we now take for granted but that, before 1976, had not been sharply articulated: nostalgia, ambivalence, regret, pity, ambition, loss.

Lettre's popularity as a "woman's novel" arises from its poignant story of marital betrayal via polygyny. The poignancy stems from the story's self-understanding as a failed romance, that failure standing in for the failure of social transformation once hoped of the decolonization process and national independence. Moreover *Lettre*'s feminism is generated and shaped precisely by what it understands as its *femininity*—namely, its investment in the marriage plot and its partner, bourgeois feminism. Through the theme of betrayal, experienced once as abandonment through infidelity and then as abandonment through death, Ramatoulaye voices a critique of Senegalese national failure using the ostensibly apolitical and insular genre of the romantic love story. Modou's second marriage so devastates his wife that this letter/ novel, written immediately after his death and five years after the new marriage, enacts her ongoing attempt to come to terms with his betrayal. Rather than narrate an openly national story through a sexualized plot, as does *Xala*, Bâ narrates a failed romance in which the betrayal of a woman by her husband stands in for the betrayal of the nation by its middle class. *Lettre* rarely speaks to national politics openly, but when juxtaposed to Sembène's film and novella, *Lettre*'s national sensibility is brought into sharp relief.[11] It slowly but surely names as political—not merely personal—Modou's act of taking a second wife, paying for her upkeep and that of her family. Ramatoulaye addresses the question of women's education and emancipation and their relation to ideologies of nationalism.

From an exploration of romance ideology and its relation to macro-politics in *Lettre*, I move to *Xala* (novella and film), which uses sex and marriage to tell an explicitly national story. *Xala* is not a romance but an anti-romance, a sexual satire that thematizes the link between commoditization and national corruption. In rewriting *Xala* into a romance, *Lettre* promotes gender from a secondary to a primary category of analysis. Sembène in turn was inspired by "Mésaventures de la conscience nationale (The Pitfalls of National Consciousness)," the most famous chapter of Frantz Fanon's most influential work, *Les damnés de la terre* (1961). All three Senegalese authors, particularly Sembène, owe an intellectual and political debt to the work of Fanon, as do many authors of postcolonial African literature. When viewed through the lens of *Xala*, Modou Fall and his disloyalty in *Lettre* look like a milder version of the antics of the anti-hero El Hadji. This perspective sharpens Bâ's depiction of the romance narrative as a reconfiguration of the national story; character failure in *Lettre* replaces the plot reversals of the satiric *Xala*. *La grève des bàttu* stands as a sibling text to *Lettre*, and like *Lettre* it is in filial dialogue with *Xala*. Unlike *Lettre* (and very much like *Xala*), *Grève*'s sense of morality avoids the sentimental and makes strong use of irony. When *Lettre* is juxtaposed against *Grève*, one result is to make visible two very different forms of response to Sembène: one exploring the communalism of Marxism and the other, his feminism.

Sembène's and Sow Fall's works are animated by a sense of public political outrage and represent social situations in a humorous way that nevertheless expresses strong judgment, and the villains or anti-heroes get their comeuppance by the end—proper endings for morality tales. Not so for Bâ. *Lettre* is far more novelistic in its exploration of character depth and ambivalence, its dwelling in the realm of the sentimental, and its refusal of satiric humor. Sow Fall remains true to the form and the spirit of Sembène's critique, and one might see her representation of communalism as a form of embracing Fanon. However, by modifying the form of her predecessor, Bâ writes a novel that is compelling enough to have caught the attention of most students of African literature. Fanon's writings allow me to pose questions about the relation of bourgeois feminism to the larger project of decoloniza- tion, positions espoused by Ramatoulaye. Bâ is the politically wayward daughter, bourgeois in her preoccupations and, as a result, more liter- arily inventive.

A Woman's Novel, a Feminine Novel

Focusing on modernist writing by European and American women at the turn of the twentieth century, Rachel Blau Du Plessis offers a succinct and convincing description of the tenets of romance as they shape and constrict women's quest for self-development, agency, and political power:

> Romance plots of various kinds, the iconography of love, the pos- tures of yearning, pleasing, choosing, slipping, falling, and failing are, evidently, some of the deep, shared structures of our culture. These scripts of heterosexual romance, romantic thralldom and a telos in marriage are also social forms expressed at once in individual desires and in a collective code of action including law: in sequences of action psychically imprinted and behaviors socially upheld. (Du Plessis 1985, 2)

Du Plessis is careful not to universalize her claims, limiting their reach to the "our culture" of the West from which she writes, meaning literary texts written in England and the United States. I suggest that the notions of romance and, especially, romantic thralldom she out- lines are more broadly transcultural. Because they are also thoroughly modern, they form an important part of the ideological skeleton of *Lettre*. Possibly because her Western education exposed her to the European novel and its sentimental tradition, Ramatoulaye is very much invested in the scripts of heterosexual romance. *Lettre* stands in contrast to *Efuru*, where Adizua's sexual transgression is considered a betrayal, but betrayal itself does not define the narrative movement. Moreover, the eponymous protagonist falls in love and unhesitatingly marries again, whereas Modou's second marriage scars Ramatoulaye for the rest of her life. She rejects not only a traditional marriage to her brother-in-law but even another, more romantic, beginning with an old suitor.

After her husband's sudden death, Ramatoulaye uses the Muslim widow's four-month-and-ten-day period of mourning in seclusion to reflect and write a "letter" to her best friend, Aissatou. Five years before his death, after twenty-five years of marriage, Ramatoulaye's husband, Modou, took as a second wife Binetou, a classmate of their eldest daughter. Ramatoulaye learned of the marriage after the fact, and although she was deeply hurt, she remained married to Modou, ignoring the advice of her daughter and the example of Aissatou herself. Some years before this, Aissatou's husband, Mawdo, had been convinced by his aging mother to take a second and younger wife, a woman from his own high caste. Aissatou's response demonstrates the other possibilities available to Ramatoulaye: she divorced Mawdo, took her four children, and left for France and, ultimately, for the United States, where at the time of narration she is working at the Senegalese embassy.

Ramatoulaye remains married after Modou's second marriage because she cannot imagine a personal credo other than one shaped by the marriage plot through which the novel is recounted. It is the primary ideological lens through which she perceives her life. Closer attention to this narrative of a family romance gone terribly awry reveals a narrative of a betrayed nation. Like the romantic discourse to which she continually professes allegiance, but that by the facts of her life she knows to be untrue, Ramatoulaye understands that her victimization is the result not only of the male-dominated social order but also of her continual complicity in the process.

Two rather different tropes help decipher this novel, one offered by the novel itself and the other invoked by the novel's Europeanist literary formation. The first is the *mirasse*, or Muslim mode of address to the dead; the second is the Greek figure of apostrophe, for more than the genre of epistolarity, the figure of apostrophe makes visible some of the novel's assumptions and conventions. Attention to it allows us to understand Ramatoulaye's textual relation to both Modou and Aissatou, the two addressees of the letter or novel. Mirasse, as I discuss later, extends beyond a judgment of Modou as Muslim and indicts him as a man for failing to fulfill his paternal or familial duties. Apostrophe, a more cloaked figure, indicts him for abandoning their love. Barbara Johnson's brief and clear outline of how apostrophe functions is helpful here:

> Apostrophe in the sense that I will be using it involves the direct address of an absent, dead, or inanimate being by a first-person speaker. . . . Apostrophe is both direct and indirect: based etymologically on the notion of turning aside, of digressing from straight speech, it manipulates the I/Thou structure of direct address in an indirect, fictionalized way. The absent, dead, or inanimate entity addressed is thereby made present, which the speaker throws voice, life, and human form into the addressee, turning its silence into mute responsiveness." (Johnson 1988, 190)

Ramatoulaye uses apostrophe to speak to both Modou and Aissatou, at different times and to different ends. Although the letter's nominal recipient is Aissatou, I read the primary apostrophic addressee to be Modou. Little of what Ramatoulaye writes to Aissatou is unknown to her friend. Moreover, Aissatou will have arrived in Dakar by the time the letter is finished. Apostrophe and mirasse allow Ramatoulaye to speak her grief over Modou's ultimate abandonment (his death), which in turn allows her to speak angrily of his earthly abandonment and destruction of their marital relation. Apostrophe itself is very much a feature of oral literature and, unlike mirasse, allows the narrative voice to address both Modou and Aissatou.

Lettre has commonly been read as a parable of postcolonialism, illustrating the devastating predicament of a woman caught between the "tradition" of Islamic polygyny and the "modernity" of monogamous romantic love. Rather than one-to-one signifiers for Africa and Europe, tradition and modernity have a flexible relation to each other in my reading. They are not strictly correlated to geography but are selectively deployed by Ramatoulaye. She uses mirasse to mobilize tradition in the service of the "modern" function of Enlightenment ideology, as insightfully characterized by Uzoma Esonwanne (1997), and her agenda includes the belief in romantic love. I depart somewhat from Esonwanne's analysis of *Lettre*'s critique of polygyny. Ramatoulaye is not a tragic celebrant of an otherwise ossified set of religious and cultural practices but a complex character who marshals arguments considered traditional toward modern ends, not least of which are a recognizably liberal feminist critique of men's privilege in both the public and the domestic social realms.

Esonwanne (1997) traces Ramatoulaye's intellectual development to her education at the teacher's training college Ponty-Ville. By elaborating the social and historical context that produced her, Eson-wanne prepares us to read Ramatoulaye as a bourgeois and liberal feminine national subject within a reading that itself embraces feminism. However, this reading castigates her celebration of education, which is always and already European. Ponty-Ville is the teacher's training school where Ramatoulaye first meets Aissatou and Modou, the novel's two most important characters: one, the nominal recipient of its epistolary address and similar in life circumstances; the other, now a permanently unavailable object of her desire and also a recipient of her address. Ramatoulaye remembers Ponty-Ville fondly as the single most important institution of change in her life. She extols the virtues of a Ponty-Ville education, celebrating the interethnic sorority of French West African girls, the gifts of knowledge, and cultural refinement it offered them all—and, above all, the preparation for their role as new *female* national citizens:

> Aïssatou, je n'oublierai jamais la femme blanche qui, la première, a voulu pour nous un destin "hors du commun." . . . Notre école, entendons vibrer ses murs de notre fougue à l'étude. Revivons la griserie de son atmosphère, les nuits, alors que retentissait pleine d'espérance, la chanson du soir, notre prière commune. Le recrutement qui se faisait par voie de concours à l'échelle de l'ancienne Afrique Occidentale Française, démantelée aujourd'hui en Républiques autonomes, permettait un brassage fructueux d'intelligences, de caractères, des moeurs et coutumes différents. Rien n'y distinguait, si ce n'étaient des traits spécifiquement raciaux, la Fon du Dahomey et la Malinké de Guinée. Des amitiés s'y nouaient, qui ont résisté au temps et à l'éloignement. *Nous étions de véritables soeurs destinées à la même mission émancipatrice.*
>
> Nous sortir de l'enlisement des traditions, superstitions et moeurs; nous faire apprécier de multiples civilisations sans reniement de la nôtre; élever notre vision du monde, cultiver notre personnalité,

renforcer nos qualités, mater nos défauts; faire fructifier en nous les valeurs de la morale universelle; voilà la tâche que s'était assignée l'admirable directrice. . . .

Comme je pense à elle! Si son souvenir résiste victorieusement à l'ingratitude du temps, . . . que le mûrissement et la réflexion dégarnissent les rêves du merveilleux, c'est que la voie choisie pour notre formation et notre épanouissement ne fut point hasard. Elle concorde avec les options profondes de l'Afrique nouvelle, pour promouvoir la femme noire.

Liberée donc des tabous qui frustrent, apte à l'analyse, pourquoi devrais-je suivre l'index de ma mère pointé sur Daouda Dieng, célibataire encore, mais trop mûr pour mes dix-huit hivernages. . . . Mais, je préférais l'homme à l'éternel complet kaki. (Bâ 1976, 27–28; emphasis added)

Aissatou, I will never forget the white woman who was the first to desire for us an "uncommon destiny." . . . Let us hear the walls of our school come to life with the intensity of our study. Let us relive its intoxicating atmosphere at night, while the evening song, our joint prayer, rang out full of hope. The admission policy, which was based on an entrance examination for the whole of former French West Africa, now broken up into autonomous republics, made possible a fruitful blend of different intellects, characters, manners and customs. Nothing differentiated us, apart from specific racial features, the Fon girl from Dahomey and the Malinke one from Guinea. Friendships were made that have endured the test of time and distance. *We were true sisters, destined for the same mission of emancipation.*

To lift us out of the bog of tradition, superstition and custom, to make us appreciate a multitude of civilizations without renouncing our own, to raise our vision of the world, cultivate our personalities, strengthen our qualities, to make up for our inadequacies, to develop universal moral values in us: these were the aims of our admirable headmistress. . . .

How I think of her! If the memory of her has triumphed over the ingratitude of time, . . . now that age and mature reflection have stripped our dreams of their poetic virtue, it is because the path chosen for our training and blossoming has not been at all for-

tuitous. It has accorded with the profound changes made by New
Africa for the promotion of the black woman.

Thus, free from frustrating taboos and capable now of discern-
ment, why should I follow my mother's finger pointing at Daouda
Dieng, still a bachelor but too mature for my eighteen years. . . . I
preferred the man in the eternal khaki suit. (Bâ 1981, 15–16; emphasis added)

The crux of Esonwanne's critique is that the Enlightenment discourse
Ramatoulaye so values is bound up with a colonial disparagement of
African cultures: "Ponty-Ville then is the crucible in which a new,
pliable postcolonial subject, the agent of social transformation, is
formed. 'Lift,' 'raise,' 'make up,' 'develop': these are stock terms of
discourses informed by the evolutionist ethos of the nineteenth century. A sense of teleological motion, of transition, pervades the verbs.
Movement from 'tradition, superstition and custom' to 'a multitude
of civilizations' is the evolutionary and successive goal, always tending toward a European norm" (Esonwanne 1997, 89). Of course,
Esonwanne is correct to read these signs of "universalism" as European in origin, and critically so, for the Enlightenment, espousing as it
did humanism and liberalism, flowered from the same tree and at the
same moment as European imperialism and its racial hierarchies.
While I agree with the substance of his critique, I would like to
temper and extend it. Whatever else one might criticize about the
redemptive language of this passage, one should also acknowledge its
high level of idealization, its hope for the future of new societies, its
celebratory account of formal education for girls, even if elite girls, all
of which contributed to interethnic harmony between young women
of different ethnic groups and potential nation-states. In fact, so
strongly does Ramatoulaye idealize "l'admirable directrice," the instrument of her education, that she sets out to emulate her.[12] Despite
the perspicacity of Esonwanne's critique, it ignores two important
facts. Historically, many, if not most, male African nationalist leaders
were educated at institutions like Ponty-Ville, and such an education
developed an intellectual foundation that then led to their anticolonial critiques.

Ponty-Ville resembles in both name and function the actual historical boys' secondary school École William Ponty, located on Gorée,

directly off the coast of Dakar, which gathered together young men from the region for service in the French West African infrastructure. Léopold Sédar Senghor was one of its most illustrious pupils. Benedict Anderson departs from his primarily Indonesian and Latin American examples to summarize this school's role in instructing the elite-to-be of francophone West Africa, sounding remarkably like Ramatoulaye: "In its heyday, the École Normale William Ponty in Dakar, though only a secondary school, was still the apex of the colonial education pyramid in French West Africa. To William Ponty came intelligent students from what we know today as Guinea, Mali, the Ivory Coast, Senegal, and so on" (Anderson 1990, 123).[13]

These were young men like Modou and Mawdo, Ramatoulaye's opposite-gender counterparts. And in that women, even elite women, were far less likely to receive an education than their male peers, Ramatoulaye's description of the fictional Ponty-Ville girls' school warrants the reader's sympathy, expressing as it does such an obvious desire for an excellent education for women. So, first, African anti-colonial nationalist leaders, who were mostly men, received similar educations to the one Ramatoulaye celebrates. Neither her desire to be redeemed nor her redemption itself is different in kind from that of her male compatriots, though, as a woman, she is expected more than men to safeguard "tradition" and embody local custom and virtue.[14]

The second way in which I diverge from Esonwanne is in understanding the complexity of being bourgeois and female.[15] The events of the novel make clear that Ramatoulaye's education, though unquestionably elite, also forms the basis for her financial independence, which even within the "traditional" logic of the novel must be read as an unqualified good, if only because it enables her to support herself and her children after Modou marries again. This latter point is made clear within the structure of *Lettre*: in narrative terms, Ramatoulaye celebrates the value of her past at Ponty-Ville directly after informing Aissatou that Moudou refused to support her and their children once he started his new family and withdrew himself emotionally and financially. Ramatoulaye's employment as a teacher appears to be the sole source of income for herself and their twelve children—an income she would not have but for her elite education.

Economic self-sufficiency is one of the few ways in which this protagonist resembles Efuru.

Esonwanne's critique of education is made on a political basis with
a particular commitment to class. Although education is not merely
instrumental, the fact remains that in this novel it is the instrument by
which both Ramatoulaye and Aissatou achieve financial independence; it their only way to earn a living once the terms of the Muslim
marriage contract are abrogated. I extend and challenge the philo-
sophical and political substance of Esonwanne's critique. His argument appears to deny the possibility that the colonized were able to
appropriate, manipulate, or otherwise transform Enlightenment or
post-Enlightenment discourses toward anticolonial ends. In almost
all respects, Ramatoulaye's actions suggest otherwise.[16]

Instead of being a passively acquiescent Muslim woman, Ramatoulaye is selective about her religious and cultural actions, appropriating
certain Islamic precepts to conform to her romance agenda and ignoring others altogether. One way by which she does this, by invoking mirasse, is discussed by Esonwanne, Stratton (1994), and others.
Mbye Cham points to the significance of mirasse as central to *Lettre*
and has shaped our understanding of the novel's rhetorical self-
positioning. Cham (1987, 91) calls mirasse "an Islamic religious as
well as juridical principle that defines and stipulates in precise mathe-
matical terms the nature of inheritance in the Islamic family, be it
monogamous or polygamous. This notion of inheritance, laid out in
the chapter on women in the Holy Qur'an, implies disclosure of all
known and unknown or secret material possessions of a deceased for
division among survivors." By extending the conceptual boundaries
of "mirasse," Cham says, Bâ is able to "undertake a comprehensive
exposition (*dépouillement*) of intimate secrets of married life with
Modou Fall, particularly his weakness as a human being and the effect
of this on their relationship" (Cham 1987, 91). And by framing her
plight within an Islamic narrative structure, I suggest, Ramatoulaye
appropriates "tradition" to make visible her victimization:

"Le Mirasse" ordonné par le Coran nécessite le dépouillement d'un
individu mort de ses secrets le plus intimes. Il livre ainsi à autrui ce
qui fut soigneusement dissimulé. Des découvertes expliquent crû-

ment une conduite. Je mesure, avec effroi, l'ampleur de la trahison de Modou. L'abandon de sa première famille (mes enfants et moi) était conforme un nouveau choix de vie. Il nous rejetait. Il orientait son avenir sans tenir compte de notre existence. (Bâ 1976, 19)

The *mirasse* commanded by the Koran requires that a dead person be stripped of his most intimate secrets; thus is exposed to others what was carefully concealed. These exposures crudely explain a man's life. With consternation, I measure the extent of Modou's betrayal. His abandonment of his first family (myself and my children) was the outcome of the choice of a new life. He rejected us. He mapped out his future without taking our existence into account. (Bâ 1981, 9)

Here I diverge slightly from Cham's reading of "dépouillement" as "comprehensive exposition" and suggest that the word denotes and, especially, connotes the more forceful sense of skinning, as in an animal, removing the covers, exposing what is underneath. "Examen minutieux (de documents)" is the second meaning the Petit Robert offers.[17] Ramatoulaye's mirasse consists in stripping away the worldly success of her dead husband, revealing both personal and political secrets. The rhetorical practice of mirasse allows her to expose Modou, to uncover how he directly violates Qur'anic law, which stipulates that a man may take up to four wives only if he provides for them all equitably.[18] She recounts how, after his marriage to Binetou, he simply stopped providing economically for his first family while lavishly spending on his second. She is justifiably incensed that he bought villas, cars, and trips to Mecca for his new wife, her parents, and her children and especially that these luxuries were financed through credit obtained against Ramatoulaye's own house, which was bought with their joint income:

Ce logement et son chic contenu ont été acquis grâce à un prêt bancaire consenti sur une hypothèque de la villa "Falène" où j'habite. Cette villa, dont le titre foncier porte son nom, n'en est pas moins un bien commun acquis sur nos économies. (Bâ 1976, 20)

This house and its fashionable contents were acquired by a bank loan granted on the mortgage of "Villa Falene," where I live. Although the title deeds of this house bear his name, it is nonetheless our common property, acquired by our joint savings. (Bâ 1981, 10, translation modified)

Modou's lavish spending limits what her family can buy, and they now have a car only because of Aissatou's generosity. Within the mirasse, stripping away includes economic arguments about Modou's failure as a father and provider for his children. Curiously, Ramatoulaye never indicates that at any time during those five years she had ever asked Modou for her share of his income, which, as a devout Muslim wife, she would have been entirely within her rights to do. The latter part of the quote—and, indeed, most of the novel—indicates that the primary thrust of her critique is sentimental; it is his emotional indifference rather than his economic irresponsibility that pains her, his abandonment of her as husband and lover rather than paternal provider that she dwells on in her lament, their marital covenant broken and she is cast aside by him.

Written from the hyper-domesticized space of Muslim widowhood and confinement, Ramatoulaye's letter appears to wish for a certain public force from romantic love. The logic of the novel suggests that sentimentalized interiority—so much a part of the European novel since the mid-eighteenth century and not much part of the early African one—is here deployed to serve a political purpose. Ramatoulaye seems to believe—or at least, to wish—that interiorized pure feeling, when openly expressed, is powerful enough to transcend the world of economic reality and public policy. Like many European novels written by women in the nineteenth century and twentieth century, which in some ways it emulates, *Lettre* is structured around competing notions of love, framing important questions in Ramatoulaye's life in terms of marriage, sexuality, and childrearing. On the face of it, then, the novel conforms to romance as its protagonist alternates between bitterness and nostalgic effusion.

Du Plessis (1985, 2) hypothesizes that romance might serve as a "compensatory social and narrative practice" when middle-class women lose economic power in the transition from pre-capitalist economies. If romance is compensatory, it is especially so at a moment of change, when the social order is shaken up. Du Plessis emphasizes the shift from feudalism to capitalism. Winifred Woodhull (1993, 11) has noted in the context of Algerian independence and its aftermath that women themselves embody conflicting forces that simultaneously compose and disrupt the nation. The Senegalese moment of social upheaval here is the shift from colonialism to independence, or, as we shall see, "postcolonialism." Conjugal love is the telos in this novella, and development of the heterosexual love relationship is the defining goal of both Ramatoulaye's life and the novel's organization. Du Plessis (1985, 5) continues: "As a narrative pattern, the romance plot muffles the main female character, represses quest, valorizes heterosexual as opposed to homosexual ties, incorporates individuals within couples as a sign of their personal and narrative success. The romance plot separates love and quest, values sexual asymmetry, including the division of labor by gender, is based on extremes of sexual difference, and evokes an aura around the couple itself."

   After Modou dies, Ramatoulaye again resists a traditional life path by rejecting a marriage proposal from Modou's brother, Tamsir, who stands to inherit her as the widow. Earlier, when she asks herself why she remains married to Modou even though she deplores his second marriage, she answers that she is too old to find someone else. She describes herself pathetically as "abandonée: une feuille qui voltige mais qu'aucune n'ose ramasser (abandoned: a fluttering leaf that no hand dared to pick up)" (Bâ 1976, 70; 1981, 53). Soon after she declines Tamsir, Daouda Dieng proposes. That he wants her enough to ask again after having been refused twenty-five years earlier proves that she is still an object of desire and produces some of the most euphoric language of the novel: "J'écarquillai les yeux, non d'étonnement—une femme peut infailliblement prévoir une déclaration de ce genre—*mais d'ivresse*. Eh oui, Aissatou, les mots usés qui ont servi, qu'on sert encore, avaient prise en moi. *Leur douceur, don't j'étais sevrée depuis des ans, me grisait: je n'ai pas honte de te l'avouer* (I opened my eyes wide, not in astonishment—a woman can always predict a declaration of this kind—*but in a kind of giddiness*. Ah yes, Aissatou, those well-worn words, which have for long been used and are still being used, had taken root in me. Their sweetness, of which I had been deprived for years, intoxicated me: *I feel no shame in admitting it to you*)" (Bâ 1976, 95 [emphasis added]; 1981, 65 [emphasis added and translation slightly modified]). She refuses Daouda in part, she says, because he also is already married, but primarily because she does not love him. Her impassioned response to Tamsir is revealing for what it says about her understanding of love and marriage:

> Tu oublies que j'ai un coeur, une raison, que je ne suis pas un objet que l'on se passe de main en main. Tu ignores ce que se marier signifie pour moi: c'est un acte de foi et d'amour, un don total de soi à l'être que l'on a choisi et qui vous a choisi. (J'insistais sur le mot choisi.) (Bâ 1976, 85)

> You forget that I have a heart, a mind, that I am not an object to be passed from hand to hand. You don't know what marriage means to me: it is an act of faith and of love, the total surrender of oneself to the person one has chosen and who has chosen you. (I emphasized the word "chosen.") (Bâ 1981, 58)

The novel instructs us to attend to the word "choisi," and so I do. Ramatoutlaye tells us that the protection and companionship provided to a married woman are insufficient. She requires the full gift of self to the beloved, and the gift must manifest itself in monogamous romantic love or she will have nothing at all. Her earlier passivity regarding Modou's unequal distribution of material resources between his two wives becomes all the more telling for its contradiction of her generally assertive behavior. *Lettre* tells and retells a story of true love and its betrayal as the narrator alternates between bitterness and nostalgic effusion. Ramatoulaye's narrative position as a heroine of elevated sensibilities is supported by what appears to be a fairy-tale courtship and marriage, that of a man and woman destined for each other. In her critique of the novels in popular culture, Rosalind Coward (1985, 178) says that "the domestic sphere could . . . be represented as the realm of pure feeling—borne by the woman—where men's true identity could be expressed.[19] Novelistic conventions contributed to the rigid separation between the public economic sphere and the private domestic space." Historically, readers of African and postcolonial novels have read this particular novel naively, as Coward suggests, as a private and domestic tale.

Consider the description of Ramatoulaye's feelings the first time she meets Modou. For her, it is love at first sight. Although the novel is generally presumed to be addressed to Aissatou, the following

passages are addressed to Modou himself, an apostrophic address
that is in keeping with the elegiac sentimentality of the language:

> Modou Fall, à l'instant où tu t'inclinas devant moi pour m'inviter à
> danser, je sus que tu étais celui que j'attendais. Grand et athlétique-
> ment bâti, certes. Teint ambré dû à ta lointaine appartenance mau-
> resque, certes aussi. Virilité et finesse des traits harmonieusement
> conjuguées, certes encore. Mais surtout, tu savais être tendre.
> Tu savais deviner toute pensée, tout désir . . . Tu savais beaucoup
> de choses indéfinissables qui t'auréolaient et scellèrent nos relations.
> (Bâ 1976, 24)

> Modou Fall, the very moment you bowed before me, asking me to
> dance, I knew you were the one I was waiting for. Tall and athlet-
> ically built, of course. Olive-coloured skin due to your distant Moor-
> ish blood, no question. Virility and fineness of features harmoni-
> ously blended, once again, no question. But, above all, you knew
> how to be tender.
> You could fathom every thought, every desire. You knew many
> undefinable things, which glorified you and sealed our relationship.
> (Bâ 1981, 13)

Her parents object, preferring the older and wealthier Daouda Dieng,
but in a markedly willful act, eighteen-year-old Ramatoulaye defies
them and marries Modou. Instead of simply ignoring Islamic wedding custom, she flouts it:

> Notre mariage se fit sans dot, sans faste, sous les regards désap-
> probateurs de mon père, devant l'indignation douloureuse de ma
> mère frustrée, sous les sarcasmes de mes soeurs surprises, dans notre
> ville muette d'étonnement. (Bâ 1976, 28–29)

> Our marriage was celebrated without dowry, without pomp, under
> the disapproving looks of my father, before the painful indignation
> of my frustrated mother, under the sarcasm of my sisters, in our
> town struck dumb with astonishment. (Bâ 1981, 16)

Ramatoulaye's description of their conjugal life invites comparison
between their spartan beginning as a couple, adorned only with the
idealism and hope of young love, and Modou Fall's overly elaborate

and expensive funeral, with which the novel opens. In contrast to their ascetic beginning, Modou's ceremonial departure seems vulgar and consumerist, indeed.[20]

Ramatoulaye wishes to believe her love powerful enough to transcend the exterior world of economic realities and public politics. A feminist reading makes visible her oscillation between Coward's description of the intensely privatized idiom of sentimentality and a more public critique. The letter that constitutes this novel, after all, is written during the Muslim widow's period of physical confinement. The traditional and religious convention of mirasse authorizes a critique whose force is not religious but primarily individual. Within the affective register of romance, *Lettre* secures a vantage point from which to critique modern bourgeois marital relations and, by clear implication, national politics. Ramatoulaye's critique extends beyond Modou's disloyalty to herself as his wife, even if now only his first wife, and their family to encompass his disloyalty to the entire country. Here the domestic sphere of their marital life stands allegorically for the public one.

Intertextuality and the Making of National Conversations

Florence Stratton (1994) insightfully notes the dialogic relation between Bâ's and Sembène's novellas, a relation she registered as early as 1988 in her article "The Shallow Grave." For Stratton, *Lettre* functions as a rejoinder to the novella written by men, thereby illustrating a certain corrective value of feminism. The relationship between the two is "partly confirmatory," says Stratton (1994, 137), for, like Sembène, Bâ is critical of the Senegalese bourgeoisie.

Both *Xala* and *Lettre* use the institution of polygynous marriage in Senegal as a premise for their narratives: Sembène, to tell the story of a bloated and corrupted bourgeoisie engorging itself on its malnourished brothers; Bâ, to testify to how immorality within the family is replicated in the national polity. For both, polygyny stands synecdochically for larger social problems—namely, the tendency for one group to betray another. Both texts name as decadent the marriage of a beautiful but impoverished young girl to a wealthy man old enough to be her father. In *Xala*, this is the husband's third marriage; in *Lettre*, it is his second. Both texts, then, condemn polygyny, though few commentators acknowledge this of *Xala*. Rama, El Hadji's militant daughter and one of *Xala*'s most sympathetic characters, tells her father that all polygamists are liars, and he slaps her for saying so. El Hadji and Modou Fall share a class origin and a rise to power synchronized with decolonization in Africa: both were trade union organizers actively involved in the independence movement; both become corrupt at about the time of independence, exchanging their early political idealism for excessive material comforts. *Xala* tells the story of El Hadji's downfall due to graft and greed. Modou Fall's dishonesty in *Lettre* appears to be less flagrant, perhaps because Bâ engages national politics indirectly or perhaps because he cannot be too soiled if he is to remain an object of Ramtoulaye's love. Nevertheless, much like El Hadji, who spends himself into bankruptcy and is impoverished at the film's end, Modou dies in debt, also due to the excesses of his last marriage.

The two girl brides, N'Goné and Binetou, marry to improve their families' fortunes; moreover, both are explicitly called "victims" by the first wife. In *Xala*, Awa says to her daughter, Rama: "Cette N'Goné a ton âge, c'est vrai! c'est une victime (It's true N'Gone is your age. But she's only a victim)" (Sembène 1973, 26; 1976, 13). Ramatoulaye says of her co-spouse, "Binetou est un agneau immolé comme beaucoup d'autres sur l'autel du 'material'" (Bâ 1976, 60), and "Victime, elle se voulait oppresseur" (Bâ 1976, 72). "Binetou, like many others, was a lamb slaughtered on the altar of affluence" (Bâ 1981, 39) and "A victim, she wanted to be the oppressor" (Bâ 1981, 48). The passivity and willing objectification of the new, young wives are counterpoised to the liberated rebelliousness of El Hadji's and Modou's daughters, Rama and Daba. Both daughters, eldest children of the first wife, are close to their mothers and outspoken toward their fathers, and within the larger frame of the narrative, they represent hope for a better future. Both novels detail the excess of material consumption in the society at large, and both blame it for the commodification of virginal and youthful female bodies. In *Xala*, the wedding is celebrated ostentatiously; the new car N'Goné receives stands as explicit exchange for her virginity. (In the film, El Hadji even fingers the car key as he leaves N'Goné the morning after.) The wedding with which the filmic action begins in *Xala* is celebrated as flamboyantly as is the funeral of Modou, which inaugurates the novelistic action in *Lettre*.

However, Stratton does not make any of these claims. Her primary interest seems to lie in interpreting Bâ's text on the axis of how it "deals with the issues that Sembène suppresses" (Stratton 1994, 137–38) rather than for what Bâ replicates of Sembène's work, as well as for what she obscures; how this text arises from dialogue with Sembène, as well as how it is driven by its own preoccupations or interests—in short, for how Bâ's conception of liberal and feminist politics rewrites Sembène's forthright Marxism. Directed primarily against Sembène, Stratton's criticism appears to follow directly from his gender identity: "Sembène is not . . . interested in the problems created by polygyny for either men or women. Rather, he exploits them for their metaphorical potential in elaborating his theme of the bankruptcy of Senegal as a neo-colonial nation" (Stratton 1994, 137). Despite her insight into the intertextual relation, Stratton's own representation of Sembène as yet another literary patriarch reveals an identitarian position that continues to plague some varieties of feminist criticism. Her assumption seems to be that only female authors can progressively depict feminism or women's suffering under patriarchy. This interpretive style, so strongly oriented toward affirming women, perceives metaphor as intrinsically limited and the opposite of affirmative representation. Therefore, a biting satire about an impotent man, one who is of the postcolonial elite, cannot be feminist because the author neither imagines nor depicts agency on the part of the women. Such a perspective not only ignores the fact that Sembène's novella and film represent many of the female characters as trapped within difficult sexual circumstances of a man's making, circumstances that are also explicitly linked to Sembène's critique of class and colonialism, but it must ignore the sharp irony of the film's title and the protagonist's frantic quest. While she perceptively notes the influence one literary text might have on another, Stratton uses a reading strategy that can speak neither to the dialogue between Sembène and Bâ nor to how Sembène's *Xala* might have had a catalyzing influence on *Lettre*.

In a different vein, Abiola Irele, who puts forth a persuasive reading of *Xala* as partaking of what he calls a new realism in African literature, conflates the text's implicit critique of El Hadji with that of his wives: "The incidental critique of the abuse of polygamy by the men is joined here to a portrayal of the false consciousness of the women characters, who give their assent to the degradation of their gender in exchange for material benefits" (Irele 2001, 223). The only one of whom an assent might be accurately claimed is Oumi N'Doye, the vulgar and modern second wife; it is appropriate to neither the first nor the third wife, for the third wife says almost nothing in film or novel, as I elaborate later. The first wife, Awa Adja Astou, is not a developed character in the film. In the novel, from which Irele draws his analysis, Awa Adja's back story tells of her origins as a Christian from Gorée who converts to Islam and risks alienating her beloved father when she falls in love with the man we now know as El Hadji. (In a different manner but bespeaking a similar strong-willed femininity in the face of love, Ramatoulaye of *Lettre* risks her family's wrath to marry the man she loves instead of the one her mother prefers.) Awa Adja responds to her husband's second marriage, which, it is suggested, is painful to her, by immersing herself into her new faith and by undertaking the Hajj.

Irele says that *Xala* "draws its inspiration from popular belief and from the African tradition of the morality fable" (Irele 2001, 221). I agree and suggest that *Lettre* accepts and begins with the morality fable as critique, although morality fable—as exemplified by *Xala*, at least—is itself significantly modified. *Lettre* underplays *Xala*'s biting representation of class relations and elaborates on what Sembène ignores: an affective rather than analytic response to polygyny that foregrounds the domestic realm of social relations. Ramatoulaye frames her critique morally, using a rational and humanist logic, but she might be said to name that morality in relation to the woman rather than to the nation. Bâ does not simply express an early feminine voice; she does this in a discursive domain dominated by orthodox nationalism, which she challenges as she privileges the domestic over the public realm.

In this sense, Bâ's novel squarely embodies my thesis that politics in novels written by women are expressed micro-politically and that the micro-politics warrant closer investigation as an allegory of the larger, macro-political world. Moreover, Bâ illustrates that women-authored or feminist representations are not inherently more progressive than men's representations. The national failures and bankruptcy *Xala* castigates within the public social realm are relegated to the margins of Bâ's work; the family drama of the domestic social realm occupies center stage in *Lettre*. (This is due not to a change of focus, as is the case with *Nervous Conditions*, as I illustrate in the next chapter, but to an explicit ideological commitment to one realm over the other.)

Bâ appears to diagnose the nation's ills as stemming not from social structures, but from the individual venality of powerful men with insufficient love for the country's people. In short, the same traits that allow Modou to betray Ramatoulaye also enable him to betray the nation. Whereas Sembène gestures to radical or revolutionary change as redemption, the only redemptive mechanism within Bâ's novel is education. It functions as the powerful—and unique—means to respectable women's empowerment and employment. Moreover, the individual stories of both Ramatoulaye and Aissatou strongly make this argument because it is only because of her education that each can materially provide for her children. Aissatou's presumably greater earning power, such as her ability to give her friend a car, is related to her further education as well as to the strength of the dollar over the CFA franc. For Sembène, modernity is not something that comes only from Europe. For example, El Hadji's daughter, Rama, advocates and practices reclaiming indigenous languages along with her secular university education, and the text offers little to counter this position. Bâ's Ramatoulaye, herself a more ambiguous embodiment of these apparent antinomies, espouses the belief, as I read her, that modernity—meaning women's education, the entrance into the public civil sphere, and professional employment—comes only with colonialism. Reading these two texts both allegorically and genealogically recasts the seemingly apolitical *Lettre* as a novel that quietly but clearly speaks to issues of national policy in postcolonial Senegal.

In the reading I have outlined thus far, Bâ retells Sembène's story by giving voice to Awa, El Hadji's noble and long-suffering first wife. A twist in the retelling appears to be the use of the heterosexual romance as a vehicle for the national narrative of post-independence Senegal. *Lettre* articulates its politics, both individual and national, in terms so compelling that by the end (and despite Ramatoulaye's own claims to the contrary), one is left believing that the prevailing family structure is as bankrupt as the nation-state run by the native elite. Bâ takes up her narrative as if from the position of Adja Awa Astou, El Hadji's dignified first wife in *Xala*. Sembène describes Awa as a former Christian, a woman who fell in love with and married El Hadji when he was a mere teacher, forsaking her family and converting to Islam for him. Like Awa, Ramatoulaye stolidly accepts, or appears to accept, the new marriage. When the outspoken daughters of both first wives demand that their mothers divorce, both mothers respond that they are too old to try again at marriage. Unlike Awa, however, Ramatoulaye is not stoic; nor does she suffer her fate quietly. Her complaint is implicit in the novel's epistolary form. Rejection of stoicism and an incessantly complaining tone also characterize El Hadji's brazen second wife, Oumi, suggesting to me that, in rewriting the narrative, Bâ imbues Ramatoulaye with aspects of both tradition and modernity, although the modern aspects frequently have been overlooked.[21]

Lettre implicitly, if not wholly successfully, contends that romantic idealism and faith in and practice of true love is the only way out of the brutal economy of commodification, the buying of labor and traffic in desire, an economy that finds its strongest expression in Sembène's film and novella, with which *Lettre* is in dialogic response. The confidence in the authenticity of sentiment and high-toned feelings over vulgar materialism and constant talk about money has its roots in Bâ's response to Sembène's sharply critical portrayal of neo-colonial Senegal.

Ramatoulaye's and Modou's romance dominates the novel, which itself is sentimental in tone. Their courtship, as well as that of their alter egos, Aissatou and Mawdo, begins at Ponty-Ville during the period of high Senegalese nationalism and idealism at the moment of independence. Both couples see themselves as the vanguard of an emerging utopian, nationalist order. As Stratton has noted, the dissolution of both marriages parallels a period of national disillusion: "The undermining by bourgeois materialism of the nationalist ideals of liberty and equality serves as a vehicle to illuminate the compromising by women as well as men of the feminist ideal of a marriage contract based on parity between the sexes" (1994, 159). Ramatoulaye narrates the vanguardist idealism of the young bourgeoisie into a romance plot.

According to this logic, the cynicism so many people feel as post-independence Senegal reveals itself to be just another neocolonial state is translated in her discourse into inherent masculine faithlessness. Although Bâ does not indict Modou Fall the way Sembène does El Hadji Abdou Kaber Baye, Modou certainly resembles the sort of national bourgeoisie so scathingly described by Fanon. As a young man courting Ramatoulaye, Modou idealistically prefers work that is "moins rémunéré mais constructif pour [son] pays (less well paid but constructive for [his] country)" (Bâ 1976, 24; 1981, 14). As time passes, however, he derives increasing financial benefit from his role as a union advocate.

In fact, Ramatoulaye refers several times to Modou's "practical attitude" of asking for his unions "only what was possible" and continually working with, rather than against, the government, a position hardly associated with idealism and the struggle for justice:

> Sa promotion au rang de conseiller technique au Ministère de la Fonction Publique, en échange de laquelle il avait endigué la révolte syndicale, disent les mauvaises langues, n'a rien pu contre la marée enlisante des dépenses où il se débattait. . . . Quatre millions empruntés avec facilité, vu sa situation privilégiée, et qui avaient permis d'envoyer Dame Belle-mère et son époux acquérir les titres de Hadja et de El-Hadj à la Mecque; qui permettaient également les changements continuels des "Alfa Roméo" de Binetou à la moindre bosse. (Bâ 1976, 19–20)

> His promotion to the rank of technical adviser in the Ministry of Public Works, in exchange for which, according to the spiteful, he checked the trade union revolt, could not control the mire of expenses by which he was engulfed. . . . Four thousand francs borrowed with ease because of his privileged position, which had enabled him to pay for Lady Mother-in-Law and her husband to visit Mecca to acquire the titles of *Alhaja* and *Alhaji*; which equally enabled Binetou to exchange her Alfa Romeo at the slightest dent. (Bâ 1981, 9–10)

Having become co-opted by the wealth available to those who work with the government, Modou serves as intermediary between government institutions and metropolitan capitalism, on the one hand, and the masses of the African population, on the other. Bâ juxtaposes his rhetoric, that of a progressive socialist in an industrially underdeveloped country, against his uncontrolled consumerism and mounting debt: three villas, at least three cars, and trips to Mecca. In this context, Modou's grumbling at government expenses seems hypocritical:

> Il maugréait d'argent contre l'installation hâtive de nombreuses Ambassades, qu'il jugeait coûteuses pour notre pays sous-développé. Avec cette saignée pour la gloriole et bien d'autres, telles les invitations fréquentes d'étrangers, que d'argent perdu! (Bâ 1976, 25)

> He cursed the hasty establishment of too many embassies, which he judged to be too costly for our under-developed country. This bleeding of the country for reasons of pure vanity, among other things, such as the frequent invitation of foreigners, was just a waste of money. (Bâ 1981, 40)

This, then, is power of the mirasse again: it allows Ramatoulaye to use a traditionally sanctioned religious protocol to sharply criticize Modou's political compromises and financial excesses in public and macro-political terms.

Lettre's constellation of desires, wishes, and frustrations throws up one last expressive flare before the novel ends. If, as Pierre Macherey (1978) suggests, one of the great moments of a text's ideological negotiation is to be found in the choice of a narrative resolution, then this novella's penultimate pages, which build to an emotional crescendo, have to be read as the textual contortion necessary to negotiate closure. The impending arrival of Aissatou puts into sharp contrast the two women's earlier similar circumstances and different choices, and, in response Ramatoulaye affirms her belief in couple and nation:

> Je reste persuadée de l'inévitable et nécessaire complémentarité de l'homme et de la femme. L'amour, si imparfait soit-il dans son contenu et son expression demeure le joint naturel entre ces deux êtres. . . .
> C'est de l'harmonie du couple que nait la réussite familiale, comme l'accord de multiples instruments crée la symphonie agréable.

Ce sont toutes les familles, riches ou pauvres, unies ou déchirées, conscientes ou irréfléchies qui constitutuent la Nation. La réussite d'une nation passe donc irrémédiablement par la famille. (Bâ 1976, 129–30)

I remain persuaded of the inevitable and necessary complementarity of man and woman. Love, imperfect as it may be in its content and expression, remains the natural link between these two beings. . . .

The success of the family is born of a couple's harmony, as the harmony of multiple instruments creates a pleasant symphony.

The nation is made up of all the families, rich or poor, united or separated, aware or unaware. The success of a nation therefore depends inevitably on the family. (Bâ 1981, 88–89)

This language stands in sharp contrast to the general feeling of pain, wounding, and occasional humiliation that has until now dominated the text. Ramatoulaye has just told a tale of national betrayal and familial abandonment, yet she affirms the possible success of the nation. Why, then, the effusion? The sentimental excess contrasts sharply with her bitter and blunt description of Modou's funeral at the very beginning of the novel. Now she affirms the nation and family emphatically and elegiacally. The monogamous marital couple, of which there are none in the novel, is the locus of all happiness.

Ramatoulaye's story of a love gone awry standing as a national story has much in common with the model of national romance that Doris Sommer developed to great effect in her reading of nineteenth-century Latin American novels (Sommer 1991). Indeed, the very story of Ramatoulaye and Moudou, Aissatou and Mawdo stands as the sort of coming together through erotics that Sommer finds as a resolution to various ethnic and racial complexities. Rama meets Modou while at Ponty-Ville in that heady moment when, along with independence, everything seems possible. Aissatou and Mawdo also meet at that moment, their love story involving the additional twist of defying caste barriers, a trope Sommer develops. Sommer's model ends in marriage, that eventful moment that resolved most novels written by women in the British, American—and French—traditions. The Senegalese novel, however, tells of the marriage of equals (Modou to Ramatoulaye and Mawdo to Aissatou) and sharply contrasts that historical moment with both men's second marriages, especially of Modou's to Binetou, saturated as it is in Modou's narcissism and Binetou's commodification. *Lettre*, the novel written by a woman from Senegal, resists the neater, narrative resolution that Sommer sees in Latin American novels of the nineteenth century written by men, a fact that has much to do with the national moment at which it was written.

Bâ's morality tale looks very different from Sembène's. While *Xala* castigates the moral bankruptcy of the elite and their draining of precious national resources into their own bank accounts, *Lettre* muffles the class critique in favor of gender critique. Sembène uses polygyny to stand for concentrated wealth held by a few individuals at the top: one man with several partners. Bâ, by contrast, emphasizes the emotional charge of the act of disloyalty. She recounts the single act of betrayal by one man of one woman through sanctioned infidelity within several marriages: that which Modou inflicts on Ramatoulaye; that which Mawdo inflicts on Aissatou; and the extramarital relations imposed by Samba on Jacqueline. For Sembène, the betrayal centers not on sex but on power, and the betrayal is of the people rather than of a single beloved. Ramatoulaye is the primary victim of Modou's betrayal, whereas in *Xala*, the victims are legion, diverse, and often unseen. The Marxist texts of Fanon and Sembène represent the problems structurally; the liberal feminist depicts them interpersonally: only men are at fault.

Before engaging at greater length the similarities and differences between Bâ's female feminism and Sembène's male Marxist feminism, I will push the genealogical reading further back by taking up Sembène's own predecessor, Fanon. Closer attention to *Xala* reveals the strong influence of Fanon's *The Wretched of the Earth*, from which Sembène drew the dominant quality of the work's tone. *Lettre* is formally shaped by and thematically responsive to *Xala*; in turn, *Xala* constitutes Sembène's largely uncritical rendering into narrative of Fanon's essay.

Published in 1961 at a time that most African states were just establishing themselves as independent, "The Pitfalls of National Consciousness" retains an extraordinary power to explain the failures of decolonizing nationalism. Fanon's essay is a trenchant critique of the

nationalist bourgeoisie as it emerges into its glory after independence. Freed from the shackles of colonial restrictions, Fanon warns,
the native middle class will prosper after independence—and it will
do so at the expense of the peasant and working classes, bringing to
an end the progressive cycle of upheaval wrought by the independence movement. Fanon (1968, 152) upbraids the bourgeoisie:

> For them, nationalization does not mean governing the state with
> regard to the new social relations whose growth it has been decided
> to encourage. To them, nationalization quite simply means the
> transfer into native hands of those unfair advantages which are a
> legacy of the colonial period.

Instead of completing the transfer of power begun by the national
liberation movement, the bourgeoisie arrests that momentum, claims
victory upon independence, and inhibits the equitable redistribution
of wealth. Relying on a hollow nationalism, it claims that because
capital is now in black or brown hands, the revolution is complete.
Fanon continues:

> The native bourgeoisie which comes to power uses its class ag-
> gressiveness to corner the positions formerly kept for foreigners. On
> the morrow of independence, in fact, it violently attacks colonial
> personalities: barristers, traders, landed proprietors, doctors, and
> higher civil servants. It will fight to the bitter end against these
> people "who insult our dignity as a nation." It waves aloft the notion
> of nationalization and Africanization of the ruling classes. (Fanon
> 1968, 155)

Willingly exacerbating racially or ethnically based divisions in the
name of nationalism, this bourgeoisie mediates between metropolitan capitalism and the masses of the African population. Unlike its
European counterpart, this native bourgeoisie has no autonomous
power, either economic or political, except as bequeathed to it by the
colonizer:

> Neither financiers nor industrial magnates are to be found within
> this national middle class. The national bourgeoisie of underdevel-
> oped countries is not engaged in production, nor in invention, nor
> building, nor labor; it is completely channeled into activities of the

intermediary type. Its innermost vocation seems to be to keep in the running and to be part of the racket. The psychology of the national bourgeoisie is that of the businessman, not that of a captain of industry. (Fanon 1968, 149–50; translation modified)

Here Fanon takes the obverse side of Marx's representation of the dynamism of the bourgeoisie in *The Communist Manifesto*. Unlike its European counterpart, this African bourgeoisie lacks both the capital and the historical dynamism to develop a significant industrial base. Calling it "senile before it has come to know the petulance, the fearlessness, or the will to succeed of youth," Fanon says that it "follows the Western bourgeoisie along its path of negation and decadence without ever having emulated it in its first stages of exploration and invention, stages which are an acquisition of the Western bourgeoisie whatever the circumstances" (1968, 153). "Since the bourgeoisie has not the economic means to ensure its domination and to throw a few crumbs to the rest of the country; since, moreover, it is preoccupied with filling its pockets as rapidly as possible but also as prosaically as possible, the country sinks all the more deeply into stagnation" (Fanon 1968, 165).

We know from the unfortunate examples of many Latin American, African, and Asian states that Fanon was altogether too prescient. Despite evidence to the contrary, he also believed, however, that the masses would respond to and overcome the greed and corruption of the national bourgeoisie: "The scandalous enrichment, speedy and pitiless, of this caste is accompanied by a decisive awakening on the part of the people, and a growing awareness that promises stormy days to come" (Fanon 1968, 167). The assumption here is that the people will arise and throw off the yoke of neocolonial subjugation. My brief reading of *Xala* shows that Sembène illustrates all of the major aspects of Fanon's polemic, down to the increased awareness and agitation that the dispossessed make visible.

Sembène filmed *Xala* some thirteen years after *Les damnés de la terre* was published. According to Noureddine Ghali (1987), he wrote the novella from his screenplay while awaiting funding to produce the film.[22] Moreover, like *Les damnés de la terre*, *Xala* instantiates a Marxism that simultaneously borrows from and distances itself from Europe. The historical materialist paradigm of the fiction brings together two axes of power: the relation between colonizer and colonized and the relation between native well-to-do and native poor. Gender serves as fulcrum metaphor that keeps the two sets of oppositions intact and opposed.

The narrative opens as El Hadji Abdou Kader Beye, a prosperous, middle-aged businessman (Fanon's term), is about to celebrate his financial success by taking as his third wife a beautiful young woman the same age as his eldest daughter. Accompanying him to the celebration that follows the marriage are his first two wives, the senior and "traditional" Awa and the more "modern" second wife, Oumi, neither of whom approves of this new development. On his wedding night, El Hadji experiences *xala*, which in Wolof means sexual impotence. Believing himself to be cursed, he frantically consults with various marabouts, neglects the daily running of his business, and fails to extricate himself from financial difficulties. As a result, his business fails, and he is drummed out of the Groupement des Hommes d'Affaires (Chamber of Commerce and Industry). As the story makes clear, he is forced out *not* because he stole thirty tons of rice two weeks before his new wedding—a theft that made possible the opulent reception and the purchase of a new house, car, and presents for the bride—but because his embezzling was so excessive that he encroached on the graft of his confrères. Only at the novel's end, after he is forced outside the power structure, is El Hadji given to understand that his xala constitutes a retribution, a spell cast on him by one of the beggars of Dakar whose clan was cheated out of its land many years earlier in one of El Hadji's first acts of thievery. The beggar promises that El Hadji will regain his manhood if he strips and is spat on by a crowd of beggars. El Hadji agrees, and the film culminates in a carnivalesque orgy of spitting.

El Hadji's Chamber of Commerce and Industry is introduced on the first page of the novella in language that is entirely in keeping with Fanon's descriptions of the national bourgeoisie.[23] The following passage constitutes most of the novella's second paragraph:

Venus individuellement d'horizons différents, ils avaient formé un "Groupement des Hommes d'affaires" faisant front à l'afflux des entreprises dirigées par des étrangers. Leurs ambition était de prendre en main l'économie du pays. Cette velléité de constituer une couche social les avait rendus très combatifs, avec même un relent de xénophobie. . . . leur manque d'avoir bancaire avivait, aguisait un sentiment nationaliste auquel ne manquait pas quelque rêve d'embourgeoisement. (Sembène 1973, 7–8)

They had come together from different sectors of the business community to form the "Businessmen's Group" in order to combat the invasion of foreign interests. It was their ambition to gain control of their country's economy. Their anxiety to constitute a social clan of their own had increased their combativeness, tingeing it with xenophobia. . . . Their exclusion from the banks had first stimulated then sharpened a nationalist feeling from which expectations of improved social status weren't entirely absent. (Sembène 1976, 1; translation modified)

In both novella and film, the reason for the opening celebration is that for the first time the Chamber of Commerce and Industry is to be headed by an African. In the film in particular, the rites and ceremonies marking the transfer of economic power from Europe to Africa are reminiscent of the transfer of state power upon independence. Europeans in business suits hand over briefcases filled with cash to "natively" dressed Africans who, in all subsequent filmic scenes, appear in business suits identical to those of the Europeans. Two of the characters, "M. le Président" and "M. le Deputé," whose very names suggest the juridical power of the legislature as well as the economic power of the Chamber of Commerce, play important secondary roles. In the novella, Sembène's language telescopes the hopes of independence and the corruption of neocolonialism into a single semiotic field, lambasting the bourgeoisie for their parasitism:

(En fait il est bon de savoir que tous ces gens qui s'étaient arrogés le droit à l'appellation pompeuse d' "Hommes d'affairs" n'étaient que des intermédiaires, des commis d'une espèce nouvelle.) Les anciens comptoirs de l'epoque coloniale, réadaptés à la nouvelle situation des Indépendances africaines, leur fournissaient des marchandises pour la revente, détail et demi-gros. (Sembène 1973, 94)

(It is perhaps worth pointing out that all these men who had given themselves the pompous title of 'businessmen' were nothing more than middlemen, a new kind of salesman.) The old trading firms of

the colonial period, adapting themselves to the new situation created by African Independence, supplied them with goods on a
wholesale or semi-wholesale basis, which they then re-sold. (Sembène 1976, 55)

This national bourgeois anti-hero is almost formulaically Fanonian.
Beginning as a teacher during the colonial period, El Hadji then
becomes involved in union organizing, a typically formative African
anticolonial activity. After losing his job because of his political sym-
pathies, he becomes an "intermédiare dans les transactions immo-
bilières (a middleman in real estate transactions)" (Sembène 1973, 10;
1976, 3; translation modified). It is as middleman that he secures his
financial toehold, functioning exactly in the manner Fanon derides,
for he produces neither new goods nor wealth but profits well from
their exchange. When Senegalese independence is declared, he is
poised to ascend to prominence, having accumulated so much money
that he can think about taking yet another wife: "Cette troisième
union le hissait au rang la notabilité traditionnelle (This third marriage raised him to the rank of the traditional nobility)" (Sembène
1973, 12; 1976, 4). Later, when he has been expelled by the "businessmen's group" (and is replaced with a petty pickpocket-cum-entrepre-
neur), El Hadji offers some sharp parting words to his former cohort
that echo those of Fanon about that class:

> Qui sommes-nous? De minables commissionnaires, moins que des
> sous-traitants. Nous ne faisons que de la redistribution. Redistribuer
> les restes que les gros veulent bien nous céder. Sommes-nous de
> Hommes d'affaires? Je réponds, pour ma part: non. Des culs-terreux.
> . . . Les banques appartiennent à qui? Les assurances? Les usines?
> Les enterprises? Le commerce en gros? Les cinémas? Les librairies?
> Les hôtels? etc., etc., etc. De tout cela et autres choses, nous ne
> contrôlons rien. Ici, nous ne sommes que des crabes dans un panier.
> Nous voulons la place de l'ex-occupant. Nous y sommes. Cette
> Chambre en est la preuve. Quoi de changé, en général comme en
> particulier? Rien. Le colon est devenu plus fort, plus puissant, caché
> en nous, en nous ici présents. (Sembène 1973, 138–39)

What are we? Mere agents, less than petty traders! We merely re-
distribute. Re-distribute the remains the big men deign to leave us.

Are we businessmen? I say no! Just clodhoppers! . . . Who owns the
banks? The insurance companies? The factories? The businesses?
The wholesale trade? The cinemas? The bookshops? The hotels?
All these and more besides are out of our control. We are nothing
better than crabs in a basket. We want the ex-occupier's place? We
have it. This Chamber is the proof. Yet what change is there really in
general or in particular? The colonialist is stronger, more powerful
than ever before, hidden inside us, here in this very place. (Sembène
1976, 83–84)

Sembène extends and embellishes Fanon in a sympathetic rewriting.
The style of "The Pitfalls of National Consciousness" is both polemical and predictive. It does not—indeed, cannot—also include the
expression of the disenfranchised on whose behalf it speaks. It can be
their advocate, but apparently it cannot represent them as actors or
agents in a story.[24] The agents in Fanon's story are the national
bourgeoisie, and the action looks to be one-sided—the national Senegalese bourgeoisie resembling the European bourgeoisie of *The Communist Manifesto*, those who, up to this point, are the real agents of
history. By exploiting the representational power of fiction, Sembène
incarnates Fanon's "wretched" in the persons of the beggars who are
everywhere in both film and novella. Their raggedly clothed, de-
formed, and malodorous bodies contrast sharply with the well-
fed, overdressed, and perfumed wedding guests and businessmen.
And they offer a corrective view of the national populace. Indeed, the
beggars' sharing of food and other scarce resources and their collective action at the end suggest an indigenous and resisting socialism,
one that during the early 1970s must have seemed very far from
experienced life. Their final act of spitting—both punishment
and cure—suggests the redemptive power of collective action on the
part of the people in the face of political paralysis and corruption.
The beggars stand for a more legitimate example of national community, one without the hollow revolutionary language of the Chamber
of Commerce gentlemen. In a narrative sense, moreover, they are
critical to the plot. An unnamed one of their number is responsible
for the curse that drives the action—and who drives El Hadji to
his ruin.

The point at which Sembène departs from Fanon interests me even more. Unlike the vast majority of African male writers of the 1950s to the 1970s, Sembène does not displace onto women the anxiety about colonialism or about the entrance of the colonized into postcolonial modernity in *Xala*. Instead, he thematizes assumptions of decolonizing nationalism about gender. An impotent man as figure of the nation overturns the familiar sign of woman as nation in the service of a nationalist agenda. Bâ, however, narrates the nation obliquely. In *Lettre*, the domestic betrayal that polygyny means for the narrator itself produces a background of the political betrayal of the nation.

By yoking sex–gender politics to Fanon's critique of economic and political corruption, Sembène highlights the deeply ingrained tendency to tell national stories in sex-gender terms. An impotent man as symbol of the African nation-state not only substitutes a male figure for the usual female one but, through this substitution, calls attention to the common use of women as national symbols: fertile woman and woman as victim of masculine violence. Instead of reiterating the gendered nostalgia at the heart of orthodox cultural nationalism, *Xala* deconstructs that sign by collapsing signifier and signified. El Hadji occupies the position of both actor and symbol simultaneously: he is author of his own downfall, having engineered his own financial ruin, and even of his xala, by cheating the beggar's family; he is also sign of the nation, his class-determined impotence standing for the paralysis and sterility of neocolonialism. Thus, within a context highly over-determined by the sign of woman and nation, *Xala* rather extraordinarily avoids representing woman as nation while still narrating a parable of sexual and national power.

In contrast to the conventional male cultural nationalist position wherein sexuality is a transparent signifier that references either the nobility or baseness of women, Sembène shifts the nature and meaning of sex while continuing to use both genders in his symbology. (He does so, of course, without abandoning an investment in progressive nationalism; in fact, *Xala* unambivalently celebrates national consciousness that stems from the common people.) Impotence, the central sexual sign, is revealed and is also revealing; its arrival catalyzes the unfolding of a national narrative of class complicity, for to regain and protect his failed manhood, El Hadji exposes his complicated system of graft, bribery, and narcissism.

While impotence is the single most important signifier in the text, sexuality in general serves as a sign for diverse problems that plague contemporary Africa. The commodification of women's bodies is emphatically conveyed through the beautiful and desirable N'Goné. Although she registers a powerful visual presence in the film, for example, she never speaks.[25] The camera lingers much more on the poster of her posing half-naked than on the actual woman herself, drawing attention to her role as a simulacrum of desire rather than as a person in her own right.

Instead of being relegated to the status of symbols or even spurious national actors, all of El Hadji's women emerge simultaneously as victims of men's narcissism and greed *and* as actors in their own right with complex and opposing interests. His daughter, Rama, represents the ideal national actor, a synthesis of indigenous culture and modern values, the chance for an egalitarian relationship with one's partner and, therefore, the best hope for the future of Africa. Sembène's text nevertheless deploys that same over-determined analytic through which contemporary African women are articulated: the Mother Africa–prostitute binary, or that of (a good) tradition versus (a bad) modernity. The first wife, Adja Awa Astou, stands for an idealized sense of tradition. She is devout, stoic, dignified in demeanor, and modest in dress, and she remains with El Hadji to the very end, even staying in the room with him during the spitting. Diametrically opposed to her is the second wife, Oumi N'Doye, who represents the coarseness of a certain modernity in her taste for European magazines, furniture, and cuisine; her aggressively expressed desires for sex; her conspicuous consumption; and her constant demands for goods and money. She becomes a prostitute in an attempt to retain her comfortable lifestyle after El Hadji loses his money.

Aminata Sow Fall's second novel, *La grève des bàttu*, was published the same year as *Lettre*. Like Bâ, Sow Fall garnered critical acclaim for her novella. It was placed on the short list for the Prix Goncourt and won the Grand Prix Litteraire de l'Afrique Noire in 1980. In both tone and structure, *Grève* resonates more with Sembène's narrative than does Bâ's. The resemblances to Sembène are visible in the satiric form and ironic twists of fate. *Grève* is a novella short on characterization and long on biting humor. The novel's premise is that, having been beaten and otherwise mistreated by the government bureau-crats who administer The City, the local beggars decide to act collectively and go on strike. They refuse to beg in the city and move to the hinterland, where they accept money and food from those who come to them. This turns into a crisis because, as it becomes clear midway through the novel, the beggars serve a critical function in the transmutation of spiritual good into material wealth.

Sow Fall's novella would seem to begin from the filmic scene in *Xala* where the beggars, having been rounded up and chased out of town by the police, form an ad hoc community. In an astute reading of the differences between the filmic and novelistic versions of *Xala*, Ken Harrow (1980) addresses what he perceives to be the film's far greater political power of representation. He contrasts the single complaint the novelistic El Hadji makes to the president that the beggars should be locked up with what, in the film, turns into a more elaborate event. In the film, we witness El Hadji phoning the president, who in turn phones the chief of police, after which we see the beggars being forcibly removed. In contrast to the novel, says Harrow (1980, 185), the film gives greater emphasis to the presence of the beggars:

> We are always aware of the poor people in the streets, from the opening shot to the wedding reception, to El Hadji's return to his shop. They gather in crowds when there's an accident (and even to see the film being made!). We see them shipped to the barren plains outside of town, returning painfully to the streets by crawling and dragging themselves back in the heat of the day. It is their presence, so much less visible in the novel, which goes far in defining the character of the film's setting and its atmosphere.

The novel offers a more complete back story to the primary and secondary characters, including the story of Awa Adja Astou. The film, however, powerfully captures the mass of humanity who go without while simultaneously (i.e., at the same filmic moment) El Hadji's chauffeur washes his Mercedes with Evian, imported French bottled water. The first two sentences of *Grève* make its focus clear and repeat the novel's subtitle, *Les déchets humains*, which I read as an echo of Fanon's *Les damnés de la terre*:

Ce matin encore le journal en a parlé: ces mendiants, ces talibés, ces lépreux, ces diminués physiques, ces loques, constituent des encombrements humains. Il faut débarasser la Ville de ces hommes— ombres d'hommes plutôt—déchets humains, qui vous assaillent et vous agressent partout et n'importe quand. (Sow Fall 1979 [2001], 11)

This morning there was another article about it in the newspaper: about how the streets are congested with these beggars, these *talibés* [begging mendicants], these lepers and cripples, all these derelicts. The Capital must be cleared of these people—parodies of human beings rather—these dregs of society who beset you everywhere and attack you without provocation at all times. (Sow Fall 1981)

Like the other two novellas, *Grève* centrally locates a rich and powerful male character who, on achieving success after independence, becomes corrupted and forgets the condition of his less fortunate neighbors and compatriots. True to form, Mour Ndiaye undertakes an additional marriage to a much younger woman. Both Sow Fall and Bâ make the new marriage a second one rather than the third that Sembène depicts, a slight narrative restructuring that allows the female authors to illustrate more sharply the duplicity and inconstancy experienced by both first wives when they learn about the event. For all three first wives, the new marriage comes as a surprise and is announced by the husband as a fait accompli. Like his brother characters, Mour personifies Fanon's native bourgeoisie by contributing little to the country but milking it of its rewards. Unlike El Hadji and Modou Fall, Mour does not even merit a history of political action on which to base his claim to wealth; his lone anticolonial gesture consists of slapping his white boss after having been insulted one too many times. Sow Fall does represent a union-organizer-turned-anticolonial-activist but she isolates the more admirable action in another character, Galaye.

The unfortunates so memorably drawn by Sembène are elaborated and given agency in Sow Fall—in a manner ultimately sympathetic to Fanon's argument. Eschewing the sexual grammar of Sembène, Sow Fall exploits a religious one. Mour's religious practices evolve out of his personal history of good luck rather than any sense of principle, for he gives only to one marabout, Serigne Birama. Having stumbled into good fortune after befriending this marabout, he now believes himself to be a devout Muslim. Ignoring the tenets of Muslim giving, Mour practices a kind of instrumental charity—giving lavishly but only to the person he believes can improve his life. His peculiar form of aid is not known to Serigne Birama himself.

The premise of the story—a strike by those who give blessings in exchange for alms (after all, money is more abstract than the labor of a blessing)—might appear far-fetched. However, in societies where religious principles include charity as a pillar of social intercourse, where begging is an old and accepted practice, one can see the powerful effect that such a strike might have. Events in Myanmar (what used to be Burma) in 2007, when Buddhist monks refused the alms of soldiers, thereby provoking a confrontation, suggest that it is not so fantastic a tale and closer to reality than one might imagine.[26]

Sembène has suggested that the weakness of the (masculine) body is related to that of the spirit, that sexual impotence is not only synonymous with but perhaps caused by political corruption. Sow Fall refuses Sembène's explicit representation of sexuality and instead uses a religious logic to make an economic argument. The beggars become a named and visible part of the national economy. Earlier, I claimed that the polemical style of "The Pitfalls of National Consciousness" could not include the voices of the disenfranchised on whose behalf it spoke, and that Sembène's advance over Fanon was to represent the disenfranchised, many of them disabled. Although the plot of the story is organized around El Hadji, by the end the beggars have taken control of the action, and the viewing position requires some identification with them. Sembène represents the *damnés* as human beings; it requires another, subsequent narrative act to give them personality and some individuation. Making the margins come to life, *Grève* speaks to the poverty of the *"déchets humains"* as they live on the edges of the city. The novel speaks to their collectivity and, even more than does Sembène, to their dignity and agency.

Grève turns on the conceit of the strike, making visible and reframing as necessary what one might think of as merely charitable relations in a way that is much indebted to Marx. The insight of *Capital I* lay in challenging the notion that the capitalist benefited the worker more than the worker benefited the capitalist in an economic enterprise that depends on the laborer's willing, even grateful, participation in a system that always gets the better of him or her. *Grève*'s Marxist claim, which elaborates on Sembène's Marxism (although it also differs from it), makes the beggars' blessings the product and, perhaps, the convenience of their blessing the "surplus value."[27]

Sow Fall's novella engages Sembène's novella and film through its plot. In contrast to the sincerity and sentimentality of *Lettre*, *Grève*, like *Xala*, is sharply satirical. It tells a different morality tale, replacing Sembène's sexual economy with one where exchange itself is more explicitly thematized and religion, that which Marx deemed an opiate and for which Sembène has no use, appears to offer the base for a politics of socialism. Although Sow Fall's novella contains a strong-willed female character, the story does not focus on feminine empowerment or emancipation but, rather, on religiosity as a means by which an exchange of morality for worldly goods might be justified.

Lettre mediates *Xala*'s sexual satire by telling a sentimental and intimate story of personal tragedy. Bâ translates *Xala*'s sexual topos into a romantic tale gone awry. In contrast, Sow Fall refuses the sentimental altogether. Rather than a character-driven story like *Lettre*, she opts for a plot-driven one, telling a differently moralistic fable. As with *Xala*, the characters in Sow Fall's novel are caricatures; they are not fully interiorized, realist characters. In both *Xala* and *Grève*, the elite man, the text's anti-protagonist, is brought down by beggars, those whom Sow Fall names in the novella's subtitle "*les déchets humains.*" These are the very people whom the main characters seek to eliminate or dispose of to continue their climb to the heights of power. In *Xala*, the beggars stand for the nation dispossessed by its own elite, as well as by European colonizers. In *Grève*, Sow Fall uses the beggars to put Islamic tenets in dialogue with African socialism. Sembène satirizes the national bourgeoisie by narrativizing Fanon's admonitions about economic impotence at the level of class into the biting tale of sexual impotence.

Beginning with *Lettre*, I have read in reverse chronological order to explore the complex ties that bind this early women's-feminist work to *Xala*. I then attend to the more straightforward linking of *Xala* to Fanon's essay. In the process of rewriting Sembène's novella, Bâ promotes gender from a secondary to primary level of analysis.

Lettre tells the tale of a romance gone wrong, a failed version of precisely the sort of relation Sommer charts in Latin America. Reconsidering this most canonical of novels written by women from Africa makes visible an intricate—and deeply ambivalent—relation between the novella itself and the polemical Marxist essay to which it is in some manner indebted. By giving up on the collective, by understanding or representing only the promises of the past, and by rejecting a sense of outrage that fuels Sembène and Sow Fall, Bâ makes a place for herself (and for female authors who come after) to speak in favor of romance, of individuality, of feminine selfishness, of individual desire. *Grève* uses almsgiving as a requirement of Islam to illustrate the basis for a monetary, moral, and human economy; Sow Fall's unsentimental and sharply humorous portrayal of neocolonialism takes up the other side of *Xala*'s Marxism and stands in sharp contrast to the sentimental feminism of *Lettre*.

3. Bildung in Formation and Deformation

Dangarembga and Farah

The happiest women, like the happiest nations, have no history.—GEORGE ELIOT, *The Mill on the Floss*

The next two chapters of this book move in a direction some-what different from that of the previous two. The chapters on Nigerian and Senegalese novels focus particularly on charting national literary histories and are organized as a set of interdiscursive readings. This chapter and the one that follows attend less to the question of beginnings than to that of the formation of the individual subject or character, the development of interiority, the relation of the individual to the group—and they take up these questions through the genre of the Bildungsroman.

The Bildungsroman, or novel of education, tells a story of character development and emotional maturation. Naive, often young protagonists encounter various trials that enable them to test their mettle. They undergo apprenticeships in the lessons of life and emerge older and wiser. The most conventional understanding of the genre has some form of test involving alienation from the group and, by the novel's end, reintegration into it. The genre is understood to have originated with Goethe's *Wilhelm Meister* (1796). Partly because it came into being in Europe in the late eighteenth century, it is also understood to be the bourgeois novel par excellence. Emerging out of a context of self-improvement, the genre's early form was well suited to serve the interests of that audience. By celebrating the individual's potential for development, and by projecting a final harmony between self and society, it promised a sunny end to an economic revolution.[1] As it developed, responding to and producing changes in reception patterns, the Bildungsroman increasingly came to expose contradictions in the ideology of individualism. As I explore in this chapter, the genre operates within an implied teleology that, when examined closely, it only imperfectly fulfills.

On the one hand, the Bildungsroman is understood to be nation-specific in origin, coming out of a period of identity consolidation in mid-eighteenth-century Germany and representing that nation's unique cultural and ethical sensibilities.[2] It has, nevertheless, migrated to other parts of Europe and even elsewhere in the world. On the other hand, as it moved, it continued to speak a relation to nationalism. If now no longer uniquely German, it remains a genre that is defined by the interrelation of self-development and national development. Subject-formation is enacted within a national frame: the growth and maturation of the individual, often explicitly and almost always implicitly, tells of the growth and maturation of the nation. What happens, then, when national development and individual growth are expressly de-linked? Or, as I ask here, what happens when the allegorical relation is maintained but either tenor or vehicle is held to be perverted or morally bankrupt?

This chapter examines the development and undoing of individual character and the national imaginary through a reading of two quite different novels written in English and published in the late 1980s, both of which bind the relation of the decolonized nation to that of individual growth and the development of the individual subject. *Nervous Conditions*, by the Zimbabwean Tsitsi Dangarembga (1988), and *Maps* (1986), by the Somali Nuruddin Farah, were published within a few years of each other outside the countries of their authors' origin. *Nervous Conditions* was the first novel of a then unknown female writer born in 1959. When it could not find a Zimbabwean publisher, it was picked up by feminist presses in the United States and the United Kingdom and has since become a mainstay on postcolonial syllabi. *Maps* has a somewhat different history: it is the sixth novel by an established writer who was born in 1945 and has not lived in his country of origin for more than a few years since he left to attend university because his critique of corruption in the regime of Somalia's longtime dictator, Siad Barre, was so explicit. *Maps* was first published by Pantheon in 1986, went out of print in the early 1990s, and in 2000 was reissued by Penguin Books. The juxtaposition of novels produces a conversation that explores yearnings and anxieties that speak to gender, decolonization, and independence in europhone African novels. Both novels demonstrate conventional Bildungsroman lineaments. Each focuses on character development and emotional maturation. Each is self-reflective and retraces the development of a somewhat problematic self. Each speaks to the importance of formal schooling, and each makes central the complex negotiation of family relations that form a part of growing up in a late-colonial and postcolonial world. In both, personal growth is a problematic enacted within the narrator's discursive self-understanding rather than merely consisting of the events that the hero experiences. Sexual development, critical to the development of individual characters and an important feature of the genre, is obscured in both novels, though the reasons for this differ and have to do with the gender of the protagonist, as well as with the type of psychodynamic model of human understanding each novel advocates.

Maps and *Nervous Conditions* are novels of contemporary history, which in this case means that they are set ten to fifteen years before the time of their writing and publication.[3] Moreover, both novels are explicitly feminist, invested in the condition of women, whether they are educated urbanites or illiterate villagers, modern and upwardly mobile or workers of the land, "traditional," superstitious, and poor. On first encounter, the primary difference between the two novels appears to be stylistic. *Nervous Conditions* is straightforwardly realist, while *Maps* is ludic in its movement between modernist disruption of linear narration and postmodern self-referentiality.

The question of form is very much part of my reading; however, I initially examine the particularities of each novel through theme or content. First and most important is the relation of the Bildungsroman to nationalist and feminist politics. The typical European and masculine hero of the Bildungsroman undertakes his quest alone. In these African novels of development, however, the protagonist is doubled or mirrored—indeed, one might suggest that each novel has two protagonists. The character through which the narrative is focalized, Tambu or Askar, exists in a form of diacritical relation to another, Nyasha or Misra, and the tension between each pair of characters drives the narrative.[4]

One of the most important similarities between the novels is that in both, the development and maturation of the Bildung protagonist is predicated on the abjection of the other character. Abjection itself is differently structured in each text. While Tambudzai succeeds in entering the world after having completed her education, the state of Nyasha's health remains unclear. Askar appears to have failed: he is directionless; Misra is dead, possibly by his hand, and the story he tells is as narrated to a police interrogator.

The two novels take different—even opposing—positions on narrating the nation, on the relation of gender to nationalism, and even on the question of the nation itself as a site of hope or productive politics. Moreover, though written within a mere two years of each other, they exemplify my claim that male authors, even feminist men, address the nation openly, while female authors speak to it in oblique, indirect terms. *Nervous Conditions* almost perfectly illustrates my thesis about national narratives in need of illumination through feminist reading. A national tale is told without ever naming the nation. The word "Zimbabwe," for example, never appears in the novel. Rhodesia is mentioned only once, at the end and in the negative, as is the United Declaration of Independence, which remains the acronym UDI.[5]

In sharp contrast, *Maps* names the nation as an ideological and political category of identity and by the novel's end has renounced that category entirely. The actual nation-states Somalia and Ethiopia, as well as the contested border region, the Ogaden, are named as such and central to the plot and characterization. Askar's visible failure to normalize and become a man and a productive Somali citizen results from the novel's having forced the question of reconciliation of national and progressive politics, as well as the production of identity cohesion, within a context where none can take place. By the novel's end, national identity is revealed to be hollow, bankrupt, useful only as an instrument of violence and death, and not as a valid category of analysis or political action.

Surveying a number of Bildungsromane from Western Europe of the late eighteenth century to the early twentieth century, Franco Moretti (1987, vi–vii) outlines three important mechanisms by which the hero is manufactured. They involve (1) the expansion of subjective time, or "making narratively interesting the bland rhythm of everyday reality"; (2) the shrinking of historical time, or "keeping history at a safe distance, separating the destiny of the individual from the great collective waves of the nineteenth century"; and (3) conversation or anxiety about class movement. The third point, for Moretti, means the threat to the aristocracy is contained by the bourgeoisie but for our purposes is more productively understood as a certain form of Westernization or, on the part of the African subject, the movement from village to town, toward the modern and individualizing and away from "tradition."[6]

Using Moretti's mechanisms for the production of socialized individuals as a guide, one sees that *Nervous Conditions* conforms to all three categories by which human potential is circumscribed or remains unexploited, but *Maps* conforms to only one. For both *Maps* and *Nervous Conditions*, the everyday advancement and growth of their protagonists constitutes the primary novelistic drama, illustrating Bildung as "calm passion" (v). The second significant generic characteristic, the one that enables the Bildungsroman to naturalize the making of social conformity or responsible adults, requires characters who willingly renounce individual "freedom" to taste the pleasure of social cohesion or "happiness." One might translate the other half of this dialectic into the "mastering" of historical time," which is to say, keeping the great sweep of history at enough distance to focus on the maturation of a single individual.

Contrasting the genre's opposing drives of individuation or self-expression, on the one hand, and normality or the necessity to conform, on the other, Moretti suggests that, to achieve conformity, the Bildungsroman cannot appear to be simply compliant with authority but must narrate that compliance as "*symbolically legitimate*" (16). Modern bourgeois society cannot simply subdue the drives that oppose the standards of "normality." As a "free individual"—not as a fearful subject, but as a convinced citizen—he or she should perceive the social norms as his or her own. This logic does much to illuminate *Nervous Conditions*, for by the novel's end, Tambu has entered Sacred Heart, accepting the not-so-subtle racism that will allow her to pursue her beloved education, and like her uncle and aunt before her, she stands poised to become part of the national elite. The compromise Tambu makes and Nyasha refuses might be compared with those made by Hilaal and Salaado in *Maps*. The Somali novel, however, never legitimizes that exchange even while continuing to depict sympathetically the characters that make it. Rather than make the act of compromise symbolically legitimate or represent a character who successfully sublimates his desires or ideals toward the compromise, *Maps* relentlessly pursues the cost to conscience, the price of freedom that is the price of "normality" or social cohesion. Askar's new sense of himself as a man and a Somali produces confusion within. It contradicts his childhood loyalties and understanding of love. To shore up his fragile sense of identity, he gives in to ugly assertions of and demarcations about who and what makes a Somali. Having posed different questions that challenge the belief that a national sensibility is an unquestioned good, the novel produces a massacre, then a rape and murder, all wrapped in the enigma of identity. Is Askar Misra's son? Is he her betrayed lover? Or is she for him the antithesis to a national motherland? And if she is the latter, why? By posing developmental question in psychoanalytic terms and by making the protagonist's early childhood years the ones in which he had the best and clearest understanding of his relation to the world, *Maps* refuses the compromise integral to successful maturation.

In an important but little known essay on the Bildungsroman, Frederic Jameson claims that the genre solves a particular problem within postcolonialism and implies a dialogue with the question of the national allegory. Jameson's essay serves as another point of entry into the sets of questions these novels pose.[7] My earlier engagement with the national-allegory essay should testify to the importance of Jameson's work for me. I have sought to illustrate that his early forays into thinking about the Third World or Global South have large blind spots but even more important insights. The essay "On Literary and Cultural Import-Substitution in the Third World" is much less known and, although it was published almost a decade after the notorious national-allegory essay (1986) it appears to have been drafted at about the same time.[8] Jameson does not precisely return to the topic of the national allegory, although he continues to work within the frame of that earlier essay by putting the First World and Third World into political dialogue via the form of their literature, particularly their prose narratives. Though he continues with and expands on the same teleological argument wherein he is accused of making the Third World appear belated to the First World, Jameson is much more careful here to couch his developmentalism in terms that move between the First World and the Third World and, especially, that speak to differences within the Third World itself. By naming two forms of Bildungsroman—one conventional and Western, and the other simultaneously postmodern and archaic—Jameson acknowledges different generic structures and different expressions of ideology while continuing to give pride of place to his strongly idealized Third World cultural space. Moreover, he tackles the question of Third World belatedness, or uneven development, when he suggests that development is itself ideologically overvalued. The alternative Marxist formulation, or uneven development, is curiously dealt with only at a conceptual level here. Jameson compares the importation and making of naturalist novels to the making of cars or films (Jameson 1996, 177).

Jameson locates the Bildungsroman centrally in the history of the novel, its particular formulation named as not merely exemplary but causal, that which allows the novel to first come into being. The development of the Western novel might be read through the genre of the Bildungsroman "if we substitute the Lazarillo de Tormes for the Quijote as the formal ancestor and if we take the European eighteenth century as its [the novel's] paradigmatic moment" (Jameson 1996, 174). Re-plotting the story of the novel in this manner shifts attention away from Germany at the beginning of its national tradition. Moving the novel's origin to Spain, moreover, makes more direct and natural its link to both Latin America and the rest of the Third World. The novel of development itself is "a formal solution of historical significance" and therefore, as a genre, the epitome of highly charged technological innovation. Its technological innovation is as a machine for producing subjectivity.[9]

For Jameson, the genre enacts a negotiation between the protagonist and family: "What the new narrative format seems to do is to pry the nascent text away from the social substance of the family itself and allow the novel—as the registration of the new and the unique—to come into being as though for the first time. This is also sometimes known as the emergence of subjectivity or individualism. Something is also implied about the family, as an institution about which 'individualistic' stories of that kind cannot be told, except in the hapless efforts of its various members to free themselves from it" (Jameson 1996, 173). The genre's value as social document lies in its performance of the weaning of the individual from the family; it thereby makes visible the coming into being of the narrative self.

Jameson insightfully recognizes that as an institution, the family mediates between the coming into individualism of the self and the public sphere of the collective or group in the Third World, something that I have claimed has explanatory value for novels written by women in particular. His blindness lies in seeing the making of individuality, or the entrance into history, as something that emerges from the timelessly primeval muck of the family, which in this respect puts him in the same league as African and other decolonizing cultural nationalists. For example, having claimed that Naguib Mahfouz's novels display a "virtually Hegelian opposition between the chthonic substance of the family and the public realm of history and business," he then asserts that "what is even more interesting about them is the formal or narrative problem they thereby act out before our very eyes—how to wrest the novelistic (in some henceforth Western sense) from this archaic family or clan material.... My hypothesis is this: that the moment of the childhood novel—the attempt to construct a Western-style bourgeois subjectivity, including 'personal identity' and the temporality of memory—breaks down and gives way to two distinct and antithetical strategies: the one openly Westernizing, if I may put it that way, the other archaic (but also postmodern in its way)" (Jameson 1996, 173–74). Both *Maps* and *Nervous Conditions* provide ample narrative material to refute Jameson's a-historical representation of the family, but, as will become clear, each does so in a different way. Both illustrate that family itself is not limited to a nuclear configuration, that extended families are no less familial (nurturing, loving, or threatening and violent) than are biological families or those in which the protagonist spends his or her formative years.

Jameson rightly focuses on the formation of the individual out of and through the family. He points to how, in the process, the narrative self comes into being for the first time via the interiority developed in opposition or distinction to the family. Both novels seem to elaborate on—and contradict—this point. In *Nervous Conditions*, it is the extended family that provides Tambu with the means for upward mobility, and it educates her in more than just an institutional way. Tambu flees her suffocating nuclear family and its burdens of poverty and brute patriarchy and is rescued by another branch, that of her paternal uncle and aunt. Like Askar's aunt and uncle, Tambu's aunt and uncle, Maiguru and Babamukuru, are both imperfect, possibly even inadequate to the task of bringing up a young person in a colonial or neocolonial world. Nevertheless, both sets of family units embrace the protagonist as their own child, enabling Askar and Tambu each to give form to the Bildungsroman's teleological spirit. For Tambu, the nuclear family remains important by way of negative inspiration; for Askar, the initial family is that for which he longs and to which he fears to return.

Neither Jameson nor Moretti gives much thought to the different sorts of development experienced by male versus female characters, and for this I turn to an early and important statement of the female Bildungsroman. The social constraints on women's maturation produce conflicts, which, while not unique to female characters, are more relentlessly explored there, say Elizabeth Abel, Marianne Hirsch, and Elizabeth Langland in the introduction to their classic collection on the women's Bildungsroman: "Repeatedly, the female protagonist or Bildungsheld must chart a treacherous course between the penalties of expressing sexuality and suppressing it, between the costs of inner concentration and of direct confrontation with society, between the price of succumbing to madness and of grasping a repressive 'normality'" (Abel, Hirsch, and Langland 1983, 12–13). Feminine sexuality, women's engagement with dominant structures of power, and the looming specter of psychological instability are the three primary motifs by which the girls engage the world and enter adulthood.

Like South Africa, Rhodesia was dominated by an intransigent white settler colony. The state of Rhodesia came about after the breakup in 1963 of the colonial entity the Federation of Rhodesia and Nyasaland, wherein Northern Rhodesia and Nyasaland became, respectively, the independent states of Zambia and Malawi. Southern Rhodesia became Rhodesia, and under Ian Smith's prime-ministerial guidance, declared independence from England in 1965 in putting forth the UDI. Within this frame, sovereignty was for whites only; the majority black population had very limited access to economic power and could not vote. The period between the UDI and the late 1970s represents one of the bleakest periods in the nation's history. Black enfranchisement came about only after a protracted guerrilla war (Chimurenga) fought by the Zimbabwe African National Union (ZANU) and the Zimbabwe African People's Union (ZAPU), the two most important wings of the Zimbabwean liberation movement. ZANU won, and in 1980 the new nation was renamed Zimbabwe.

In many respects, *Nervous Conditions* is a conventional Bildungsroman and seems to exist in marginal relation to fictions of the nation as told by the male writers Chenjerai Hove and Shimmer Chinodya. *Bones* (1988), by Hove, and *Harvest of Thorns* (1989), by Chinodya, are dissimilar from each other in form and subject matter; nevertheless, both represent and engage the Zimbabwean struggle for liberation in a direct manner. For all of the formal innovativeness that garnered it the Noma Award in 1989, at the level of theme *Bones* rewrites the clichéd figure of Mother Africa through its violated heroine, Marita. *Harvest of Thorns* more closely resembles *Nervous Conditions* in its realism and in that at least one section conforms to the genre of Bildungsroman. Part of *Harvest*'s interest lies in its narration of the impossibility of objectively recounting war experiences. Problematized and self-consciously depicted though *Harvest* makes that representation, the fact remains that it exists. The war is in some manner represented via language, although the language is never fully adequate to the experience. In contrast, *Nervous Conditions* charts a less direct and far more conflicted route of narrative and character development. Part of that conflict stems from its critical attention to gender, which on first reading implies that decolonizing nationalism subsumes feminism into its overarching agenda. In a classically realist mode of narration, this novel tells the story of a black Rhodesian girl whose quest for an education takes her to the home of her more urbanized and Westernized aunt and uncle and from there to an elite convent boarding school. Recounted in the first person at a moment of thoughtful reflection after Tambudzai Siguake successfully integrates herself into the socius, it exemplifies many aspects of the typical Bildungsroman, narrating the unfolding of an individual in all of his or her complexity and richness. It is at the level of form that I pursue my discussion of the novel. The novel's focus on the burgeoning strength of its female narrator is paralleled by the diminishment of the other major female character. This dual move troubles its form and brings it up against the limits of its own narrative project, that of embourgeoisement.

The conventional understanding of realism is that it presents concrete, individualized, non-elite figures embedded in the context of particular places at particular times, its impression of fidelity to life stemming from figural individualization and particularization. The epitome of the classical realist form is the Bildungsroman, which in psychological terms represents the development of an interiorized subjectivity and in social terms represents the consolidation of the lone, bourgeois, and usually male character who takes up a place in (or outside) society. Tambudzai appears to be the traditional Bildungsroman protagonist, who, in a manner consonant with the European tradition, develops during the course of the novel into an individualized and bourgeois subject. By illustrating the values of thrift and hard work, her story charts a course compatible with the European and male prototype, illustrating the topoi of self-discovery and self-consolidation in a genre that poses as seamless.

The Berlin Conference of 1884–85 famously parceled off most of the African continent to European colonial nations. Berlin enacted on Somalia a miniaturized version of the partition of the rest of the continent. Unlike Ethiopia, Greater Somalia had never existed as a state. Dividing it between Ethiopia, England, Italy, and France, however, served to consolidate Somali nationalism in anticolonial response. Djibouti, the former French colony, opted for its own independence, which left four of the five parts of Greater Somalia: British Somaliland, Italian Somaliland, a portion of northern Kenya, and the much contested Ogaden.[10] By the early twentieth century, the three European nations and Ethiopia had all laid their claims; pan-Somali organizing efforts intensified after 1945. Britain, which controlled the rest of Somalia in 1960, ceded the Ogaden as well as part of what is now northern Kenya to Ethiopia shortly before Somali independence. The year 1960 ushered in national independence, but 1969 brought the assassination of the first prime minister, Ali Sharmarke; it also meant the ascendance of Siad Barre, who would hold power for almost twenty-five years. Farah's vigorous criticisms of dictatorship constitute a response to the tight grip on cultural, economic, and social power wielded by Siad Barre, and through Farah's exile one sees that Somalia has responded in return. "In 1977 Siyad Barre invoked the nationalist dream of unifying Greater Somalia by lending government support to the independent Western Somali Liberation Front, committed to reclaiming the Ogaden from Ethiopia, a move that initially strengthened his popularity among the Ogaden clan" (Alden and Tremaine 1999, 25). Military success was short-lived, for the Soviets used the occasion to switch their support to Ethiopia, whose Marxist revolution had come in 1974. Siad Barre immediately accepted Western patronage to replace that of the Soviet Union, but the exchange did not bring him significant military assistance, and Ethiopia drove the Somali army out of the Ogaden in 1978. Patricia Alden and Louis Tremaine (1999, 25–26) put it sharply: "That defeat on the battlefield (the most important battlefield of all for Somali nationalists), the resulting flood of refugees, and the ease with which Siyad Barre had bent his knee first to one superpower and then to another fed the already growing disillusionment with the revolutionary government. In the wake of an abortive military coup in April 1978, two opposition groups formed, significantly allied with two different clans who felt excluded from power."

In contrast to James Joyce's *The Portrait of the Artist as a Young Man*, which uses increasingly complex linguistic structures to reflect the burgeoning intellect of Stephen Daedalus, the story of the national man child in *Maps* unfolds through degeneration, not of language, but of the symbolic system of thought. Askar's newly acquired sense of himself as a man and a Somali produces confusion and ambivalence because it contradicts his childhood loyalties and notions of love. As his intellectual faculties mature and his sense of political affiliation sharpens, the linguistic structure moves from the discrete and sensual to the conceptual and abstract. At the same time that Askar matures, Misra, who is associated with the earth, becomes less and less significant to his story of the national subject, the story of himself as told by himself. Misra's and Somalia's respective corporeal and national bodies stand in metonymic relation to each other, one diminishing while the other increases in importance in narrative space. *Maps* does not just tell an elaborate narrative of the past from a present-tense place of reflective self-understanding. Rather, the novel often states that its own past-tense narration is unreliable, as Askar cannot remember crucial events.

Maps bears stronger affinities to *Wide Sargasso Sea* (1966) by the Dominican expatriate Jean Rhys. Both are anti-Bildungsroman, and both refuse the genre's teleological orientation. They both lack what Rita Felski (1989, 80) has called "cultural confidence in the reproducibility of an objectively present world." Posing questions through form allows them to expose the foundations of the reigning social order. The particular modernism in *Wide Sargasso Sea* links the larger colonial enterprise with the challenge to individual development. Colonialism and, especially, the institution of slavery in the Caribbean determine and over-determined Antoinette's degeneration. In *Maps*, colonialism's legacy of decolonizing nationalism accounts for the protagonist's radical alienation from his past and uncertainty about the future. It produces a protagonist whose maturation into a national citizen makes him either a matricidal renegade or so alienated from himself as not to know where he was at the time of Misra's death.

Unlike *Nervous Conditions*, which when interpreted reveals or produces a national allegory, *Maps* refuses an allegorical reading by foregrounding the already allegorized figure of woman as mother of the nation.[11] Representing Misra as so maternal as to embody Mother Africa works at one level to flatten her as a character; it requires that an allegorical reading be refused or, at the very least, deferred to a level of greater remove. Reading her allegorically requires that the allegory function at third level of reading. The following plot summary must reduce the non-chronological narrative recounting: *Maps* alternates regularly between first-person, second-person, and third-person narration, all focalized through the consciousness of Askar, a seventeen-year-old Somali boy at the time of the telling of the story, though at times in the story he is seven and occasionally younger.

The story begins with the mysterious circumstances of Askar's birth in the Ogaden, a region disputed by Somalia and Ethiopia. Askar's mother dies when he is a newborn, and he is brought up within the village of Kallafo by Misra, an Ethiopian woman of somewhat inde- terminate origin. The relationship between these two oddball charac- ters (he, a funny orphan with a penetrating stare; she, an ethnic outsider and unmarried mother) is rendered as profoundly intense, practically visceral; their need for each other so primary that it resem- bles that for bodily sustenance or sex. Askar's paternal uncle Qorrax, an important citizen of Kallafo, protects Askar with his name. Qorrax permits the child to remain with Misra, who is a foreigner and a poor woman, in exchange for her sexual favors. Misra agrees in order to keep the child.

Askar is circumcised at five and lives in the same house in Kallafo with Misra until he is seven. But meanwhile (in 1977 in historical time), tensions between Somalia and Ethiopia concerning the Ogaden erupt again, and Somalia temporarily wins control over the region. Later that year, Askar is sent to Mogadiscio, where he lives with his maternal uncle Hilaal and Hilaal's wife, Salaado. They are both profes- sionals, educated and liberal in their gender politics. Not only does Hilaal cook and Salaado drive, but when they learn that Salaado cannot bear children, Hilaal has a vasectomy in solidarity with her. Salaado is Askar's formal teacher, but Hilaal soon becomes a role model and his best interlocutor. Askar continues his studies while living with them; he becomes integrated into mainstream Somali culture and deeply interested in nationalist politics. His decision at the moment of narration is whether to join the Western Somali Liberation Front or to continue in his studies and become an aca- demic. At the same chronological, though not narratological, mo- ment, Misra comes to Mogadiscio looking for him. Ethiopia has retaken military control over the Ogaden (it is now 1978), and Misra has fled Kallafo amid rumors that she has betrayed 603 Somali sol- diers and civilians to a young Ethiopian officer with whom she was having an affair. Askar, now openly nationalist and obsessed with boundaries, is distant toward her, and it is left to his aunt and uncle to welcome her into their home. Misra denies the rumors of the betrayal and recounts the violent punishment, a gang rape, she was meted out by some villagers. Sick with breast cancer, she is taken to the hospital, and while recuperating from a mastectomy she is kidnapped from the hospital, never to be seen alive again. Her body is found days later at the local morgue. Before her death, her heart had been torn out. The implied question with which the novel closes is whether Askar participated in this murder. Although he does not confess to it, there are enough narrative gaps and enough partially articulated reasons for this to be a credible surmise. At the novel's end, he is arrested and taken by policemen for interrogation; Hilaal and Salaado are made to accompany him. We are then left with a series of questions. Did he kill her? And if he did, was it because of his own jealousy at her having taken a lover who was not him? Or were his emotions stirred because he believed she was party to a national slaughter?

The novel operates via a series of symbolic binary oppositions that it repeatedly establishes and undermines. Askar, the citizen of Somalia, narrates his coming-of-age story, which is obviously also a national Bildung. He is the son of nationalists, both of whom die in the Ogaden, one as a guerrilla fighter. Askar does not succeed in becoming a productive member of the nation, or even a full adult. Even before the question of Misra's murder is raised, it becomes obvious that his life is at an impasse. He cannot decide between becoming an intellectual in the service of the state or a revolutionary on behalf of the Somali nation. Misra, on the other hand, embodies the national subject, even though she is not a citizen. More than any other character, she enacts the selfless devotion of a woman of the nation. She agrees to a sexual relationship with the tyrannical uncle Qorrax to continue to care for the national man child. Her undiminished love for Askar fulfills nationalist stereotypes of self-sacrificing women and mothers nurturing in the service of the nation. Against Askar's legal right to citizenship, which is an abstraction—though one with tangible consequences—is juxtaposed Misra's material and organic connection to the land of Somalia. She is rendered in physical, sensual, concrete terms. She is frequently dirty from the labor of cleaning the floors or butchering a chicken; she sweats and gives off odors. She practices divination with animal organs and has an abortion, which is explained to Askar as the result of her not bleeding as she ought. Askar later recalls that her name is supposed to mean "the foundation of the earth" (Farah 1986, 177).

Askar and Misra share hauntingly similar tales of growing up. Both are taken from their childhood homes at seven because they are orphaned. Unlike Askar's, Misra's move is forced: she becomes the booty of a warrior. Ten years later, she, like Askar, confronts a momentous shift in her understanding of sexuality when she is compelled to marry the man who brought her up and whom she had thought of as her father. Askar is not forced into a sexual relation with Misra. Indeed, that she voluntarily takes at least two lovers during the course of the novel suggests that the text opens a crevice of narrative doubt large enough to allow the reader to perceive the story we have as not seamless, to read against the novel's own powerfully sexualized tone. The sensuality of the characters' relation and Askar's fierce jealousy of Misra's lovers throws them into the Oedipal drama. The text addresses these strong ambivalences by pointing to the violence by which Misra ends her family relation with her father-turned-husband: "In the end, the conflicting loyalties alienated her, primarily from herself. And she murdered him during an excessive orgy of copulation" (Farah 1986, 69). Does Askar's narration of Misra's story serve to foreshadow what will happen to her later, and by the hand of her own foster son? More than half of the novel is devoted to Askar's early life with Misra, an emphasis that signals the importance of the mother–child bond and that cries out for a psychoanalytic reading. *Maps* describes the period from Askar's birth to age seven and scants the ten-year period of formal education in Mogadiscio with Hilaal and Salaado. In addressing the question of the unconscious, the relation of the body to psychic urges, Farah engages in a reconfiguration of Freudian and Lacanian models. He takes from them both the notion that the ego does not have an a priori existence; that it comes into being historically. For Freud, the ego is illusorily produced as a whole and unified self in a stage that begins at about six months. For Lacan, the equivalent of coherence production, or the phase of primary narcissism, is called the mirror phase. Like Freud's, Lacan's story has the child entering the world of selfhood, here called the symbolic order, at great cost to itself. From its onset, subjectivity depends on the recognition of the distance between self and other, a recognition only achieved through alienation, through loss of numerous "parts" of itself that are relegated to the status of objects (here, importantly, including the foreskin at circumcision). For Lacan, however, selfhood depends on the perception of the self as not-Other, a moment of alienation from the mother's voice or breast or from its own feces.

Farah modifies the psychoanalytic model to produce two distinct stages commensurate with rituals and education in rural Somalia. The first stage is the acquisition of oral language (Somali) and a consciousness of self. Having acquired the ability to symbolize, Askar becomes aware that he has rivals for Misra's affections. In this period, he imagines himself as an additional breast in response to the "third leg" Aw-Adan presents to Misra. Askar's initial separation from Misra begins when he is taken away to study, when he first has access to the written word:

> Her body (or should I speak of her bodies: one of knowledge, another of immortality; one I knew and touched and felt, the other for others such as Aw-Adan and Uncle Qorrax) anticipated my body's needs (because I was a child, I had only one body, with hardly a shadow to speak of, this shadow being the size of a bird's dropping whenever I looked for and found it) only to satisfy them. If I couldn't pluck a fruit off a tree Misra's hand reached out and got it for me, and when I couldn't soap the small of my back, her palm was there to scrub it. Likewise, when I couldn't move my obstinate bowels, it was her applying massage or kneading techniques which helped me do so.
>
> Then I remembered the first painful separation: when I was sent to the Koranic school run by Aw-Adan. I was very, very unhappy. For some inexplicable reason, it felt as if, between my feet and the rest of my body, there existed an unfillable space. It was only much, much later that I rationalized that perhaps this was the unused space (previously Misra's) which had surrounded me for years but wasn't there anymore. (Farah 1986, 79)

Until this chronological moment, Misra looms large and comfortingly in Askar's life. She meets his physical needs fully, feeding, bathing, and nurturing him, despite the occasional intrusions of her lovers. Although he resents the intrusion by the men, Askar does not have to fully distinguish himself from Misra until he begins his formal education. As a baby, Askar knows himself to be whole when Misra is in the room, and he learns of his aloneness in her absence. Farah illustrates the larger Freudian axiom that subjectivity is produced through alienation; that only with the loss of the other comes apprehension of the self, and that these losses are experienced retroactively, from a position within the symbolic. For Farah, Askar's cultural identity requires this separation, and because his own status as a Somali is in some doubt, he must lose the object entirely. The pain of this loss and the nostalgic desire for its return constitutes most of the compelling material of the novel.

The second stage takes place when Askar is about five and is produced out of two important social acts: the acquisition of written language, Arabic, and circumcision, which makes of him a man and a Somali.[12] In associating the acquisition of masculinity with physical pain, Farah diverges sharply from both Freud and Lacan, for whom these forms of pain are entirely psychic. In telling of the physical pain associated with learning to write, Askar describes one facet of his entry into the symbolic, a register that also serves to mark his difference from Misra. Askar expresses bitter anger with both Aw-Adan and his poor memory for not recollecting why he could not speak Somali correctly:

> The letter alif, because I was hit by Aw-Adan and I bit my tongue, became balif; and ba when struck again sounded like fa; whereas the letter ta, now that my mouth was a pool of blood, was turned by my tongue into sha. (I can't explain why, but for a brief period that no one but me remembers, I had difficulty pronouncing the letter ta, which is rather odd, given that I could actually pronounce the letter that, as in the English word "thorough," and also fa.) Mind you, it wasn't because my upper, front teeth were missing or anything, no. It was as if the sound t was altogether absent from the repertoire of sounds I could make. (Farah 1986, 86)

Separation anxiety and the pain of losing the mother in learning language is here made literal and corporeally internalized. More important, as we soon learn, the psychic separation process is interrupted by the social factors of national or ethnic identity or affiliation.

Benedict Anderson's often quoted *Imagined Communities* schematizes some of the fundamental precepts of nationalism; the logic of the novel works against all of Anderson's forms of definition in a manner that illustrates the profound anti-nationalism of *Maps*. Anderson's most innovative contribution is his claim that nationalism is best understood through the register of kin relations rather than as an ideology.[13] Three additional characteristics of an imagined community involve allegiance to people one will never see; the Benjaminian concept of the national experience as "homogeneous empty time," wherein secular, calendrical relations supersede religious ones; and finally, and most important for these purposes, the community made possible by a shared vernacular language.

Maps's representation of the concept of a shared national language most strongly exposes the force of its anti-nationalist sensibility.[14] Hilaal, the person Askar most respects in the world and, within the novel, a person of independent authority, defines Somali identity through linguistic ability rather than blood or parentage and in terms that ultimately are deeply disturbing:

> "A Somali," said Uncle Hilaal, "is a man, woman or child whose mother tongue is Somali. Here, mother tongue is important, very important. Not what one looks like. That is, features have nothing to do with a Somali's Somaliness or no. True Somalis are easily distinguishable from other people, but one might meet with foreseeable difficulty in telling an Eritrean, an Ethiopian or a northern Sudanese apart from a Somali, unless one were to consider cultural difference. ... Somali identity ... is one shared by all Somalis, no matter how many borders divide them." ... [When Askar asks about Somalis in the Somali Republic and those in the Ogaden, Hilaal replies:] "The Somali in the Ogaden, the Somali in Kenya both, because they lack what makes the self strong and whole, are *unpersons*." Silence. Something made me not ask, "But what is an unperson, Uncle?" Now, years later, I wish I had told him I didn't understand the concept. Years later, I find it appropriate to ask, "Is Misra a Somali?" "Am I a refugee?" "Am I an unperson?" "Is or will Misra be an unperson—if she comes to Mogadiscio?" (Farah 1986, 174–75; emphasis in original)

Closer inspection reveals why Hilaal's description might frighten Askar so. In this passage, Hilaal describes, in what seems to be an affirmative manner, the way national identity works. Identity is not visible, he says, and in the face of the vulgarly race-based nationalism of most of the world, this seems remarkably enlightened. It is not race, skin color, or phenotype that determine Somaliness—but then, self-identification, cultural and political embrace, and even the rejection of another nation or state do not do so, either. Rather, national affiliation is determined through speech, through grammar and pronunciation; as such, speech should be able to be learned. Hilaal's first few sentences are ultimately less disturbing than the succeeding one.[15] In a passage shortly before the one quoted earlier, Hilaal asserts to Askar that there are states such as Germany that recognize as citizens people who were not born within its borders. Hilaal's statement about those who are "unpersons," then, may well refer to Somalis from the Ogaden or from northern Kenya, who, because they have no money or family connections, become nonentities to the state. Askar's fear, always present, bubbles to the surface when he hears this, for he is intimate with an unperson; he has been brought up as her son. Moreover, Hilaal's logic easily leads one to believe that Askar's having learned Somali from Misra compromises his status as a Somali. Because of his geographic distance from the Somali language and having been educated by a non-Somali, Aw-Adan might himself be an unperson. The novel's third-person voice suggests that, by this logic, he has reason to fear: "For years, he had enormous difficulties pronouncing his Somali gutturals correctly, since he had learnt them wrongly from her; for years he mispronounced the first letters of the words in Somali for 'sky' and 'earth'—just like she did" (Farah 1986, 56). Rhonda Cobham (1992, 92) suggests that "from Askar's perspective Misra's culture is identical to his own. Thus he reasons, she too could qualify for Somali citizenship. . . . Hilaal's caveat [that those from outside the Somali Republic are 'unpersons'] throws him along with Misra outside the circle of national certitude, and Askar is left as confused about where to draw the national boundaries around himself as it were unless he can find a way to distinguish between himself and Misra."

Askar comes from the Ogaden, as Cusmaan's ridiculed tutor comes from Tanzania or Kenya. The grammatical missteps by Cusmaan's tutor are a running family joke. Askar's own early linguistic deficiencies, his distant birthplace, and his mockery of Cusmaan's tutor allows us to perceive him as anxious and as distancing himself from Misra as a means of denial. His ultranationalism comes about, then, because of fear of exclusion from the circle of his family and friends.[16]

Modernist works often call attention to their form, and form is one of the first things the reader of *Maps* notices. The novel jumps about sharply in chronological time and is narrated in three voices. It alternates regularly between second person, first person, and third person, in that order, all emanating from Askar's voice or focalization. The shifting perspectives speak to uncertainty about acts undertaken as well as positions held. The tripartite form of narration allows for the recounting of Askar's different—and conflicting—motivations. The reader is rocked about, shaken, and jostled in the constant movement from one point of view to another.

The novel begins in the somewhat startling second-person point of view: "You sit, in contemplative posture, your features agonized and your expression pained; you sit for hours and hours and hours, sleepless, looking into darkness, hearing a small snore coming from the room next to yours" (Farah 1986, 3). Because English, unlike French, does not have much history of avant-gardist writing in the second person, this literary style jars and appears hostile.[17] Cobham (1992, 88–89) calls the second-person voice in *Maps* "judgmental" and "accusatory"; in her opinion the second person self-interrogates rather than describes. Francis Ngaboh-Smart (2001) suggests that the second person is a skeptical voice, with which I am more in agreement. After all, it is in the second person that the novel first describes Hilaal and Salaado in their progressive glamour.

It is in the second person that Hilaal's letter of advice to Askar, written late in the chronological story but narrated at the novel's beginning and introducing Hilaal as mentor, makes itself known. The second person is the voice in which the most conventional relation Askar has with a person his own age in Mogadiscio, the almost girlfriend Riyo, is represented. And, of course, the second person interrogative interrupts Askar regularly to enquire about his relation to Misra, repeatedly asking, "Do you remember?" (Farah 1986, 215–16).

Ngaboh-Smart (2001, 79) claims that first person is the voice of African nationalism. I am inclined to agree, with the qualification that the first person presents nationalism's best face in the novel—and not the one that ultimately most defines it. He rightly notes that the first person narrates Askar at his most naive and vulnerable. It is from this point of view that Askar first recounts his forced separation from Misra to learn Arabic at the hands and stick of Aw-Adan (Farah 1986, 79); he tells of his dual, and doubly painful, entrance into the symbolic order, enduring both fearful separation and impotence, the inability to speak, and tongue biting. The first person tells of Askar's circumcision; his journey through what he calls "the geography of pain." Finally, as we have seen, first person is the voice in which Askar inquires of Hilaal about his status as a refugee or real Somali and in which he comes to learn that, although he has an identity card, his situation bears frightening resemblances to that of Misra, whose life hangs precariously in the balance between state indifference and individual violence.

Ngaboh-Smart suggests that the third-person point of view might best be read as a glimpse into Hilaal's perspective. I disagree wholeheartedly. The third person is far less friendly than Hilaal or the other two points of view; in it we encounter the most alienated and asocial Askar. This point of view is first introduced via a nightmare. Askar is in flight (for six or seven pages) from something he does not know. Moreover, it is this voice that later recounts his involvement in childhood guerrilla gangs, which Cobham rightly sees as the first step in his distancing himself from Misra (Cobham 1992, 141; Farah 1986, 100). This is the voice that takes over after the fearful first-person point of view of the circumcision. The frightened boy is replaced by the fearless nationalist warrior in a voice that itself easily substitutes an idea for a person:

> What mattered, he told himself, was that now he was at last a man, that he was totally detached from his mother-figure Misra, and weaned. In the process of looking for a substitute, he had found another—Somalia, his mother country It was as though something which began with the pain of a rite had ended in the joy of a greater self-discovery, one in which he held on to the milky breast of a common mother that belonged to him as much as to anyone else. A generous mother, a many-breasted mother, a many-nippled mother, a mother who gave plenty of herself and demanded loyalty of one, loyalty to an ideal, allegiance to an idea, the notion of a nationhood —no more, and no less. (Farah 1986, 100)

Above all, it is in the third person that Askar recounts his own detach-
ment in response to what he considers Misra's betrayal of 603 Somali
soldiers (Farah 1986, 195). Misra tells Hilaal and Salaado her version
of how the soldiers came to die, but feeling betrayed for reasons he
does not fully understand, Askar does not believe her. Most important, and somewhat surprising given the novel's strong protocol of
focalization, is that Askar is narratively absent from this key scene
(third-person limited becomes third-person omniscient here; Farah
1986, 205). Moreover, after Misra's body is discovered, the events are
recounted in a neutrally toned third-person voice, and it is in this
voice that he makes clear that he neither helps with the burial prepa-
rations nor attends the funeral.

The strong position of negation in *Maps* is based in resistance or
objection to telling a tale that ordinarily falls within a genre defined as
developmental. It puts into question the most typical modern narrative of social identity (that of the national collective), and in a tightly
coordinated metaphoric logic it undermines an otherwise typical
modern novel of individual progress, the Bildungsroman. What might
appear to be a novel with allegorical possibilities here turns into an
explicitly allegorical novel. It violates our sense of causal relations and
natural setting. Discussing the relation between narrative and allegoresis in a different context, Michael O'Connell (1990, 18) says that
it "forces us to unify what we read according to some other standard:
we search for its meaning. Hence allegorical narratives are often, in
Aristotelian terms, badly constructed: paratactic, digressive, episodic,
and replete with iconographic details that have nothing to do with the
story." *Maps* deploys the national allegory explicitly, though in some
curious ways. It turns allegorical figures of fable, such as Mother
Somalia and the national man child, into fuller characters to drive a
story about individuation and psychological development. Such a
strategy brings into conflict several systems of meaning. It also means
that allegory loses some of its force as a vehicle by which to tell two
stories simultaneously.

   Not only does this novel cast doubt on whether societies or individuals improve over time, it also asks—and answers—the sharper question of whether groups or individuals can be said to possess any kind

of continuous identity over time, which is in part suggested by the constant shifting among three narrative voices. All are presumably narrated by or focalized through the same person, but the shifts in tense and the occasional uncertainty of narration as expressed by the narrator, along with a few discrepancies in the plot, cast doubt on certainty. Attentive reading of the novel reveals a doubly anti-teleo-logical stance; both national and individual histories unfold as se-quences of rupture and loss of separate and disjunctive states.

Rather than tell a familial story that can be read as an allegory of national politics, *Maps* tells a national story that obliquely addresses the unspeakable in family relations: desire between family members, as well as its opposite, repulsion. In the novels by women I look at here, such as *Une si longue lettre*, *Nervous Conditions*, and, in the next chapter, *Ombre sultane*, the nation that is unspoken as such is made visible by reading the family as nation. When nation is thereby made to come into view, it often appears as a potential site of progressive political action. Not so in *Maps*. Nations, and the question of identi-fication with them, are always highly visible; in fact, they are inescap-able. Moreover, nations as nations wreak havoc on human relations, forcing some people together and driving many others apart. *Maps* takes pains to suggest that the family need not be limited to blood relations and might be configured in any of several ways; nor is the family idealized or represented as always nurturing. (Uncle Qorrax, whose name and money protect Askar in his youth, is suspected of regularly beating his wives; he is certainly unfaithful to them and divorces and remarries regularly.) Nevertheless, family is depicted here as a smaller, less dangerous group, allowing its more dispos-sessed and marginal characters room to maneuver. Rejecting the An-dersonian formulation of nations as kin groups, Farah adopts the constructed family as a working metaphor of collectivity. It is the family unit that offers the greatest potential site for intimacy, hope, and political possibility.[18]

Unlike Buchi Emecheta's *The Joys of Motherhood*, which keeps family and nation in narrative tension, *Nervous Conditions* appears to efface the story of Zimbabwean nationalism entirely, emphasizing instead the personal travails of two black Rhodesian girls as they arrive at womanhood. *Nervous Conditions* is set a couple of decades earlier than its 1988 publication date, beginning in 1968 and continuing into the 1970s. Despite the difference in time of almost twenty years, which might constitute space for reflection, the novel makes almost no reference to the Chimurenga, or guerilla war, which would have been raging at the time and in the location of the story. In its apparent silence on the question of the black independence struggle, *Nervous Conditions* differs sharply from *Bones* and *Harvest of Thorns*.

The novel narrates the struggle for self-determination of two teen-age girls, Tambudzai and Nyasha Siguake, yet it never risks trivializing their problems or making either girl a simple icon of the nation. I believe that these departures from convention—rendering full and complex female characters against a literary background populated by Mother Africa and prostitute figures—explain why *Nervous Conditions* has not yet been read as a national parable. Since the political practices of African novels written by women are not always visible, readers must devise new forms of literacy, new and informed ways to understand how these texts represent politics. Tambudzai and Nyasha Siguake function as two aspects of Zimbabwean subjectivity as the new nation emerges from and against Rhodesia. In Tambu, the novel depicts the making of one subject whose evolution is not particularly heroic and, in fact, only comes about with the help of the female community in whose custody she comes of age. *Nervous Conditions* does something else: it explicates a decolonizing nationalism that it understands as bound up with domestic relations and claims that such a literary politics becomes evident only through a thorough reconsideration of Nyasha's place and function.

The interplay of structures of family and nation, domestic and public spheres, even the discursive constructs of tradition and modernity, becomes legible in *Nervous Conditions* through a corresponding legibility of history and literary history. Following Pierre Macherey's notion of the "not-said" (Macherey 1978), I suggest that the nationalist story of *Nervous Conditions* remains invisible, obscured by the feminist, until the facts of Zimbabwean history and theories of decolonizing nationalism are juxtaposed against it. These discourses bring to light what the text cannot speak about itself. The "discontinuity," in Macherey's terms, is an investment in feminism at the expense of decolonizing nationalism, which here is combined with a critique as expressed by Nyasha of bourgeois complacency.[19] My reading considers the novel's deployment and revision of generic conventions. I read this Bildungsroman in relation to literary theories of realism, as well as in relation to the political theory of Frantz Fanon. Attention to both structure and theme unearths a more complex narrative, illustrating how the micro-political and macro-political spheres are allegorically represented. The public political import of Dangarembga's text becomes legible only when the critical apparatus for interpreting it is revised or reconsidered. Although the fact of Tambu's gender powerfully determines the content of narration (the desire of a poor girl to acquire an education, which, as a girl, she would not otherwise have), in structural terms Tambu's personal story reaffirms the Bildungsroman as a narrative of uplift. Her quest for advancement is preceded a generation earlier by that of her uncle, Babamukuru. Early on, the novel establishes Babamukuru's journey as the paradigmatic story of advancement through merit, scholarship, and hard work. This is the story Tambu prepares herself to emulate: "It was truly a romantic story to my ears, a fairy-tale of reward and punishment, of cause and effect. It had a moral too, a tantalizing moral that increased your aspirations, but not beyond a manageable level" (Dangarembga 1988, 19).

Through her own industriousness, Tambu earns money for the school fees her parents cannot afford, taking on the additional task of growing mealies, or maize, for sale in the tuck shops or local vendors of prepared foods. Though she is almost thwarted by her brother in this enterprise, she continues undaunted, and with the help of a kindly teacher she takes her mealies to Umtali, a nearby city. She earns enough money to secure Babamukuru's notice and, ultimately, a prized education at his mission school.[20] Her real path toward maturation begins with her move to the mission school and to the home of Babamukuru and Maiguru, a move that, not coincidentally, corresponds with the generic convention of the move from country to city. Under the watchful eyes of her uncle and aunt, she gains a more rigorous formal education, as well as the material means (books, time, and artificial light) by which to acquire it, and she is exposed to Northern, or European, ways, such as eating with a knife and fork and sampling non-Shona foods. Above all, as she assures us, she begins to examine social values. In particular, her cousin Nyasha encourages her to think critically about the books she reads, as well as about the means by which her education is made available. At the end of the novel, having completed her schooling at the Sacred Heart convent and grown into an adult, Tambu stands poised to enter the Zimbabwean elite.[21]

Nyasha, on the other hand, incarnates all of the problems with women's access to development. She is the exceptional woman—or, in this case, girl—doomed either to transgress and be punished or to suffer a life in which she does not believe. Tending toward transgression, Nyasha frequently challenges her parents' authority, especially that of her father, Babamukuru. She pays the price for open defiance with her mental and physical health and even at the novel's end persists in an unstable, uncertain psychological state. By applying pressure to sites of narrative tension that highlight the novel's expression of divergent positions, we can make visible some of the mechanisms that form the basis of Tambu's developmental success and Nyasha's undoing.

Tambu's and Nyasha's parallel stories illustrate the argument of Abel, Hirsch, and Langland (1983) that feminine fictions of development reflect tensions between the assumptions of a genre that evolved representing the growth of male characters, on the one hand, and the often conflicting aspirations of female protagonists, on the other. Reading gender and genre as intertwined makes visible the Bildungsroman's legacy of representing woman as a sign of the sexual for male protagonists, and it highlights the fraught terrain of sexuality for female protagonists. Indeed, that novels written by women have tended to represent narrative resolution for female protagonists as a choice between marriage (success) or death (failure) has become axiomatic within feminist criticism. Penny Boumhela (1988), Rachel Blau Du Plessis (1985), and Rita Felski (1989) agree that romance usually complicates and sometimes co-opts the Bildung's quest course with the marriage plot to inhibit or contain the aspirations of the female characters.

Consequently, some feminists have asserted of the genre that, unlike in the process of masculine development, sexuality in and for itself rarely plays a central role in women's processes of self-discovery.[22] Felski (1989, 132) claims that "erotic passion, by its very intensity, can sabotage the protagonist's struggle to strengthen an often precarious sense of independent identity." And Du Plessis (1985, 1), to whose exposition of romance I am much indebted, begins with: "Once upon a time, the end, the rightful end, of women in novels was social— successful courtship, marriage—or judgmental of her sexual and social failure—death." In the case of *Nervous Conditions*, romance and its conventional outcome, the marriage plot, are juxtaposed against sexual self-expression uninhibited by wedlock and its goal of procreation. Instead of inverting the conventional logic of woman as a sign of the sexual by representing a male figure as sexuality incarnate, as, for example, Sembène does in *Xala, Nervous Conditions* displaces sexuality from the female body into one of two feminine discourses. In the prototypical Bildungsroman, the male hero negotiates his path to adulthood by—and through—at least one debased and one exalted female character. *Nervous Conditions* rewrites the cliché of the sexualized woman by using its two main characters to explore two stances on sexuality, all the while refraining from depicting actual objects of interest on the part of either female character. Tambu, the successful protagonist, has faith in the romance plot, and Nyasha, her resisting counterpart, issues challenges to it.

Given my earlier claim that Tambu's narrative exemplifies Bildung as a story of uplift, it is noteworthy that romance is the single major aspect of the "masculine" Bildung that remains undeveloped in her story. Sexuality, even curiosity about sexuality, is absent from Tambu's maturation, having been quashed early on the homestead, as this description of her love of dancing illustrates: "My early childhood had been a prime time for dancing. As I had grown older and the music had begun to speak to me more clearly, my movements had grown stronger, more rhythmical and luxuriant; but people had not found it amusing anymore, so that in the end I realised that there were bad implications in the way I enjoyed the rhythm. My dancing compressed itself into rigid, tentative gestures. I did not stop completely, but [family] gatherings were much less fun after that and made me feel terribly self-conscious" (Dangarembga 1988, 42). Later, when at the mission school, Tambu admits to being thrilled when male preceptors dress formally and even considers Nyasha's brother, Chido, handsome and dashing. None of these potential objects of desire ever seriously engages her attention, however, and her libido is represented as diffuse and unformed. Unlike Nyasha, she does not question the value of marriage and, indeed, apparently continues to believe in its value even in her older and wiser narrating voice. Not coincidentally, the primary difference between Tambu's story and that of the prototypical man is that this novel specifies that its hero is desexualized, partaking neither of the Scylla of the romance narrative nor of the Charybdis of unsanctioned sexual desire for its own sake.[23]

Tambu's hazy vision of romantic love throws into sharp relief her cousin's open curiosity about sexuality for its own sake. Nyasha shocks her parents by reading *Lady Chatterley's Lover* and by even unselfconsciously bringing it to the dining table. Later she proclaims to Tambu that she would rather give up her virginity to a tampon than a womanizing man. In fact, when Tambu begins to menstruate, Nyasha teaches her slightly scandalized cousin how to use tampons and assures her that Maiguru will supply them with the expensive products: "Although Maiguru knew that tampons were offensive, that nice girls did not use them, she would be pleased enough to know we were not pregnant to be persuaded to provide. [Nyasha] chuckled. 'No, really,' she conceded. 'Mum's quite sensible underneath all the feathers.' That cousin of mine! Shocking and funny; disrespectful and irrepressible" (Dangarembga 1988, 96). Because she continually challenges the authority of the conjugal love plot for herself, for Tambu, and, perhaps most important, for her own mother, Nyasha runs the risk of becoming a "bad girl," the youthful equivalent of a "fallen woman," a conceit that the narrative deploys to illustrate the function of gendered relations of power and simultaneously exposes as false.

This setting frames the tumultuous events of the night of the school dance. Most commentators rightly interpret Nyasha's and Babamukuru's battle as one about power and patriarchy. Few acknowledge that it takes place on the field of sexual expression. The miniskirt Nyasha wears, which has been approved by her mother, rankles her father when he sees her in it before the dance. Afterward, her tarrying behind Chido and Tambu with one of the Baker boys to learn new dance steps provokes the notorious fight:

> "No decent girl would stay out alone, with a boy, at that time of the night," Babamukuru was insisting in a quavering tenor. "But you did it. I saw you. Do you think that I am lying, that these eyes of mine lie?"

Nyasha, unfortunately, was still unrepentant. "What do you want me to say?" she asked. "You want me to admit that I'm guilty, don't you. All right then. I was doing it, whatever you're talking about. There. I've confessed."

"Do not talk to me like that, child," warned Babamukuru. "You must respect me. I am your father. And in that capacity I am telling you, I-am-telling-you, that I do not like the way you are always walking about with these—er—these young men. Today this one, tomorrow that one. What's the matter with you, girl? Why can't you behave like a young woman from a decent home? What will people say when they see Siguake's daughter carrying on like that?"

I like to think that Nyasha really believed that the confrontation had taken a conciliatory turn. She smiled that the number of her male acquaintances was the one thing that should put her father at ease. "You know me," she told him, but of course she was mistaken. "You've taught me how I should behave. I don't worry about what people think so there's no need for you to." She did not know her father either, because anyone who did would have retreated at that stage. . . .

"You, Chido, keep quiet," Babamukuru snapped. "You let your sister behave like a whore without saying anything. . . ."

Nyasha grew uncharacteristically calm at times like this. "Now why," she enquired of no particular person, "should I worry about what people say when my own father calls me a whore?" She looked at him with murder in her eyes. . . .

"Chido, I have told you to keep out of this," reminded Babamukuru, gathering himself within himself so that his whole weight was behind the blow he dealt Nyasha's face. "Never," he hissed. "Never," he repeated, striking her other cheek with the back of his hand, "speak to me like that." (Dangarembga 1988, 113–14)

Though mere steps behind her companions, Nyasha and her actions are interpreted by her father as breaching propriety, and his response quickly escalates from verbal to physical retribution. Instead of accepting the name calling and blows, Nyasha fights back and even punches him once, a response to paternal violence I have never before encountered in an African novel. That it comes from a daughter is even more shocking. Babamukuru pummels her fiercely for this. The altercation marks the beginning of Nyasha's mental and emotional troubles. Although her analysis remains sharp throughout the novel, she never emerges from this emotional decline.

In the passage, the novel blurs the distinction between discipline and punishment, between Babamukuru's benevolent paternalism and the malevolent consequences of sexual permissiveness against which he positions himself. That is to say, the father's desire to protect himself from shame becomes inseparable from his anxiety about protecting his daughter from public sexual mistreatment and thereby takes the form of the violence and humiliation he enacts on her. The passage echoes an earlier one: as a youthful narrator welcoming her seven-year-old cousin Nyasha, Chido, and their parents back from England, Tambu quietly disapproves of Nyasha because she wears a short skirt. That some years later, in the fight after the dance, Babamukuru begins his repudiation of Nyasha with an objection to the length of her skirt is not narratively coincidental. Skirt length, then, is just one of the many circuits through which sexual control is exercised, not only by men or by those in the previous generation, though to be sure they have greater power and are represented as blinded by it. The novel alleges that by Babamukuru's own standards of moral virtue, the fears he harbors about his daughter's sexual expression, prove groundless. Fourteen-year-old Nyasha's chastity is secure; no particular boy even holds her interest. What is more, Tambu understands that the regulation of sexuality constitutes one form of control, and sometime in the brief span between the child's experience and the adult narration, she recognizes that such regulation focuses on women's bodies, but by then it is too late to intervene on behalf of her cousin. In direct contrast to the policing of Nyasha's friendships, Chido is allowed to maintain a form of close rapport with the missionaries' daughter, Nyaradzo Baker, sister of the boy with whom Nyasha dallies after the dance. This friendship, though known to their age mates and parents alike, does not come in for censure.[24]

Desire itself is never narratively represented; sexuality functions as its metaphor. As vehicle, sexuality illustrates women's engagement with dominant structures of power, illustrating the risks of openly challenging patriarchy, and as tenor, it serves to catalyze the moment of Nyasha's psychological instability. Nyasha and Tambu occupy structurally divergent narrative positions that should be understood as investment in or refusal of the romance narrative. Tambu maintains an ideological commitment to romance while refusing to partake of it herself. At the same time, Nyasha demonstrates curiosity about one of the transgressive aspects of romance—sexuality—which in all of its menacing aspects becomes the sign and catalyst for her undoing.

Because the analysis of the feminine Bildungsroman by Abel and colleagues (1983) is conducted at the level of individual psychology rather than at that of a dialogue between the psychological and the social, it tends to represent gender as fixed, largely unaffected by history, class, or culture.[25] Their advocacy of the simple inclusion of gender and sexuality as categories of analysis unintentionally occludes a more complex understanding of narrative mechanisms. I wish to be clear about the limits of my literary assertions: *Nervous Conditions* neither constitutes a radically new genre nor does it lay claim to the conscious resistance to a humanist ideology of the literary that John Beverley (1992) declares on behalf of the *testimonio* narrative.[26] This Zimbabwean novel stretches the boundaries of the genre bound up with embourgeoisement, and it thereby articulates a different literary politics. That the novel renders two female protagonists in lieu of the typical lone male serves to unsettle the genre's unproblematized terms of selfhood.

In both formal and thematic terms, *Nervous Conditions* rewrites the "classic" Bildungsroman's extreme emphasis on self-creation, and it downplays what Fredric Jameson has called the genre's "overripe subjectivity" in favor of a mode that underscores the role of the collective in producing the individual (quoted in Beverley 1992, 96). On the one hand, *Nervous Conditions* affirms convention by affirming Tambu's identity. Through Nyasha's unmaking it also exposes the genre's avowal of a seamless and unified self. On the other, the very manner and reasons for Nyasha's unmaking link the critique of bourgeois consolidation with a critique of the imperialist enterprise in Africa, a point to which I return.

One important difference between *Nervous Conditions* and the orthodox Bildungsroman's assumption of autonomous and heroic self-making can be seen in the relationship between individuality and collectivity. The novel tells the story of the formation and dissolution of subjectivity through Tambu and Nyasha. At a primary level of explication, the novel explores the conflict between the desire for feminine self-realization versus the virtually universal understanding of womanhood as living for others, and it endorses the former position through its assertion and celebration of Tambu's arrival at adulthood. At a secondary level, however, the older Tambu perceives her psychological development and social success as having been made possible through the community of women in whose company she came of age; she says so explicitly on the novel's first page. The myth of the exceptional woman is doubly put into question: first by the open acknowledgment that she was produced by a collective, and second, by the parallel unraveling of her narrative counterpart. Nyasha, the unmade girl, is herself instrumental to Tambu's formation, helping to shape her cousin socially and responsible for her critical acuity. She exposes Tambu to a library beyond the limited one of the Mission School and frequently prods her cousin's increasing awareness of patriarchy and colonialism.[27] Felski contends that the female community serves a mediating function that shapes the cautiously positive conclusion of the feminist Bildungsroman. The female community "functions as a barrier against and a refuge from, the worst effects of a potentially threatening social order by opening up a space for nonexploitative relationships grounded in common goals and interests. The feminist Bildungsroman thus combines the exploration of subjectivity with a dimension of group solidarity which inspires activism and resistance rather than private resignation, and makes it possible to project a visionary hope of a future change" (Felski 1989, 139).

Several women contribute to the making of Tambu, both directly and by example. Despite her constant exhaustion and wariness about cultural alienation, Tambu's mother quietly encourages her eldest daughter to pursue her scholarly ambitions. She persuades her husband, Jeremiah, to allow their daughter to use maize seeds to grow crops for sale. As if taking a leaf from her own life's book as an example, she also warns her daughter not to expect too much from life, lest she be disappointed.[28] More than that of any other character, Mainini's personal identity is obscured by the burdens of her maternal and wifely status. Tambu's grandmother contributes the land and agricultural skills that equip Tambu to grow maize for sale to earn her school fees, but her most important legacy is that of providing—and, indeed, embodying—a different history.

It is from her grandmother, with Nyasha's later and next-generation reinforcement, that Tambu learns a counter-discourse to the colonial history taught in school. Tambu's aunt Maiguru, of course, exemplifies the kind of woman Tambu would like to become. Tambu's growing realization of the nature and number of sacrifices her aunt makes, however, prompts a reconsideration of this path from the perspective of the older narrator, and for the reader, it prompts a reconsideration of modernity as the corrective for feminine ills: "I felt sorry for Maiguru because she could not use the money she earned for her own purposes and had been prevented by marriage from doing the things she wanted to do. But it was not so simple, because she had been married by my Babamukuru, which defined her situation as good. If it was necessary to efface yourself, as Maiguru did so well that you couldn't be sure that she didn't enjoy it, if it was necessary to efface yourself in order to preserve his sense of identity and value, then, I was sure, Maiguru had taken the correct decisions" (Dangarembga 1988, 102).

Illiteracy and lack of training virtually ensures servitude for a woman in colonial and postcolonial times. The squalid conditions under which Tambu's mother lives testify to this. But education does not necessarily liberate women, as the example of Maiguru indicates. Although she has a master's degree, like her husband, and is a teacher, the text offers no information at all about Maiguru's accomplishments outside the home or the domestic world she supervises at the homestead. Her educational achievements are unknown to most. She gives over her salary to her husband to spend on his extended family. Her personal narrative is organized around her worries about Babamukuru's eating and the Herculean task of food preparation that she takes on each time she and her family visit Tambu's nuclear family on the homestead. The novel describes her, as it does Mainini, in terms of organizing and preparing domestic arrangements.

For both "traditional" and "modern" women, identities as housewives dominate the narrative horizon. Lucia, the only unmarried adult woman besides the servant, Anna, is free precisely because she is not responsible to a husband and as a "barren" woman is not hampered by the burdens of reproduction.[29] These facts, normally considered severe limitations in the African context, enable her to have a sexual life based primarily on pleasure, and she is the only woman who does. The female community provides a mediating force between the female protagonist and the burdens of the society she struggles against; moreover, it offers a communal counter-icon to the African family, the conventional emblem of group solidarity and resistance. In the novel's oft-quoted first paragraph, the African family is dethroned and replaced by a female community:

> I was not sorry when my brother died. Nor am I apologising for my callousness, as you may define it, my lack of feeling. For it is not that at all. I feel many things these days, much more than I was able to feel in the days when I was young and my brother died, and there are reasons for this more than the mere consequence of age. Therefore I shall not apologise but begin by recalling the facts as I remember them that led up to my brother's death, the events that put me in a position to write this account. For though the events of my brother's passing and the events of my story cannot be separated, my story is not after all about death, but about my escape and Lucia's; about my mother's and Maiguru's entrapment; and about Nyasha's rebellion— Nyasha, far-minded and isolated, my uncle's daughter, whose rebellion may not in the end have been successful. (Dangarembga 1988, 1)

Most readers in most contexts would find striking the thinly veiled hostility of this introductory paragraph. Dangarembga is one of the rare anglophone African novelists who baldly represents the family as coercive and occasionally violent, not just hierarchical but patriarchal and gerontocratic.[30] And she has been understood to be unusually critical. In an interview with Dangarembga, the noted Africanist and Caribbeanist scholar Kirsten Holst Petersen revealed her disapproval by asking in the first question: "Do you find that your main character is justified in harboring such an unnatural sentiment?" (Petersen 1994, 345). Peterson's question illustrates that within the europhone African novel, the effect is heightened, for rarely do African novels begin by eschewing all pretense at harmonious tranquility within family relations.[31] In subsequent pages of *Nervous Conditions*, Nhamo reveals himself to be lazy, as is his masculine due, as well as frequently cruel toward his younger sisters; moreover, he commits the unpardonable sin of trying to foil Tambu's attempt to earn money for school fees, money he does not himself have to earn. The introductory paragraph allows Tambu to protest her brother's privilege and to refuse to feel sad or guilty about his death because, as we later learn, he actively opposed her attempt to acquire an education. Within the first two sentences, in fact, she represents her narration as depending on—not simply following—his death: "Therefore I shall not apologise but begin by recalling the facts as I remember them that put me in a position to write this account."

Although she does not kill Nhamo, she harbors murderous thoughts toward him, as Charles Sugnet (1997) points out, and, like Nyokabi of *The Graduate*, Tambu is willing to accept her brother's death as the price of her freedom. Perhaps most important, Nhamo's death serves a structural as well as a rhetorical function. Rhetorically, it captures the reader's attention (Sugnet claims that Dangarembga takes some pains to wrench the narrative around to begin this way); structurally, however, because Tambu's ability to narrate is openly and gratefully predicated on her brother's demise, the novel offers no narrative space for grief or, in fact, for any response but a certain relief.[32] In form and content, then, Nhamo's death serves as the catalyst to the story of Tambu and, as she has told us, about the story of the women who produced her. Through its men, the African family is portrayed as a network of power relations that almost always work against its most disadvantaged members: children and, particularly, women. Examples of masculine offenses within this network include Jeremiah's laziness, Nhamo's malicious rivalry, Takesure's philandering, and Babamukuru's benevolent domination. So instead of a domestic collectivity based on biology or kin to nurture her, the text tenders its protagonist one based on women's shared experience of oppression or persecution. The female collective Tambu celebrates in the novel's first paragraph is placed in ideological and functional opposition to and takes the place of the African family. The family serves to oppress her, Nyasha, Maiguru, Mainini, and Lucia. Similarly, if one of the most important moments of ideological negotiation occurs in the way a novel resolves loose ends and achieves closure, as Macherey suggests, then it is remarkable that Tambu ends by repeating her testimony that her own story overlaps with those of the women. The last line, in fact, is: "The story I have told here, is my own story, the story of the four women whom I loved, and our men, this story is how it all began" (Dangarembga 1988, 204).

Deepika Bahri (1994, 83) notes that Babamukuru's objection to his daughter's reading *Lady Chatterley's Lover* marks the first time that Nyasha rejects food. As the novel proceeds, and as Nyasha more openly asserts her individuality and her politics, Babamukuru more openly monitors her eating. After he thwarts her outright refusal of food at the dining table, Nyasha moves to a more covert form of resistance by using a toothbrush to induce vomiting after the meal. When, later in the novel, Tambu visits the mission after taking up her studies at Sacred Heart, Nyasha explains to her cousin her fights with her father about food, conceding that the subtext is his ability to control her sexuality: "Imagine all that fuss over a plate of food. But it's more than that really, more than just food. That's how it comes out, but really it's all the things about boys and men and being decent and indecent and good and bad. He goes on and on with the accusations and the threats, and I'm just not coping very well" (Dangarembga 1988, 190). While the novel depicts Nyasha performing bulimic acts, the manner in which she manifests her eating disorder departs from the common pattern of excessive eating and then vomiting associated with many teenage girls.[33] Instead, Nyasha abstains, or attempts to abstain, altogether from eating in a manner that more closely resembles a hunger strike.

Food and education have a complex relationship in *Nervous Conditions*, sometimes metaphorical, sometimes metonymic. Nyasha displaces her struggle with her father about control over sexual expression into the realm of food consumption. And consumption, whether of food, of a colonial education, or of the romance narrative, is itself an object of thematic exploration in the novel. Nyasha's refusal to consume either the food or the colonial culture forced on her exists in structural and ideological relation to Tambu's hunger for knowledge and her ambition to escape the homestead, where lack in general and worries about food in particular are constant features of daily life.

Because Nyasha's eating disorder fuels the narrative trajectory of the second part and looms over the ending, *Nervous Conditions* has frequently been interpreted as a simple parable of deracination and cultural alienation. Closer inspection reveals that figures of eating and control are to be found everywhere in the novel and that they are frequently expressed in discursive tension with education. Nyasha's anorexia and bulimia are given the most attention, but she is not the only female character to stop eating, or even the only African casualty of "nervousness." Babamukuru also experiences anxiety, poor eating habits, and "bad nerves" because of his position as colonial intermediary (1988, 102). Mainini's illness and hunger strike is yet another example. Toward the middle of the novel, Tambu's mother refuses food in part because she becomes fed up with her family's mistreatment and in larger part in protest against Tambu's decision to attend the Sacred Heart convent. Toward the novel's end, Maiguru stops performing domestic duties, both material and symbolic, in particular refusing to cook for her family and to nurture them, and even leaving her house in protest against her husband.

Alienation in the broadest sense, rather than deracination or cultural purity, is at issue. The novel explores a complex interrelation between food and instruction. Both are consumed or ingested, and both function as a means of providing for oneself or one's family. Food preparation is accomplished largely through manual labor; achieving an education is accomplished largely through mental effort. While the "masculine" register of formal schooling requires time and space for solitary reflection, the "feminine" registers of food cultivation, preparation, and even consumption has a built-in social component. Neither solitariness nor sociality is intrinsic to education or food production, respectively, but they are the primary ways in which each is manifested. On the symbolic level, education is associated with the consumption of new ideas and with cultural estrangement. This logic underlies Mainini's bitter condemnation of Babamukuru and Maiguru when Nhamo dies; she accuses them of having exposed her son to alien and therefore poisonous ways, killing him in the process. And she strongly objects when Tambu decides to attend Sacred Heart and thereby remove herself even more from the world of the homestead.[34] The relationship between eating and education is also straightforwardly material: having an education gives one upward mobility and enables one to eat more and better food, which explains why Tambu so craves to attend school in the first place.

Tambu knows from her parents' generation that Babamukuru's and Maiguru's education translates into having food and a comfortable home and, perhaps most important, that one does not have to engage in backbreaking work even when old. It also enables possession of a certain leisure available only to men on the homestead. Tambu's mother understands her daughter's desire for both and intervenes early on when Jeremiah would prevent Tambu from growing maize to pay for school fees—that is, producing foodstuffs to finance her primary schooling. Nevertheless, later, when Mainini chastises her daughter for craving the material gain and social prestige education brings, she does so using the metaphor of eating, making it stand in for cultural estrangement: "If it is meat you want that I cannot provide for you, if you are so greedy you would betray your own mother for meat, then go to your Maiguru. She will give you meat. I will survive on vegetables, as we all used to do. And we have survived, so what more do you want" (Dangarembga 1988, 141).

Mainini rightly believes that the ideas Tambu will consume at Babamukuru's home will make their shared life on the homestead even more alien to her daughter. Moreover, the quoted passage precedes Mainini's own hunger strike. When, against her mother's wishes, Tambu decides to attend the elite school in which she will be only one of a handful of Africans, her mother stops eating and withdraws from her family responsibilities. In an insightful reading of food's symbolic and social value, Heidi Creamer (1994, 354) outlines Mainini's resistance to her daughter's perceived assimilation into European culture as well as the recuperation of her resistance by the familial structures to which she is bound: "Lucia brings Mainini back to health. . . . [She] also incorporates the symbolic power of food into her healing; she insures that Mainini eats meat and milk which are usually served only to men during holidays." At a socio-symbolic level, eating or not eating signifies control over one's limited resources. Nevertheless, the novel does not lose sight of the brute fact that, historically, food cultivation and preparation are women's work.[35] In the case where a woman is unfortunate enough to have a man who does not provide food, as Mainini does in Jeremiah, she has the additional burden of providing the uncooked comestibles before preparing the meal. The novel offers several accounts of the feminine time and labor required of the girls and women who feed the rest of the African family. The examples of gatherings at the homestead are particularly appropriate:

> Counting Nyasha, Anna, Netsai, Rambanai and myself, there were twenty-four people altogether on the homestead, which was twenty-four stomachs to fill three times a day. Twenty-four bodies for which water had to be fetched from the Nyamarira daily. Twenty-four people's laundry to wash as often as possible, and Tete's youngest was still in napkins. Now, this kind of work was women's work, and of the thirteen women there, my mother and Lucia were incapacitated a little, but nevertheless to some extent, by pregnancy. Tete, having patriarchal status, was not expected to do much and four of us were only ten years old or younger. So Maiguru, Nyasha, the three helping girls and myself were on our feet all day. (Dangarembga 1988, 133)

The relation of the novel's female community toward food preparation and consumption is deeply bound up with control over self and with the daily grind of food acquisition and preparation. In the novel's first part, when Tambu lives on the homestead, endless references are made to the difficulties of procuring food and to how her father's laziness forces her mother to both provide and prepare the meals. Moreover, as is made clear, girls have far less time to study if cooking and cleanup are an assumed part of their duties. At the mission school, the physical work load is far less severe, though women still bear the responsibility for feeding and nurturing, and, as Maiguru illustrates, nurturing is frequently accomplished via food. (She ritually feeds and attends to Babamukuru at dinnertime, makes *sadza* and other familiar dishes to ease Tambu into her new life, and worries about Nyasha's inadequate eating.) Above all, although she is her husband's equal in education, she is not his equal in status. On their visits to the homestead, it is Maiguru whose high status means she must take responsibility for feeding the extended family:

> Maiguru worked harder than anybody else, because as the senior wife as well as provider of the food to cook, she was expected to oversee all the culinary operations. It was ceaseless work and unwise

to delegate, because she had to make sure that the food lasted until the end of the vacation. With thirteen extra people to feed—and the lot of us devouring seven loaves of bread and half a pound of margarine each morning . . . Maiguru had to be strict about sharing out the food, and this made my mother irritable. . . . [Later, some of the side of beef Maiguru brings spoils due to lack of adequate refrigeration; the lone woman in the patriarchy, Tete Gladys, insinuates that the meat is inedible.] This threw my aunt, who was a good woman and a good wife and took pride in this identity, into a dreadful panic. She took to cooking, twice a day, a special pot of refrigerated meat for the patriarchy to eat as they planned and constructed the family's future. (Dangarembga 1988, 135–36)

More than the simple gendered division of labor, this passage implies that gender supersedes class in determining one's labor. Manual work, such as food preparation, is performed by women; mental work, such as the patriarchy's decision making, is performed by men. Education and food themselves function as signifiers of modernity and tradition, respectively—as non-fixed symbols of women's (and men's) status under colonialism and, in developing countries, as signifiers of cultural authenticity and tradition. Education is bound up with the imperatives of decolonizing nationalism. Although one of the promises this nationalism makes is to create the New (and educated) Woman, education itself is usually seen as the province of men.[36] Food, of course, usually constitutes part of the domain of women; it has a powerful connection to the notion of cultural authenticity and, as such, haunts women, especially the educated and modern woman of the new nation-state.

So when Nyasha describes to Tambu her understanding that Babamukuru's policing of her eating constitutes his displaced disapproval of her sexual expression and appropriate femininity, she calls on a range of complicated references wherein eating and education echo the familiar idioms of tradition and modernity, masculinity and femininity. The consumption of food and formal education have an intricate relation of displacement and substitution. Tambu's appetite for education, the discourse that dominates the first part of the novel, is structurally replaced by Nyasha's self-starvation in the second, as Nyasha's increasingly precarious state interrupts the telling of the securely plotted path of Tambu's development. In brief, Tambu consumes education not only for spiritual or mental self-improvement but also to have greater access to more food and greater wealth in general. That form of consumption produces the proper young lady ready to claim her place in the ranks of the black bourgeoisie. Tambu's narrative meditation is not simply about successful integration into the socius; in actual historical terms, it is also the moment that immediately precedes real independence.

While Tambu embodies the development of the new national bourgeoisie and the hope of the New Woman in particular, Nyasha's tragedy evokes the unfulfilled promise of the persecuted nation. To Tambu's matter-of-fact striving is juxtaposed Nyasha's heroic pathos; to Tambu's repression, Nyasha's frank curiosity about sex. Like Tambu's narrative, Nyasha's is teleological and filled with obstacles. Unlike Tambu's narrative, Nyasha's is—at a certain level at least—a story of miscarriage in that, by the novel's end, the survival of its protagonist is not at all assured. At the level of surface representation Nyasha's personal struggle against her father's benevolent tyranny might have failed. However, closer inspection illustrates that Nyasha's very failure as a coming-of-age subject raises a set of questions about subjectivity, power, and control that go beyond the private domain of home and family to the public one of nation and state, that pose public questions via the private domain. This linking of domains belies the received wisdom, first, that decolonizing nationalism only asks questions about the public, and second, that female writers usually leave such questions unanswered. As I have argued, it is female authors who by and large have illustrated the deep interpenetration of both domains.

Nyasha's unrelenting search for Truth, coupled with the register in which she articulates her objections to her father, moves the novel out of a single-minded feminist politics, such as the exercising of minute control of the body, to suggest an interrelation between the politics of anticolonialism and feminism. This move seems to confirm the notion that, while the genre of the Bildungsroman involves a progression or quest in the development of the self, that quest need not only entail the making of individual subjectivity. It might also encompass self-realization in the service of a collectivity. Nyasha's search for a "higher truth" makes manifest her interpellation in the psychological and physical violence of a triumphant colonialism, and her crusade for self-control serves to expose the self's identity as colonized (as a "mimic," to appropriate the appropriation of Fanon by Homi Bhabha [1984]). As a failed Bildungsideal, Nyasha highlights the novel's powerful, if buried, black nationalist agenda.

In contrast to Tambu, who frequently shows uncertainty about her relation to the public political arena, and to Babamukuru and Maiguru, who assume positions of "responsibility," which means dismissing what they consider to be their daughter's foolhardy criticisms, Nyasha is unhesitatingly and passionately interested in politics, both local and global. She frequently pushes Tambu to situate her enthusiastic discovery of the cultural sphere within a larger geopolitical one. Moreover, with the exception of the girls' shared grandmother, it is Nyasha who voices the novel's most stringent and consistent critique of colonialism. When her father forces a Christian wedding ceremony on Tambu's indigenously married parents, Nyasha responds: " 'It's bad enough,' she said severely, 'when a country gets colonized, but when the people do as well! That's the end, really, that's the end' " (Dangarembga 1988, 147).[37]

As Sugnet astutely notes, *Nervous Conditions* makes only three "direct references to . . . [national political] events . . . , and they are brief and passing." I am indebted to Sugnet for cataloging these references and for his perceptive reading of the novel in general, and I agree that "there may be a complex, partly subterranean relationship between it and the struggles of the young Tambudzai against the immediate manifestations of patriarchy in her life" (Sugnet 1997, 34). However, I disagree with his appraisal that "*Nervous Conditions* contains enough chronological specifics so a reader familiar with Zimbabwean history will know that the novel's period encompasses . . . landmark events in the national narrative as the founding of ZANU and ZAPU, the ten-year detention of Robert Mugabe and Joshua Nkomo, Ian Smith's Unilateral Declaration of Independence, and the officially celebrated 'first battle' of the chimurenga war on April 28, 1966" (Sugnet 1997, 34). That is to say, a reader already familiar with Zimbabwean history might be aware that a historical narrative runs parallel to the more literary tale of Tambu and Nyasha. But none of these historical or political events rises to the novel's surface. The reader has to labor to discover and then trace a relationship between them, so elliptical are the allusions. There is a connection between the character of the political palimpsests and the individualist narrative, but it requires some elucidation.

Nervous Conditions directly ascribes to Nyasha two of the three national political allusions, and the remaining one appears to result from her influence. All three illustrate my assertion that the novel represents public and private spheres as interpenetrated and interdependent. In the first instance, Nyasha insists on knowing "exactly why UDI was declared and what it meant" (Dangarembga 1988, 93); she refers here to the United Declaration of Independence by which white Rhodesians declared their sovereignty from Britain and enshrined black disenfranchisement. The reference appears in the paragraph immediately following Tambu's elated description of her personal blossoming under the superior education at the mission school: " 'So,' [Nyasha] advised, concerning my fairy-tales and my reincarnation, 'enjoy it while you can. These things don't last' " (Dangarembga 1988, 93). On the face of it, Nyasha's admonition functions to temporarily halt the Bildung's normative and nearly narcissistic tendency of acclaiming self-development to the exclusion of all else. On closer inspection, the admonition functions to draw attention to how the process of self-development in the colonial Bildungsroman must take extraordinary steps to ignore the worldly conditions under which it is produced.

The second reference, which involves only Tambu and Maiguru, is undoubtedly prompted by Nyasha's influence. Tambu has just discovered that her aunt has a master's degree and that she is as well educated as her husband but does not keep all her money: " 'What happens to your money?' I asked. 'The money that you earn. Does the Government take it?' For I was beginning to learn that our Government was not a good one" (Dangarembga 1988, 101). Although the novel makes plain that Maiguru's money enables Babamukuru's largesse toward his extended family, without which Tambu would not have her education, it nevertheless simultaneously compares Maiguru's economic subordination to her husband with that of blacks to the white government. The third and final reference comes toward the end. As in the previous examples, the text places public, national, and "important" concerns against those private, domestic, and mundane ones that shape their everyday lives:

> Beside Nyasha I was a paragon of feminine decorum, principally because I hardly ever talked unless spoken to, and then only to answer with the utmost respect whatever question had been asked. Above all, I did not question things. It did not matter to me why things should be done this way rather than that way. . . . I did not think that my reading was more important than washing the dishes, and I understood that panties should not be hung in the bathroom where everybody could see them. . . . I was not concerned that freedom fighters were referred to as terrorists, did not demand proof of God's existence nor did I think that the missionaries, along with all the other Whites in Rhodesia, ought to have stayed home. (Dangarembga 1988, 155)

Under the pressure of Nyasha's relentless interrogation, the public and private spheres make themselves visible as overlapping and deeply political. The passage constitutes one of the most powerful challenges to the received understanding of late colonialist politics as explicated in this novel. Because Tambu recounts Nyasha's stinging denunciation of colonialism; because the novel makes its most explicit reference to the Chimurenga war here and suggests, albeit obliquely, that an end is in sight; and above all, because missionary work, from which Babamukuru has benefited and that he promotes, is represented as part and parcel of the colonialist enterprise. This textual moment occurs shortly before Nyasha becomes manifestly unstable.

If Tambu's developmental success can be read through the Bildungsroman, an understanding of Nyasha as anti-Bildungsheld benefits from an intertextual reading of Fanon's political theory. The link between *Nervous Conditions* and Fanon is apparent from the novel's title, which originally comes from Jean-Paul Sartre's preface to *The Wretched of the Earth* (1968). Although Sartre remains curiously unmentioned, that the phrase derives from *Wretched* is made clear in the epigraph to Dangarembga's book: "The condition of native is a nervous condition." When read through the lens of Fanon's critical theory, the subtle and complex investment in decolonizing nationalism in *Nervous Conditions* is thrown into relief, and we see that, despite

R. Radhakrishnan's gloomy pronouncement, it is possible to express in literary form a public politics of the nation grounded in feminism (see Radhakrishnan 1992).

Sugnet (1997, 35) observes of Dangarembga's appropriation of Sartre that she "seized on this particular phrase for her title because her novel redefines Fanon's insights and because she wanted the slight double meaning in 'nervous' in the ordinary sense of anxious, uneasy or worried, but also in the formal medical or psychiatric sense of 'so-and-so suffers from a nervous condition,' " such as Nyasha's anorexia nervosa. I agree that Dangarembga redefines Fanon and would add that she rewrites Sartre's singular "nervous condition" into a plural formulation. Elaborating on Sugnet's point, I suggest that Dangarembga is interested precisely in the move from ordinary to medical nervousness, just as she is interested in the relationship between small and big collectives, "minor" and "major" political questions.

The title's plural form signifies the complexity of Nyasha's anxiety; it also suggests that more than one character in the novel suffers from it. Any reading of "nerves" or "nervousness" should begin with Nyasha but should then extend beyond her. As discussed earlier, although Nyasha is the narrative's central and most tragic casualty of colonial violence, all of the colonized Africans around her suffer different forms of its consequences—and in a similar register of consumption, refusal, and nervousness. Furthermore, the title proposes an association between anorexia nervosa as a quintessentially feminine disorder and the colonized as disempowered or feminized by virtue of their subordinate position. Among those afflicted with anorexia—typically teenage girls—one reason for its onset is as a response to lack of agency or power, a point Fanon makes repeatedly with regard to the colonized in *The Wretched of the Earth*.

The afflicted exert control in the limited ways they can, and inhibiting eating or controlling the body is a common way. *Nervous Conditions* lends itself to an ironic reading based on this: one might well see Babamukuru's assiduous and patently patriarchal attempts to supervise the sexuality (both in the budding form of his daughter and in the more mature and non-monogamous forms of Lucia and Jeremiah) as a metaphor for the actions of the disempowered. The harmful repercussions of Babamukuru's humiliation of Mainini and Jeremiah via the Christian marriage he imposes, his acute repression of Nyasha via sexuality, and his compelling her to eat are obvious at the surface level of story. At a further level, however, that a colonized adult would seek to control what bodily practices he can through benevolent tyranny serves to underscore his own powerlessness in a system in which he is ostensibly a star product and emblem of power, itself a tragic effect. A primary sympathetic resonance between the novel and Fanon's work lies in the shared assumption that the native is not born but made: "For it is the settler who has brought the native into existence and who perpetuates his existence" (Fanon 1968, 36). Echoes of a shared existentialist tradition can also be heard in Simone de Beauvoir's earlier assertion, "One is not born, but rather becomes, a woman" (de Beauvoir 1953, 267). *Nervous Conditions* illustrates both principles equally well. It illustrates the formation of one member of the new nation's bourgeoisie in the person of Tambudzai, the country cousin whose education and upward mobility results in the ability to narrate this tale in reflection, as well as the undoing of elite status and the challenge to that class as posed by Nyasha, the urbanized and Westernized cousin whose criticism and encouragement shape Tambu's self-awareness, but whose insight leaves her vulnerable to incapacitating moral indignation and anxiety.

One important similarity between Nyasha and the prototypically male Fanonian protagonist lies in their shared anxiety and unease, a discomfort that constitutes the physical and psychological response to a system whose violence must remain unseen for its illusion of naturalness to hold sway; this similarity is thematic. Nyasha also bears a resemblance to the Fanonian narrator at the level of form or style, particularly in the tone of her incorrigible and startling pronouncements. Nyasha's honesty and irrepressible personality, manifested partly in her practice of scandalizing her family, interfere in the dynamic of the imperialist enterprise; her more youthful pronouncements early in the novel might be read as an intervention intended to shock them out of their complacency as part of the native bourgeoisie.

This sort of intervention is audible in the inflection and tone of Fanon's most polemical texts, *The Wretched of the Earth* and *Black Skin, White Masks* (1982). Paradoxically, the psychological hypersensitivity or "nervousness" shown by both Nyasha and the Fanonian native are precisely the attributes denied the native by colonialism. "The psychiatrist [to whom Nyasha's parents take her after her final outburst] said that Nyasha could not be ill, that Africans did not suffer in the way we had described. She was making a scene. We should take her home and be firm with her." Nyasha, for her part, "begged to see an African psychiatrist" (Dangarembga 1988, 201).

While it adheres to the main points of Fanon's indictment of colonialism, Dangarembga's forthright feminism combined with her practical elision from her story of the guerrilla struggle that Fanon so values might be read as riposte to Fanon's own elision of gendered politics from his analysis.[38] The novel adheres firmly to the anticolonial aspect of Fanon's politics. Nevertheless, it also implicitly indicts Fanon for writing the anxiety of colonialism as a lack of masculine agency, since he occasionally betrays the belief that the colonial subject is exclusively masculine: "The first thing the native learns is to stay in his place and not to go beyond certain limits. This is why the dreams of the native are always of muscular prowess; his dreams are of action and of aggression." And again: "The look that the native turns on the settler's town is a look of lust, a look of envy; it expresses his dreams of possession: to sit at the settler's table, to sleep in the settler's bed, with his wife, if possible. The colonized man is an envious man" (Fanon 1968, 52). Fanon's celebration of muscular aggression as a form of rebellion against alienation has been celebrated in literature by many male African writers, including Ayi Kwei Armah, Ngugi wa Thiong'o, and, in a different vein, Ousmane Sembène. Dangarembga tellingly recasts the Fanonian protagonist's masculine-coded desire for aggression and agency as a teenage girl's suffering from an eating disorder, the very opposite of muscularity at the most literal level, thereby exposing the Fanonian protagonist as (universally) male.

The genre of the Bildungsroman illustrates the making of a nonnative national subject in Tambu; the political theory of Fanon explains the construction of the native in Nyasha. The ideological connection between the two is that of decolonizing nationalism and feminine subjectivity. Earlier, I suggested that in psychological terms, the Bildungsroman charts the development of an interiorized subjectivity and in social terms it depicts the consolidation of the lone, bourgeois, and usually male subject. Here, via a Fanonian lens and through the character of Nyasha, one can see a similar exposition of social and symbolic activity in the service of decolonizing national-ism. Fanon's most important contribution to anticolonial theory is his claim that the violence of colonialism is not simply physical but also structural and psychological and that the threat of violence itself functions as a form of coercion of the colonial disenfranchised. In *The Wretched of the Earth* and *Black Skin, White Masks,* his most influen-tial books, Fanon devotes most of his attention to analyzing colonial-ism's repressive apparatus of psychological and institutional violence. Similarly, *Nervous Conditions* dispels the notion that, in Rhodesia, colonialism was upheld primarily through brute force, for with the exception of Tambu's grandmother's story of how the ancestral family was thrown off their land, most of what the novel narrates involves no physical political violence. The same holds true within the family, with the exception of the fight after the dance: only on that one occasion does Babamukuru strike his daughter.[39]

Jeremiah, a far weaker and less admirable man, is never shown to hit his daughter. Both men, however, actively inhibit their daughters' ambitions. And the more powerful Babamukuru also coerces Nyasha into eating or not reading forbidden books by threatening to expel her from "his" house. The buried anger of the female native erupts into violence toward the novel's end. In the following passage, Nya-sha's defiance of her father is represented as being of a piece with her defiance of the structures of colonial domination to which she per-ceives him and herself to be subject. In the following passage, the heretofore occluded apparatus of colonial subjugation is tied to the novel's more obvious mechanism of gender discrimination:

> "They've done it to me," she accused, whispering still. . . ."It's not their fault. They did it to them too. You know they did," she whis-pered. "To both of them, but especially to him. They put him through it all. But it's not his fault, he's good." Her voice took on a Rhodesian accent. "He's a good boy, a good munt. A bloody good kaffir," she informed in sneering sarcastic tones. . . . They've taken us away. Lucia. Takesure. All of us.
>
> They've deprived you of you, him of him, ourselves of each other. We're groveling. Lucia for a job, Jeremiah for money. Daddy grovels to them. We grovel to him. . . .

Nyasha was beside herself with fury. She rampaged, shredding her history book between her teeth ("Their history. Fucking liars. Their bloody lies"). . . . They've trapped us. They've trapped us. But I won't be trapped." Then as suddenly as it came, the rage passed. "I don't hate you, Daddy," she said softly. "They want me to, but I won't. . . . Look what they've done to us," she said softly. "I'm not one of them but I'm not one of you." (Dangarembga 1988, 200–201)

In the absence of an organized mode of social rebellion, Nyasha's refusal of colonialism and patriarchy first turns inward into anorexia and bulimia, a renunciation of colonial culture at a symbolic level. Later, she literalizes her objection to the consumption of colonial history; she uses her mouth not to ingest but precisely to destroy. The book with which she rampages is the history book, the icon and means by which her family and race have accepted their colonization. Spitting out the history book, Nyasha spits out the very means by which colonialism's benevolent face is made manifest (to her as well as to the "sublimate," Tambu). Not only does Nyasha object to consuming colonial history, but she names the link between that history and the hierarchy of which her father, and she through him, forms a part. Fanon (1968, 51) claims that when the native interrupts the narrative of colonization, he or she has arrived at a moment of productive crisis: "The immobility to which the native is condemned can only be called in question if the native decides to put an end to the history of colonization—the history of pillage—and to bring into existence the history of the nation—the history of decolonization."[40] Although Nyasha's story produces an ending without a positive role model, her outburst here suggests that she and through her, the reader, has arrived at such a moment of productive crisis.

The novel ends with Nyasha's mental and physical state unresolved. Nyasha's illness and uncertain condition becomes juxtaposed against Tambu's secure narrative voice and future, calling into question the closure of the classic realist novel. Earlier, I suggested that instead of a single position of character identification or reader identification, this novel deploys a set of hierarchized positions, one illustrating the coming into being of the national subject and the other, a simultaneous unraveling of the self-aware "native" whose language gives the novel its vibrancy and moral force. The realist Bildungsroman that produces its protagonist and, by extension, its readers as unified human subjects is hereby challenged. Rather than a novel that represents or fails to represent the coming of age of two girls, *Nervous Conditions* lends itself better to a reading of the struggle between the position of a "national" subject and a "native" one, and it thereby illustrates how a form normally understood to be flatly mimetic enacts its own limits and incompletions.

Teleology, the orientation of the Bildungsroman, and its perfect fulfillment necessarily raise the question of unfulfillment or failure, which Farah and Dangarembga engage differently. Dangarembga's realist novel of developmental success contains a secondary narrative of failure, while Farah's modernist novel enacts anti-teleology via its anti-hero. *Nervous Conditions* tells a story of successful development but displaces its anxiety about failure to the narrative margins and deposits it into another character. Nyasha's excessive Westernization, including her bulimia, is the novel's most honest avenue to self-knowledge and political critique. Through his membership in a collectivity, Askar gives in to the crude politics of nation that surround him everywhere and, in the process, loses all that he ever held dear. The modernist *Maps* has a different dynamic altogether. It refuses to represent a mature hero. Working within the genre's teleological structure and with the notion that individual and national stories overlap, it ultimately narrates a character whose development is aborted and whose weak sense of self becomes more vulnerable and then diminishes rather than strengthens. By naming, then frustrating, development, *Maps* explodes the national allegory and unravels rather than consolidates the story of selfhood.

4. Bildung at Its Boundaries
Djebar, Two Ways

> I need not say that what I am about to describe has no
> existence; Oxbridge is an invention; so is Fernham; "I"
> is only a convenient term for somebody who has no real
> being.—VIRGINIA WOOLF, *A Room of One's Own*

Assia Djebar, one of the most accomplished novelists Africa has
produced, illustrates in the trajectory of her writing some of the
preoccupations I have elaborated in this book: a concern with voice, as
well as voicelessness, from within the colonial paradigm; individual
women's agency and its relation to group social power. By giving special attention to how novels written by women represent their characters in relation to public-sphere activity, I claim that the strength of
expression of a public politics—in this case, the force or conviction of
female writers' representation of the African nation—is directly related to how long women had been writing and publishing novels.
Within only a few years of the first published efforts by Nwapa, Sow
Fall, and Bâ, African novels by women such as the Cameroonian
Calixthe Beyala and the Zimbabwean Yvonne Vera became increasingly visible sites for macro-political exploration.[1]

Two novels by the Algerian Djebar, *L'amour, la fantasia* (1985a) and *Ombre sultane* (1987), provide the final set of close readings of literature I explore. The novels make up two volumes of the Algerian Quartet, which Djebar has called her autobiography. They exemplify the developmental model of writing I have charted thus far, and yet they contradict some of the chronology I have proposed. The chronological challenge first: Djebar's first novel, *La soif* (1957) was published nine years before the first novels by Nwapa and Ogot, who are, respectively, the first Nigerian and Kenyan female novelists. I assign great weight to 1966, the publication date of *Efuru* and *The Promised Land*, and name Nwapa and Ogot first authors; this literary intervention makes explicit a racialization of inauguration claims. I also make explicit the fact that North Africa is frequently categorized differently, the Sahara marking a racial and geo-cultural divide between the Maghreb and the rest of Africa.[2] As to developmentalism exemplified, Djebar wrote *L'amour* and *Ombre sultane* almost thirty years into a substantial literary career, and the reception of these novels, in contrast to that of *La soif*, illustrates exactly the sort of change in literary writing and reception I have been tracing.

A melodrama of modernity and femininity, *La soif* tells the story of two Algerian women, Nadia and Jedla, in the late 1950s. Nadia, liberated and unmarried, wants to explore her romantic and sexual sensibilities. Jedla, who is married, worries about her husband's fidelity, especially when she believes she cannot bear children, which constitutes grounds for divorce. The story involves attempted suicide, intrigue against the husband, and the betrayal of one woman's trust by the other. Nadia convinces the pregnant Jedla that bearing her husband a child will not keep him faithful. Jedla is led to an abortionist and dies on the operating table. The novel makes no explicit reference to the Algerian struggle for independence, which was at its height at the time of publication.

According to the sociologist Marnia Lazreg, who is not one of Djebar's admirers, Djebar's early novels were severely criticized by Algerians for not taking into account—that is, for not registering or reflecting—the life conditions of most Algerian women. In *The Eloquence of Silence* (1994), Lazreg objects strongly to the lack of representation of the social and political conditions of life for "the common woman" in particular.[3] Evelyne Accad, an admirer of Djebar, agrees with the facts as Lazreg names them: that the political content of Djebar's first novels was limited to themes of women's development within the domestic sphere. Certainly, it contained no representation of the war. This early work constituted the beginning of a period of intellectual, artistic, and political development, says Accad, of which we have the full flower only now in Djebar's mature work. In a retrospective examination of Djebar's major works, Accad acknowledges the lack of revolutionary fervor and, especially, the negative association of *La soif* with Françoise Sagan's *Bonjour tristesse* (1954): "In fact, it may well be that adolescent rebellion and the search for identity are not the stuff of the great novels of tomorrow. . . . What matters is that these works were in many ways authentic and necessary; you must know some basic things about yourself before you can begin to write about your place in the millennium" (Accad 1996, 801–2).

I have retold the story of Djebar's controversial beginning because I wish to juxtapose it with her current reputation as the female and African member of the Academie Française.[4] Above all, I believe that the development of both themes and her prose style stand as metonymy for the development and reception of women's novelistic writing on the African continent as a whole. In other words, Djebar's own trajectory as a writer illustrates the coming into being of a feminine and feminist political consciousness in narrative, moving from an understanding of the novel as individualist and woman-centered to a vehicle for telling feminist tales of women of the nation. Within the context of African writing more broadly, it became increasingly possible as overtly political female writers began to appear to read more novels in allegorical relation to the nation. Writers such as Djebar, then, have been at the forefront exploring the writing of feminine allegories, both claiming and undoing the figure of woman as sign of the nation.

The Djebar of *Femmes d'Alger* (1980), the first written work after a decade of publishing silence, was already a writer whose grasp of and engagement with politics put her in the camp of extroverted political representation, along with Buchi Emecheta, Aminata Sow Fall, and Nawal El Saadawi. Like Emecheta's, Djebar's political universe traverses the domestic and public world; like Sow Fall, she explicitly names the nation. Her later work explores her relation to both French and Arabic, through which languages are mediated her representation of Algerian women, the idea of Algeria, the relation of speech to writing, and, most explicitly named, orality to the archives.

Djebar's writing is self-consciously interested in art, literary history, and the question of influence; it also invokes classical (Arabic), native (Berber), and colonial (French) sources and motifs. Her style is lyrical, formally complex, and sensuous, and her self-assurance allows her to explore the question of nationalism for feminism in a manner that is comparably powerful to that of Mariama Bâ and Tsitsi Dangarembga, both of whom write less explicitly about national politics and are more highly praised for their artistic accomplishments than Sow Fall and Emecheta. Like Bâ, Djebar implies a connection between the state of the home and the state of the state. Like Dangarembga, she tells the national tale via the stories of several women.

L'amour and *Ombre sultane*, the first two novels of the Algerian Quartet, begin the full flowering of Djebar's mature work and are the product of years of writing, as well as a period of reflection, a coming to terms with feminism's individualism and her own commitment to collectivity.[5] The first novel of the quartet, *L'amour, la fantasia*, explores th[...] ation of Algerian history. *Ombre su[...] etween two very different women a[...] events of the mid-1980s as backdrop[...] icular, their form strongly suggest t[...] ogue with each other as a literary p[...] r political and intellectual history.[6] [...] ence and disappearance of histories [...] attenuates their horror by mixing in personal, intimate tales of women; *Ombre sultane* alternates the stories of two very different women and thematizes storytelling itself by conducting an intertextual dialogue with the classic Arab tale *One Thousand and One Nights*. Without developing any argument concerning the relation between the two books, several critics have called the unnamed protagonist of *L'amour* Isma, which is the name of the first-person narrator of *Ombre sultane*.[7] I shall try to offer grounds for this comparison.

In her discussion of the novels' interrelation, Anne Donadey astutely points out that the same quotation by French painter and writer Eugène Fromentin inaugurates *L'amour, la fantasia* and closes *Ombre sultane*. The postscript of *Ombre sultane*, the very last words before the table of contents, consists of the reference information for an unattributed quotation that appears two pages earlier. Donadey notes that the first quotation is not exactly the same as the second.[8] She interprets Djebar's slight alteration of Fromentin's words "as a desire to remain true to the (oral) spirit of the quotation while going beyond the constraints of its (written) letter. . . . [They] seem to point to the workings of memory and transmission" (Donadey 2001, 65). Donadey is insightful in noting the discrepancy and, I believe, essentially correct about orality, although I am not so willing to read all of Djebar's efforts as entirely intended or pedagogical. Writers often quote from memory, and they are not always accurate. Donadey's insight lies in the following unanalyzed assumption: in a culture in which a written–oral interface exists, such as the French and Arabic one Djebar inhabits and attempts to bridge, the ability to recite from memory calls on one's oral skills, which themselves are made visible only in an incorrect quotation. For the purposes of my reading, the Fromentin quote serves to bookend a single text—one that is opened by the epigraph of *L'amour* and closed by the post-script of *Ombre sultane*. As Bildungsroman, which Djebar's text seems to be more than the autobiography she claims, the text's generic interests lie in the depiction of the lone individual as she negotiates family, clan, or nation; explores the relation of individual being to social being (as in *L'amour*); and discovers that sociality has a strong interior component (as in *Ombre sultane*).

Djebar has noted the difficulty of writing an autobiography because that genre values the individual over the community, because of its highly personal rhetorical form, and because even more than Algerian men, Algerian women are not supposed to make public the details of their personal lives. Given the historical and political weight behind her move to name this writing as autobiography, one might wonder how I can read it as a Bildungsroman. I do so by taking seriously the axiom that the genre of autobiography takes its mark of definition from the truth claim of the signator: neither *L'amour* nor *Ombre sultane* name an Assia Djebar or a Fatima-Zohra Imalhayène as protagonist.[9] Elements of Djebar's own life appear in the storyline of the protagonist of *L'amour*; however, *L'amour*'s protagonist does not have a name. The second novel, *Ombre sultane*, seems to move closer to autobiography through its regular use of the first-person pronominal form and by naming its protagonist. The name of the character most like Djebar's, however, is Isma, a word that means "listen" in Arabic. This meaning itself comments on the need for those who have a voice to attend to those who do not. Isma's *je* is regularly interrupted by the *tu* of Hajila, whose story Isma narrates on her behalf. The story of another woman's life is woven into the fabric of the primary narrator's life, unsettling the question of whose story is being told.

Whatever else one might say of the Algerian Quartet's increasingly autobiographical mode of self-representation, *Ombre sultane* is not ready to lay claim to a true life story or to link the character with the author. Donadey, who does read Djebar autobiographically, also believes that Djebar does not write a conventional autobiography. In a comparative reading of *Ombre sultane* with the autobiography of Ibn Khaldun, Donadey says that Djebar writes "a second-degree autobiography. . . . in other words, the autobiography of the historical character or writer rather than the person. . . . [It] also reveals very little about her personal life. In it, she mixes the story of her relation to the French language in Algeria" (Donadey 2001, 73). Neither of Djebar's novels is a conventional autobiography, which is to say that neither offers a history of one person's life as told by that person. Both tell life stories in which one of the characters resembles Djebar, and both weave history, autobiography, and imagination into a novel, the genre that most encompasses and allows the expression of heterogeneity. Moreover, both conform to the novel's reputation as a genre at the forefront of newness, change, and stylistic innovation.

The novels share a structure of alternating chapters. Both use the technique of many chapter divisions to organize the narrative's unfolding, only to suggest toward the end, at the level of both form and content, that the distinctions marked by the chapters cannot hold. At the level of story, *L'amour* tells of the French conquest of Algeria from the perspective of an Algerian reading and writing about it one hundred fifty years later using the historical records of the French and one known Algerian chronicler, Mufti Ahmad. These parts of the novel comprise military diaries, journalistic accounts, and letters home from officers.[10] They are the source materials for the author-narrator, who sometimes quotes from them and sometimes fictionalizes them by presenting their presumed thoughts without quotation marks. Sometimes the thoughts are presented in the first person in an orchestration directed by the narrator.

Theme is bound up with content, for the novel alternates chapters of conquest from between 1830 and 1852 with chapters on the mid-twentieth-century Algerian female protagonist. *L'amour* contains historical letters and documents not written by Djebar, as well, of course, as the voice of the narrator. Because of this heterogeneity and because it points to the representation of the otherwise voiceless while practicing giving voice to one character, I read it as a novel. Because its chief interest lies in the making of an Algerian woman, I read it as a Bildungsroman. Djebar incorporates the collective story of Algeria's conquest into this Bildungsroman, thereby exploring the limits of generic boundaries. Beyond the structuring into narrative and the chronological growth of a single character, *L'amour*'s force lies in its recounting the history of the nation—in particular, how the Algerian nation came to be. In *L'amour*, the unnamed girl's story is literally imbricated with a variety of stories about Algeria's military conquest and resistance. At one level, the girl stands as allegory of the nation, her story of development paralleled with that of the new nation, something to which I will return. At another level, the very uniqueness that the national Bildung figure implies is itself undermined by the multiple stories or vignettes of the many other women who populate the narrative margins.

Ombre sultane, set in the present tense of its writing—the mid-1980s—tells a more interiorized tale of the relations between two women: Isma, who is educated, Westernized, and middle class, and Hajila, who is lower middle class and accustomed to wearing the veil. Both novels are composed in three parts and juxtapose sharply divergent realms or narrative voices in the form of sketches or vignettes. Both also give over one of the three parts to the heterogeneity of women's stories or voices. In *L'amour*, parts I and II consist of sets of contrasting tales recounted in alternating sections, individual and collective; part III consists of stories of women. That is, they are stories neither of the narrator nor of members of her immediate family or circle of intimates. In fact, except for the fact that the subjects of the tales are various Algerian women (and in one case, a French woman), we know little about these characters. In *Ombre sultane*, parts I and III consist of alternating chapters focalized through Isma or Hajila. The chorus of women's vignettes comes in part II, and it resembles the tales of *One Thousand and One Nights* that the original Scheherazade tells the sultan and her sister. Individually, *L'amour* and *Ombre sultane* each recounts its own tale of the interpenetration of the public and the private; together, they offer a nuanced meditation of the relation of nationalism to feminism; of the value of gender to oral histories, class, and religious politics as played out in late-twentieth-century Algeria; and, above all, of the fundamental importance of developing and sustaining women's subjectivity that is not merely individualistic yet nevertheless includes a claim to individual rights.

The title of *L'amour* speaks via its second noun to the act of war, particularly to the Maghrebi equestrian mode of combat.[11] In the North African context, "fantasia" refers to the fierce and elegant martial dance for which Algerians were famous and by which they nobly, and often unsuccessfully, fought the French. The first of the two nouns, however, is "love," which, when juxtaposed to "fantasia," establishes an immediate set of contrasts or antinomies: love and a war dance. As the title suggests, Djebar's artistic method is formally contrapuntal and, if for no other reason than that she writes fiction with archival material, freely structured.

The story of the individual is told in chapters that alternate with those on the conquest of Algeria. The novel opens by telling the story of the girl, suggesting that the young Algerian we encounter will grow and mature. Her walk to the French school on her first day of class, hand in hand with her father, inaugurates the novel and places it directly within the generic boundaries of the novel of education and development, the Bildungsroman:

> Fillete arabe allant pour la première fois à l'école, un matin d'automne, main dans la main du père. Celui-ci, un fez sur la tête, la silhouette haute et droite dans son costume européen, porte un cartable, il est instituteur à l'école français. Fille arabe dans un village du Sahel algérien. (Djebar 1985a, 1).

A little Arab girl going to school for the first time, one autumn morning, walking hand in hand with her father. A tall erect figure in a fez and a European suit, carrying a bag of school books. He is a teacher at the French primary school. A little Arab girl in a village in the Algerian Sahel. (Djebar 1985b, 3)

The introduction promises, and the novel delivers, the story of a young girl's growth to womanhood. *L'amour*'s chapter divisions mark the passing of chronological time, each subsequent chapter telling a story from a later moment in her life. What I will call national-historical chapters are interleaved with those of the story of the girl, who is unique by virtue of having been taken at an early age to a French school by her educationally (and generally) progressive father. Girlish stories describe the cloistered world of women, domesticity, and the development of a romantic sensibility oriented toward marriage. The stories appear small and private, though the private often contains within itself a relation to the public. For example, the narrator's three girlfriends, all of whom are literate, are, unlike her, sequestered and protected from the eyes of men. Yet they shock the narrator by secretly corresponding with men from all over the Arab world, a correspondence that makes visible the power of literacy and illustrates how easily the world enters their home. The story of the French conquest of Algiers in July 1830 is told in alternating chapters, primarily through the chronicles of three French military men who witnessed the events. Archival material produced by French soldiers and officers, colonial clerks, scribes, and functionaries serve to reconstruct the events of the taking of Algiers and, later, the battles of the countryside.[12]

The substance of the Bildung genre—the development of character and ripening of individual subjectivity—is deferred until *Ombre sultane*. As a pair, *L'amour* and *Ombre sultane* function as a single (if not absolutely coherent) and flexible Bildungsroman, the first novel serving as the form or mold that manifests temporal change and the second novel, as content—or, as Franco Moretti (1987) puts it, "the fattening of particularity" that expresses individual complexity. Only when one reads *L'amour*'s successor, *Ombre sultane*, does one encounter a more complete articulation of character roundedness in its ambivalence and irrationality; this is the substance of interiority that the novel contributes to the Bildung narrative.[13] If we understand *L'amour*'s protagonist to be Isma and, therefore, *L'amour* as a frame through which to consider *Ombre sultane*, the first novel makes visible within the second a story of the contemporary national condition. The interrelation of the two novels produces a more complete narrative. The explicit feminine allegory of *L'amour, la fantasia* nudges us towards an allegorical reading of women's relations in *Ombre sultane*.[14]

Whereas *L'amour, la fantasia* might be called a Kunstlerroman, or novel of artistic formation, *Ombre sultane* resembles the "novel of awakening," under which subcategory fall many canonical novels of women's post-marital development. Many are novels of adultery, such as *Madame Bovary* and *Anna Karenina*, as well as the feminist novel *The Awakening*. Feminist literary critics for some time have celebrated novels of awakening written by women, in part because the depiction of transgression, especially sexual transgression, is itself felt to be a liberating gesture. Djebar's novel of two post-marital women certainly depicts transgression: Isma has escaped her marriage (and romantic couplehood, though she entered the state voluntarily, and there is no depiction of mistreatment), and Hajila, who is mistreated, wants to unveil, move freely, and explore her individual self (she, too, flees a marriage). Djebar's novel shares with its Western counterparts the fact of the challenge to marriage, both at the global level of institution and through the experiences of a single character, and its descriptions celebrates the pleasure in one's own body, sexual congress, and the right to be veiled or unveiled, as the woman chooses. Unlike "Western" novels of awakening, *Ombre sultane* refuses both monogamous and polygamous marriage from *within* the bounds of marital fidelity. Unveiling, while a particular sort of sexual transgression, is not bound up with infidelity. Hajila claims the right to nudity (*nue*, or "naked," is the word she uses to refer to herself unveiled), rigorously separating it from the sexual excess of adultery, a gesture of chastity that I read as a sign of cultural nationalism. More important, it serves well as riposte to the adultery that begins the cycle of *One Thousand and One Nights*. No man ends Isma's romance (indeed, the novel gives no sign of other men in her life after "the man"); nor does Hajila find herself drawn to another. *Ombre sultane* differs sharply from many other women's Bildungsromane because it puts forth a qualified rejection of development without representing either of its female characters as failed protagonists, as, for example, does *Nervous Conditions* of Nyasha or *Maps* of Askar. These recursive narrative strategies suggest different developments.

L'amour, la fantasia's startling originality lies in its linear rendering of individual maturation (the girl's first day at school and sketches of her youth, ending with the day of her marriage) while also undermining the assumption of novelistic individualism by refusing to tell a psychological tale. The very title to part I of *L'amour*, "La Prise de la Ville, ou, L'Amour s'écrit (The Capture of the City: or Love Letters) puts into play two diverging registers of human engagement that the novel holds in tension.[15] At one level, the recounting of official narratives of war in French versus the exploration of romantic intimacies in Arabic; at another level, the public conquest of Algiers in the nineteenth century as recorded in memoirs and letters to France versus the private world of mid-twentieth-century Arabo-Berber girls writing clandestine love letters to far-flung parts of the Arab world. At the level of history, Djebar juxtaposes a chronicle of conquest that is more than a century old with the reminiscences of a childhood past.

Speculating on what the archives cannot speak while simultaneously engaging what they do say is one means by which the novel represents both literally and literarily those buried by French colonialism. The narrator conveys the archives' limitations by recounting that of the thirty-seven accounts of the siege of Algiers in 1830, some thirty-two are in French, only two are in Arabic, and none are by women (Djebar 1985a, 55; 1985b, 44). One of the narrative incidents most commented on, and arguably the one that functions as the novel's climax, is a genocidal massacre, though it is not necessarily recorded as such in the annals of French history. The chapter is titled "Femmes, enfants, boeufs couchés dans les grottes (Women, Children, Oxen Dying in Caves)," which, the narrator says, speaks to the killing by smoke asphyxiation of fifteen hundred men, women, and children—the entire tribe of Oulaed Riah in 1845—by the French officer Colonel Pélissier. The narrator lavishly describes the manner in which the Ouled Riah were found after Pélissier's victorious cessation of what Djebar calls the "*enfumade*," finding its most powerful description in the language of an anonymous soldier whose letter home is published by a Dr. Christian:

L'anonyme s'attarde particulierement sur un detail:

"J'ai vu un homme mort, le genou a terre, la main crispée sur la corne d'un boeuf. Devant lui était une femme tenant son enfant dans ses bras. Cet homme, il était facile de le reconnaître, avait été asphyxié, ainsi que la femme, l'enfant, et le boeuf, au moment ou il cherchait a preserver sa famille de la rage de cet animal." (Djebar 1985a, 86–87)

The nameless writer lingers particularly over one detail:

"I saw a dead man, with one knee on the ground, grasping the horn of an ox in one hand. In front of him lay a woman with a child in her arms. It was easy to see that this man had been asphyxiated, together with the woman, the child and the ox, while he was struggling to protect his family from the enraged animal." (73)

Unlike the Arabs, who surrendered in 1830, the Kabyles or Berbers, of whom the Ouled Riah formed part, continued to fight the French well after annexation in 1848. Their last and greatest rebellion took place in the 1870s, beyond the period the novel covers.[16] When the massacre became known, Pélissier came under severe criticism by the French at home, not for having brutally and slowly suffocated women and children along with their men and cattle, but because what he wrote about the event was "beaucoup t___ ___ ___ described too much about the num___ [*Becomes*] ___ manized them excessively by outlinir___ ___ 1985a, 86–89; 1985b, 73–77). Pélissie___ ___ officer, Bugead, despite the evidenc___ ___ ers. Bugead, one of France's most im___ ___ written to Pélissier: "Si les gredins ___ aux Cavaignac aux Sbeah, enfumez ___ ds! ("If the scoundrels retreat into their caves," Bugeaud orders, "do what Cavaignac did to the Sbeah, smoke them out mercilessly, like foxes"; Djebar 1985a, 78; 1985b, 65). As the narrated events make clear, the Ouled Riah were not smoked out of the caves, rather; they were smoked in, or asphyxiated.[17]

The narrator dwells for some time on Pélissier's public exhumation of the dead. The military executioner's prose, shaped by his proclivity for detailed recordkeeping, becomes a historian's tool, and, in the hands of Djebar, archival materials combined with the imagination become the stuff by which tales of heroic people are told.[18] Two other known instances of mass death by asphyxiation of the Kabyles have escaped the archives, she says, one committed by Cavaignac before Pélissier, as Bugeaud makes explicit in his letter of instruction ("imitez Cavaignac aux Sbéah"), and one by Saint-Arnaud afterward. The third massacre, by Saint-Arnaud, of at least eight hundred Sbeahs, remains almost secret, the most difficult to document.[19] Mindful of Pélissier's problems, which resulted from the public knowledge of this spectacular form of killing natives, Saint-Arnaud does not exhume the Sbeah bodies, and they remain forever interred in the place of their suffocation. Only through indirect historical references, such as those provided by people who recorded or represented Bou Maza's lieutenant, can the historian claim as fact that these people actually did die by Saint-Arnaud's hand. Pélissier's is the only massacre to be described with any level of elaboration because it is the only one of which there is an actual record. It becomes, therefore, one of the few ways in the early twenty first century to imagine the grotesquerie of the nineteenth-century massacres by the quiet killers, Cavaignac and Saint-Arnaud:

> Je me hasarde à dévoiler ma reconnaissance incongrue. Non pas envers Cavaignac qui fut le premier enfumeur, contraint, par opposition républicaine à régler les choses en muet, ni à l'égard de Saint-Arnaud, le seul vrai fanatique, mais envers Pélissier. Après avoir tué avec l'ostentation de la brutale naïveté, envahi par le remords, il écrit sur le trépas qu'il a organisé. J'oserais presque le remercier d'avoir fait face aux cadavres, d'avoir cédé au désir de les immortaliser, dans les figures de leurs corps raidis, de leurs étreintes paralysées, de leur ultime contorsion. D'avoir regardé l'ennemi autrement qu'en multitude fanatiseé, en armée d'ombres omniprésentes. (Djebar 1985a, 92)

> I venture to express my gratitude—however incongruous. Not to the first fumigator, Cavaignac, who was forced by Republican opposition to settle matters quietly; and not to Saint-Arnaud, the only real fanatic; but to Pélissier. After the spectacular, brutal killing carried out in all naivete, he is overcome with remorse and describes the slaughter he has organized. I venture to thank him for having faced the corpses, for having indulged the whim to immortalize them in a

description of their rigid carcasses, their paralyzed embraces, their final paroxysms. For having looked on the enemy otherwise than as a horde of zealots or a host of ubiquitous shadows. (Djebar 1985b, 78)

The Pélissier narrative provides a launching point to attend to textual mediation. For example, it is within this section that the narrator explores the absence of records of the deeds of Cavaignac and Saint-Arnaud and accuses the latter of having killed so many people. By so doing, Djebar plots herself and her family into a colonial history.[20] The narrator links the killings by Pélissier with two others. Through the technique of narrative adjacency, Djebar succeeds in eliciting from one set of archival materials about one massacre information and affective response that speaks to two other massacres whose details have not been recorded by the institution of colonial bureaucracy. Several commentators have discussed the narrative force of Pélissier's atrocities, but none has noted that this "enfumade" is named by the narrator as only the most famous one of three.[21] We are told explicitly here that this is only a small portion of a much larger, unrecountable story.

> Il faut partir. L'odeur est trop fort. Le souvenir, comment s'en débarrasser. Les corps exposés au soleil; les voici devenus mots. Les mots voyagent. Mots, entre autres, du rapport trop long de Pélissier; parvenus à Paris et lus en séance parlementire, lis déclenchent la polémique: insultes de l'opposition, gêne du gouvernement, rage des bellicistes, honte éparpillée dans Paris où germent les prodromes de la révolution de 48. . . .
>   "Pélissier n'eut q'un tort: comme il écrivait fort bien et qu'il le savait, il fit dans son rapport une description éloquente et réaliste, beaucoup trop réaliste, des souffrances des Arabes." (Djebar 1985a, 89)

It is time to depart; the stench is too great. How can one get rid of the memory? The corpses exposed in the hot sun have been transmuted into words. Words can travel. The words, for example, of Pélissier's verbose report, which arrive in Paris, are read at a parliamentary session, unleash a[n] uproar of controversy: insults from the opposition, embarrassment on the parts of the government, fury of the warmongers, shame throughout Paris in which the seeds of the 1848 Revolution are germinating. . . .

"Pélissier made only one mistake: as he had a talent for writing, and was aware of this, he gave in his report an eloquent and realistic—much too realistic—description of the Arabs' suffering." (Djebar 1985b, 75)

The national chapter that immediately follows the Pélissier massacre tells the tale of the abduction of a girl named Badra. Entitled "La mariée nue de Mazouna (The Naked Bride of Mazouna)," it stands out in several different ways. First, it is the only national chapter to come directly after the massacre, and it is the penultimate chapter of part II. (Parts I and II alternate girl-to-woman stories with those of Algeria from Ottoman territory to French annexation.)[22] Like the chapter that precedes it, "La mariée nue de Mazouna" also tells a story of implicit violence, though the violence takes place on an individual rather than a mass scale. A beautiful Algerian maiden is offered in marriage by one clan to another to end internecine fighting. Her bridal procession is attacked along the way by a fantasia headed by the *sherif* Bou Maza, who was famous for his campaign against Bugead.[23] Although the violence is not as brutal here as it is in the tale of the Naylettes, which is a chapter about two women, the tale is instructive because the warring parties are not colonizer and would-be colonized but the "Algerians" themselves. "La mariée nue de Mazouma" represents violence as intimate and makes clear that the exchange of women serves as social glue for many cultures. Badra is twice said to be as old as the conquest of "El-Djezai," or Algiers; this reference names her as national allegory, though Badra herself comes from Mazouna, an interior town that did not submit to the French for some time.[24]

This last national chapter has a powerful, if heretofore unacknowledged, relation to the other main narrative: that of the Bildungsroman. Thus far, I have noted two narrative threads in *L'amour, la fantasia*: individual and national development, private and public progress. They have contributed to alternating stories of individuality and collectivity, each set unfurled with no direct connection between the two. However, "La mariée nue de Mazouna" comes immediately before the final chapter of the Bildungsroman, which constitutes another chapter on marriage, here between the unnamed protagonist and her similarly unnamed fiancé. Attention to adjacency makes visible a relation between the two sets of chapters or two realms of life. Within the classic Bildung, marriage signifies full maturity and entrance into adulthood.[25] The first mention of the Bildung protagonist in this chapter is *la future épousée*, which puts her in direct relation to *la mariée*, Badra. For a moment, in fact, the first-time reader experiences some confusion about which century she is in, which wedding is about to take place. Compounding the confusion is the fact that, in both chapters, the husband-to-be lacks a name and any discernible individuation. The narrative adjacency of the chapters and the fact of the thematic significance (marriage as a gift of self versus marriage as the exchange of wom~~ ~~ that *L'amour, la fantasia* suggests t~~h~~ ary lovers will have some aspect of ε ~~ ~~ ιe abduction of women. Djebar's n~~ ~~ ed or full heterosexual relations. Ν ~~ ~~ n and for itself (rather than for ten ~~ ~~ duction of children, or the improve ~~ ~~ nces) is challenged in both *L'amou* ~~ ~~ *sultane*. The romance plot is scrutinized a..u emptied of affective force. Both novels excise the affective content of marriage and leave behind the form. We are left with the developmental endpoint without the sentimental run-up of romantic courtship in one and with polygynous marriage without the issue of sexual jealousy in the other.

L'amour, la fantasia ends the private story of the individual (though not the novel itself) with the marriage in Paris of the young woman to her revolutionary lover. The lovers appear to be motivated as much as by their commitment to national independence as by strong feelings for each other (Djebar 1985a, 106; 1985b, 108). By organizing itself around the topic of polygyny, *Ombre sultane* treats marital relations as a given; the novel devotes itself to examining marriage in both form and ideology. As I discussed about *Une si longue lettre*, it has become axiomatic to read narrative closure in novels written by women as a choice between marriage (success) and death (failure). As a result, feminist critics, particularly of the nineteenth-century European novel, agree that romance and the marriage plot usually complicate and sometimes co-opt the protagonist's quest to inhibit or contain the aspirations of its female characters.[26] Consequently, some femi-

nists have asserted that, unlike in the process of masculine development, sexuality in and for itself rarely plays a central role in women's
processes of self-discovery.

Part III of *L'amour, la fantasia* moves away from the strict binaries
of nation and maturing individual; it contains stories of various and
diverse women, some of whom fought militarily in the twentieth-
century war of independence, and others of whom resisted at earlier
moments in history. This series of vignettes appears to be structured
as a musical composition—a fantasia, perhaps.[27] Part III itself consists
of five movements, the first four of which are divided into six subsec-
tions or vignettes. The fifth is divided only in two, and after that
comes "Tzal'rit," which is translated into French as "Finale." The first
vignette of each of the five movements is focalized through the protagonist, a Western-educated woman, her voice sounding remarkably
like that of Isma of *Ombre sultane*. Each subsequent vignette is focalized through a village woman. The lone exception is the very first
vignette of the first movement, which is about a woman who is hit by
an oncoming tram car and survives unscathed. It bears a strong
resemblance to Hajila's accident at the end of *Ombre sultane*.

The content of part III also resembles stories recounted in *La Nouba
des Femmes du Mont-Chenoua* (1979), the film Djebar directed and
produced shortly before publishing *L'amour, la fantasia*. Both film and
novel contain multi-voiced sketches of women; many tell of those who
lived and struggled through the war of independence. As other critics
have noted, many of these stories are of actual, historical women, some
of them Djebar's relatives.[28] Echoing the musical form of fantasia,
these accounts serve as a counterpoint to the two sets of alternating
tales that come before.[29]

The voices of numerous women, narrated in individual vignettes,
mediate the tension between the individual rights of a single protagonist and the necessity of thinking collectively, whether as a gender or as
a nation. One vignette tells of Cherifa, who at thirteen cradles the
body of her dead brother; another tells of Cherifa the *maquisarde* or
freedom fighter, some time later; and a third vignette, set some years
later still, has Cherifa back on the farm in a conventional and perhaps
dull marriage. Most, when put together, do not form a more complete
chronological story of a single character. A nineteenth-century sketch

from Fromentin tells of the Naylettes, two prostitutes who were killed when they attempted unsuccessfully to kill French troops who had called on them. Historical sketches are interspersed with accounts of twentieth-century women who lost all of the men in their families during the independence struggles. The voice of the Western-educated woman resembles Isma's; she speaks of telling her autobiography, one weighted down by the story of her people.

Taken together, these sketches illustrate the novel's playful establishing and undoing of national allegory as a woman. The unnamed protagonist stands as one version of Algeria, the New Woman of the nation; so might Cherifa, the peasant, stand as one of the many who worked actively in the armed struggle. Beautiful Badra, as old as colonized Algeria and vulnerable to forced marriage and rape, stands as a perfect victim—a woman in danger, as well as grace under duress.[30] The novel's end, however, suggests that, in addition to the contemporary narrator, the character who most explicitly allegorizes the nation—the character with whom the novel closes its allegorical impulses—is the historical Pauline Roland whose relation to Algeria is neither racial nor biological. Indeed, her relation is historical only by accident. Roland's vignette is highlighted by its prominent place as the final story of the final section (part III) of the book. The historical Roland was a Frenchwoman and Saint-Simonist; she was politically active on behalf of women's and workers' rights, and she played a prominent role in the Paris Revolution of 1848. In the aftermath of the failed Paris Commune, she was punished by exile to Algeria in 1852. She spent four months there, took ill, and died shortly after her return to France. Roland was famous in her time, a hero to French progressives. Victor Hugo celebrates her in the poem "Pauline Roland," bemoaning her banishment to the "unhappy Africa" to which she was sent.[31] Djebar is up to something important. She sets up a relation between the year 1848 (multiply resonant here), colonialism, and the revolutionary change—and failure—that that year meant for Europe. The year 1848 is the one in which Algeria was annexed as a formal department and thus a part of France. Rather than representing that moment in this Algerian novel as one of simple anticolonialism, Djebar chooses to represent it from within the Paris Commune and simultaneously in solidarity with the Arabs and Berbers. In telling of the end of Roland's life, the novel implies that she, a Frenchwoman, is as much "mother of the nation" as is Badra, the beautiful bride born in the year in which Algiers fell:

Elle embarquera très malade. Sur le bateau qu'elle prend, elle demeurera couchée sur le pont, souvent battu par les vagues d'une mer démontée. Débarquée à Marseille, Pauline ne peut plus se lever. . . . En fait, elle n'a plus quitté l'Algérie sinon pour délirer. . . . Notre pays devient sa fosse; ses véritables héritières—Chérifa de l'abre, La Zohra errante dans les incendies de campagne, le choeur des veuves anonymes d'aujourd'hui—pourraient pousser, en son honneur, le cri de triomphe ancestral, ce hululement de sororité convulsive!

Durant les quatre mois de ce voyage algérien, Pauline n'a cessé d'écrire de multiples lettres à ses amies de combat, à sa famille, à ses proches. . . .

J'ai rencontré cette femme sur le terrain de son écriture: dans la graise du glossaire français, elle et moi, nous voici aujourd'hui enlacées. Je relis ces livres parties d'Algerie; une phrase me parvient, calligraphie d'amour, enroulant la vie de Pauline:

"En Kabylie," écrit Pauline, en juillet 1852, "j'ai vu la femme bête de somme et l'odalisque de harem d'un riche. J'ai dormi près des premières sur la terre nue, et prés des secondes dans l'or et la soie." . . ."

Mots de tendresse d'une femme, en gésine de l'avenir: ils irradient là sous mes yeux et enfin me libérent. (Djebar 1985a, 250–51)

She is very ill when she embarks. On the boat, she remains lying on the deck, often swept by the waves of a stormy sea. When she lands at Marseille, Pauline cannot get to her feet. . . . In fact, she was delirious when she left Algeria. . . . Our country became her grave: her true heirs—Cherifa, hiding in her tree, La Zohra wandering among the fires that ravaged the countryside, the chorus of anonymous, women of today—could pay homage to her with that ancestral dry of triumph, the ululation of convulsive sisterhood!

Throughout the four months of her Algerian travels, Pauline wrote letter after letter to her friends in the struggle, to her family, her relatives. . . .

"In Kabylia," Pauline writes in July 1852, "I have seen women treated as beasts of burden, and others odalisques in a rich man's harem. I have slept at the side of the former on bare ground, an besides the latter amid gold and silk." . . .

Affectionate words from a woman, pregnant with the future: they give off light before my eyes and finally set me free. (Djebar 1985b, 223)

Having explored various forms of Algerian femininity, "traditional" and "modern," the novel moves sharply against the cultural national-ism it has so often espoused and ends with a gesture toward a universal sisterhood based on an idealized internationalism. Roland's story evokes structures of feeling between the failed utopianism of the Paris activists of 1848 and those, like the narrator's ancestors, who fought colonialism. Roland stands for potential alliances across culture, reli-gion, and geography while poignantly acknowledging that such bonds are produced only under conditions of duress and struggle.[32] The utopianism of the French radical is made maternal, the dying woman "*en gésine de l'avenir* (pregnant with the future)," makes of Roland an unlikely mother of the Algerian nation and, in particular, mother to its politically active women.[33] The vignette of Pauline Roland pushes at the limits of national and allegorical boundaries to dream a larger feminism in the service of a much larger internationalism, a bold move with which the novel ends. In this final gesture toward international-ism after having made a nationalist argument for pages and pages, one might hear an echo of Fanon's *Wretched of the Earth*.

Most remarkable to me is that, rather than depicting 1848 as the year France annexed Algeria, which it did shortly after the failed commune, *L'amour, la fantasia* shifts the perspective away from a triumphal France and an inescapable colonizer–colonized binary to a more utopian moment, albeit a failed utopianism. From a historical vantage point in 1852, the novel suggests a forward-looking and future-oriented perspective. In choosing to end with Roland, Djebar chooses to em-phasize 1848 as a moment of revolution and utopian sensibility (in France) rather than the humiliation of annexation (in Algeria).

In this respect, *L'amour, la fantasia* resembles *Maps*, and the French Pauline Roland resembles the Ethiopian Misra. Both novels make sharply political arguments through the forceful representation of woman as signifier of the nation, a female character who in biological terms cannot represent the nation. It is her actions, however, that make her maternal, that associate her with the idealism of the new nation to come.[34]

Ombre sultane pours its content, the affective material of the novel of education, into the Bildung shape of *L'amour, la fantasia*. *L'amour* provides the carapace and defers elaboration of character development until *Ombre sultane*. In turn, *Ombre sultane* illustrates that change and development on the parts of its two main characters though simple teleology is complicated by recursivity, as the novel is bound up with retelling and claiming of *One Thousand and One Nights*. The intertextual allusion only heightens the novel's most powerful questions about representation: who can represent, and how can we know the Other? The questions are posed generally through the desire for and fundamental problematizing of women's solidarity; they are posed specifically through the fact of Isma's control over the narrative and that she speaks for Hajila. *L'amour* troubles the Bildung's self-understanding as individual formation with a set of far more interesting stories about the making of a nation.

By organizing itself around the topic of polygyny, *Ombre sultane* engages both the form and the ideology of marital relations. Isma represents as voluntary and passionate a marriage that she recalls through a somewhat distant youth. The narration empties the relation of its teleological force while allowing for a nostalgic reminiscence about the power of romance. In this relation, *Ombre sultane* interrupts the question of individual maturation by using a story of parallel and non-teleological development in narrative terms. Individual development here is uncoupled from history, in contrast to the tight coupling of individual history and character in *L'amour, la fantasia*. The story of Isma and Hajila nevertheless arises out of a particular historical context, even though the novel itself does not speak history easily. In contrast to *L'amour, la fantasia*'s unnamed protagonists, all of the major female characters are named. At a primary level, *Ombre sultane* is a novel about polygyny; it also richly expresses consciousness (of one or two characters) of love, desire, sexual pleasure, violence, and emotional and mental development and strong stirrings of emotionality—in response to lovers, husbands, children, sisters, and, most important, mothers. Moreover, the interlocking stories of Isma and Hajila explicitly reverberate the literary history of *One Thousand and One Nights.*

Conducted almost entirely as a conversation of sorts between two contemporary women, *Ombre sultane* depicts macro-politics less explicitly than does *L'amour, la fantasia,* which immediately precedes it and which recounts women's participation in nineteenth-century and twentieth-century anticolonial campaigns. In its attention to the private spheres of marriage, sexuality, and the family, to the prospect of dialogue between women and the complex topic of veiling, *Ombre sultane* perfectly illustrates the porosity of public and private spheres in how it subtly, but surely, references the tensions between religious fundamentalism and Westernized feminist practices and notions of modernity that shaped Algerian politics toward the end of the twentieth century.

Ombre sultane was published two years after *L'amour, la fantasia* and before a period of intense, open, and protracted violence in Algeria, a struggle for power between militant fundamentalists, on the one hand, and the party in power, the once revolutionary Front Liberation Nationale (FLN), on the other. Those caught in between were the educated and professional class, especially secular intellectuals of Djebar's generation, who as young people had worked for the liberation of Algeria. The violence of the late 1980s and early 1990s has abated significantly, but at the moment of my writing (in 2007) it had not disappeared entirely.

Beginning in the late 1980s, Algeria experienced a sharp increase in Islamic fundamentalist activity, as well as a related spike in violent deaths, due in part to the tensions between religious and liberal-secular Algerians, a story that lurks but is not openly addressed in the novel. The rise of fundamentalism was fueled in part by economic chaos, including high unemployment rates among the male urban poor and lower middle classes. It had been helped into place, ironically, by the post-independence nationalist choice of Arabic over French as the language of the new state. One consequence was to produce a more religious youth; there was also the strong feeling among some that Algeria's national-political path requires more direct involvement of religion in daily life. For many, that involvement has meant women's wearing the hijab, or veil. The Front Islamique du

Salut (FIS) was founded in 1989 but immediately won in preliminary balloting, far ahead of the FLN. Fearing it would lose too much ground to the Islamists, the FLN banned the FIS by presidential decree; in response, FIS supporters began a campaign of violence in which militants killed several thousand intellectuals, journalists, and, especially, feminists. Like Nuruddin Farah's *Maps* (1986), *Ombre sultane* presciently outlines and engages actual nationally felt social tensions just before they exploded onto the international scene.

The novel addresses none of these issues directly. However, by juxtaposing two female characters with different backgrounds, levels of education, and, especially, attitudes toward the veil, the novel hints at tensions between Westernized feminism, on the one hand, and a landscape of economic uncertainty, high unemployment, and a shifting sense of national priorities, on the other. Although there is little personality depiction of the character "the man," his stronger economic standing is understood by Hajila's family to be part of their salvation. His assumptions that Hajila will remain at home and go out rarely and only when veiled, combined with his occasional drunkenness, hint that his great frustration and unhappiness might connect him to lower-middle-class men whose economic standing is weaker than they had expected, whose personal status has been shaken by feminism (Isma having left him and supporting herself financially), as well as general post-independence anomie.

Ombre sultane tells a double-threaded and nonlinear story of two different women who have been wives to the same man. Part I consists of chapters that alternate in focalization. Isma, the narrating voice, recounts the stories of both women using the first-person *je* in the chapters about herself and the second-person familiar *tu* in those about Hajila in a gesture reminiscent of Michel Butor's *La modification* (1957).[35] Through nostalgic reminiscences, we learn of Isma's education at an Algerian boarding school, which included being unveiled; her university days in France; her falling in love with "the man"; their marriage; and the birth of their daughter.

Such political choice, youthful rebellion, or even romantic love seems less available to Hajila, the second wife, who comes from a lower-middle-class family made poorer by the war of independence and by her father's early death. She marries "the man" well after Isma has left him, and she is installed in a modern apartment with conveniences and luxuries previously unavailable to her. While his two children are at school and "the man" is at work, Hajila begins to venture outside the apartment for walks, removing her veil in the process. She is found out by her husband and beaten. She then discovers that she is pregnant and that she does not want the baby. Part II of the novel interrupts the tale of the two women with a set of third-person narration of domestically themed *contes*, or vignettes. Part III returns to Isma and Hajila, though it seeks to break down the barriers of communication (and, one might claim, blur the lines of character differentiation) with exchanges between the characters. While they are in the public baths, Isma introduces herself to Hajila and gives her a key, enabling Hajila to escape the apartment within which she has been imprisoned. Hajila is hit by a car in the street and miscarries but is otherwise unharmed.

What follows is a schematic reading of *Ombre sultane*'s engagement with Western feminism and education, as well as with local women's emancipation. I will flag a couple of important points. In attending to literary history, I trace here an intertextual reading of *One Thousand and One Nights* that *Ombre sultane* uses as a narrative frame. Djebar engages in an act of literary-cultural nationalism by linking herself to the most famous of stories in Arabic; she also makes it yield a proto-feminist mode of storytelling. *Ombre sultane* depicts the overcoming of personal obstacles that the Bildungsroman demands. Its representation of two important characters challenges the genre's putative individualism. By refusing to gloss over the problem of class, it refuses to settle for easy answers. Perhaps most important, it makes of "the novel of awakening" a genre that fundamentally challenges the marriage plot, that quintessential feminine mode of narration for Westernized and poor Algerian women alike. The novel does not represent its female characters in adultery. *Ombre sultane* acknowledges, even emphasizes, the social anxiety about women who stray from the constraints of the home (the original sultana, Hajila when she goes out, and even Isma), the fact remains that the only characters who engage in polygamous, multiple-partner relations are men.

A full exploration of *Ombre sultane* ought to begin with some discussion of its openly declared intertext, *One Thousand and One Nights*.

With the exception of her contemporary fellow Algerian Leila Sebbar, whose Sherazade trilogy of novels thematizes French racism, colonialism, and immigrancy, Djebar's novel constitutes one of the earliest acts of recuperation of this exemplary feminine figure for a style of narration that resonates both with Arab cultural nationalism and a feminist mode of storytelling. (Rachid Boujedra wrote *Les 1001 années de la nostalgie* [1979], which, however, is not as explicitly interested in reworking the classic story for feminist ends.) *One Thousand and One Nights* consists of the narrative frame and a set of stories that are formally harmonious with the European novel and yet that developed independently from it.[36] To be sure, the Algerian novel rewrites the importance of the Arabic tale. In *Ombre sultane*, the size of the frame tale in relation to the many *contes* that come between are reversed in size and, I suggest, in importance. In enlarging the frame relative to the "nights," Djebar diminishes the masculine sphere in favor of the feminine, for the memorable tales from *One Thousand and One Nights* are paradigmatic masculine tales of adventure. In this way, we might read *Ombre sultane* against *L'amour, la fantasia* for the female adventure tales fantasia spins, in particular that of the beautiful and doomed Badra of Mazuma, a feminine allegory of Algeria whose marital journey is doomed from the start.

In brief, *One Thousand and One Nights* begins with the disillusionment of two sultan brothers, Shahzaman and Shariyar, with monogamous heterosexuality. After Shahzaman visits his beloved older brother, Shariyar, he learns that his own wife is unfaithful to him. Soon after, both brothers witness the adultery of Shariyar's wife.[37] In reaction to the adultery and other feminine licentious behavior, Shariyar decides to abandon the permanent company of women, taking a wife for one night, then executing her the next morning. This continues for some time. Over the objections of her father, the grand vizir to Shariyar, Scheherazade insists on being married to the monarch. She enlists the help of her younger sister, Dinarzade/Dunyazade, who accompanies the couple to the bedchamber, waits under the bed, then requests a story after the sexual activity is over. Scheherazade begins a tale but does not complete it before dawn breaks, and the sultan, enthralled by the not yet complete story, spares her life for that day.

In *One Thousand and One Nights*, the sisters serve as the morally upright counterweights to the pair of cuckolded sultan brothers. The classical Arabic frame tale depends on the notion of an exceptional and gifted woman, a notion that Djebar's novel works to subvert. Scheherazade does appear to be the ideal woman who prevails over the sultan through suasion rather than confrontation and restores his faith in women. She wins at the age-old game of power men and women play because she displaces seduction via sexuality with seduction via narrative, and she puts her beauty, wit, and charm at the service of the collectivity—that is, the women of the sultanate. Above all, in preoccupying the head of state and bearing him three sons along the way, she protects the heads of her countrywomen from his vengefulness.

The first three pages of *Ombre sultane* constitute a frame exterior to its three-part structure. Together, the frames set up many of the issues the novel then develops (singly and doubly), thus formally echoing the classical Arabic text's introduction of Scheherazade. The first sentence refers to the sultan's bride and her shadow, "Ombre et sultane; ombre derrière la sultane (A shadow and a sultan's bride; a shadow behind the sultan's bride)" (Djebar 1987, 1), introducing the remarkable Scheherazade alongside her sister.

The interpretive hinge on which my reading of Djebar's novels turns is this: the frame of *Ombre sultane* itself has a frame around it— that of the girl's story in *L'amour, la fantasia*. A post-Enlightenment novel with a marriage at its center will likely engage the convention of the romance plot and its permutations, and *Ombre sultane* is no exception. Rather than reconfigure the romance, this novel suggests its bankruptcy. It introduces a semi-polygynous set of relations in its storytelling about successful monogamy. Moreover, it represents as failures both the Western-style love marriage and the arranged Islamic second marriage that ends in neither procreation nor spousal affection. Isma's marriage begins in love but ends with the woman in flight. According to the conventions of the Western romance, the man begins as cold and distant but, as the story unfolds, becomes sensitized to the needs of his beloved, whereupon the match reaches fruition. Hajila's marriage, however, shows no development of knowledge or increase in intimacy between the partners. In place of romance, *Ombre sultane* substitutes women's homosociality: conversation that represents men as necessary—biologically, socially, and economically—but insignificant to their affective lives. Rather than serve as the locus of each woman's desire, making them competitors for intimacy and sexual relations (as would be the case if this were a romance), *Ombre sultane* displaces heterosexual desire onto homosociality, manifestly casting the man as the third term whose narrative function is to provide reason for the women's conversation.

The novel's second sentence, for example, reveals that both Isma and Hajila are or have been married to the same man and, moreover, that they are not rivals. It confronts the common stereotype of jealous wives competing for a husband's attention and immediately asserts a refiguration. In *Ombre sultane*, the polygynous man is never named (but is always referred to as *il* or *lui*): "Le corps de l'homme devient mur mitoyen de nos antres qu'un meme secret habite (The body of the man becomes the party wall separating our lairs, which house a common secret)" (Djebar 1987, 91; 1993, 82). In so doing, Djebar responds to the male homosocial bonding of the classical Arabic story and rewrites it with a feminine difference. How does this rewriting of the marriage plot bear on the coming into being of a fully developed feminine subject?

Through its evocation of *One Thousand and One Nights*, *Ombre sultane* also manages a complicated dance of displaced sexual and narrative desire, women's solidarity and voicelessness. The story of Scheherazade not only links sex and storytelling; it makes the narrative act necessary to women's liberation and, indeed, women's survival. It is through control over the narrative act—and control over men through narrative—that Scheherazade wins at sex. Moreover, although she is exceptional in her intelligence, wit, and beauty, Scheherazade is not a lone heroine. She clearly depends on another woman, Dinarzade, for her survival. If her younger sister did not watch for the dawn, then wake her and initiate the storytelling, Scheherazade likely would be executed. In *Ombre sultane*, Djebar makes this dependence more explicit. The Algerian novel twice states that the sisterly relation between Scheherazade and Dinarzade even threatens the polygynous structure, for a man cannot have sexual relations with the sister of a woman who is already his lover or wife:

> Pour le polygame, la consanguine de l'épouse est interdite, tout au moins tant que sa femme est vivante. . . . La loi autorise le polygame à prendre toute concubine, toute femme esclave s'il est maître, sauf la soeur de celle qu'il renverse dans sa couche. La soeur sous le lit,

peut done attendre, peut done entendre et, pour cela même, pro-téger de la mort. (Djebar 1987, 103, 108)

For the polygamist, any female blood relation of his wife is taboo, at least in the wife's lifetime. . . . The law allows the polygamist to take any concubine, any female slave of whom he is master, except the sister of the woman whom he tumbles in his bed. Thus, the sister beneath the bed can lie in wait, hearing everything, and for that very reason, shield from death. (Djebar 1993, 95, 99)

Dinarzade is protected by Scheherazade when she waits under the conjugal bed to ask for her story. She will, in turn, protect her sister by waking her. In an attempt to call on this tradition in which women's solidarity overcomes men's power, Isma collapses the distinction be-tween co-wives and sisters and refigures the relationship between Hajila and herself as that of sisters instead of wives. However, Isma's logic is incommensurable with the events of the contemporary narra-tive of which she is part. The fact is that both she and Hajila have had sex with and have been married to the same man. The relation be-tween the sisters Scheherazade and Dinarzade is what it is because it is not—and cannot be, according to law—the relation between co-wives, who are rivals. Thus, Isma's frustrated gesture toward a female literary history only foregrounds the fact that Hajila is her rival be-cause she, Isma, has herself put her there.

In *One Thousand and One Nights*, each of the two primary female characters occupies a differently signified position. Scheherazade is the narrator, the protagonist, and the initiator of action. As I sug-gested, however, she cannot accomplish her plan without her help-meet and sister, Dinarzade. In fact, as Fedwa Malti-Douglas (1991, 21) points out, although Scheherazade is the catalyst, it is Dinarzade who links sex and narration "by first witnessing the act, then requesting the story." With that in mind, Djebar's occasional representation of Isma as *both* Scheherazade and Dinarzade deserves special attention. Most of the time, Isma occupies the Scheherazade position: she initiates Hajila's marriage and her own separation from the man, and she controls all avenues of narrative discourse. Occasionally, however, Isma also occupies the ancillary position of Dinarzade, the one who waits quietly under the bed and wakes her sister:

Isma, l'impossible rival tressant au hasard une histoire pour libérer la concubine, tente de retrouver le passé consumé et ses cendres. Cette parleuse, aux rêves brûlés par le souvenir, est-elle vraiment moi, ou quelle ombre en moi qui se glisse, les sandales à la main et la bouche bâillonnée? Eveilleuse pour quel désenchantement . . . (Djebar 1987, 149)

Isma, the impossible rival, haphazardly weaving a story to free the concubine, hunts for the ashes of a past that has gone up in smoke. Is this woman who is speaking, whose dreams have been burnt up by memory, really me, or some ghost within me, who steals in, sandals in hand, and mouth gagged? To waken her sister to what disillusionment . . . (Djebar 1993, 159)

On the one hand, Scheherazade's liberation of herself and the other women of the sultanate is reinscribed into Isma's liberation of Hajila. On the other, this woman who "steals in" and awakens her sister is none other than Dinarzade. For Isma to substantiate her claim to the position of both women, she must deny the reasoning of the women's literary history offered by the precursor text that two or more women working together can outwit the patriarchal hegemony. Moreover, Isma must deny the fact that she herself imprisons Hajila (who here becomes the "concubine") before she can "liberate" her, for in *One Thousand and One Nights*, it is the sister, not the concubine, who is silent under the bed. Note also the link between Dinarzade's awakening her sister and the genre of the novel of awakening. Here, at least, wakefulness is not always a glorious experience.

According to the logic of the precursor text, it should be Isma under the bed helping Hajila. I have just pointed to a couple of instances of *Ombre sultane*'s tendency toward recursiveness, multiple figurations of the classic tale folded into the contemporary. A simpler reading of the shadow or ghost that is the "*ombre*" ("est-elle vraiment moi, ou quelle ombre en moi qui se glisse") permits Hajila a signifying space—and allows the text to slide in meaning between Isma's desire to occupy the positions of both Scheherazade and Dinarzade. Since it is Isma who narrates the often violent events of Hajila's bedroom and helps her flee house and marriage, one could assert that Isma does in fact play Dinarzade's role in a sisterly way. By pointing to some of the ways in which women can work in concert to help each other at the same time that it also problematizes the motivations of these actions, the novel suggests women's alliances involve multiply over-determined actions and desires.

Working through its many layers reveals that *Ombre sultane* is not merely rich in intertextual allusions, but, like *L'amour, la fantasia*, it frequently espouses both sides of opposing positions. Even as it offers itself as an instrument of Algerian women's liberation, the novel represents the fact of the silence and powerlessness of those very women, resisting the impulse to depict the entry of some into public space as a complete emancipatory act. It dwells on those women who remain excluded from (men's) public space and it reads (women's) private space differently. Despite the privileging of the patios and *hammam*, or baths, as sensual and safe havens for women, *Ombre sultane* nevertheless makes clear that women's free access to public space is necessary to their emancipation. Meaning here evolves out of the dialogical movement between inside and out, "tradition" and "modernity."

Within this context, the locating of *Ombre sultane*'s most forceful emancipatory act in the character of a woman with so little social or economic power suggests that the most important liberation is of those at the bottom of the hierarchy—an idealistic perspective, indeed. There is no question of challenging her marital destiny. This is significant choice of plot lines within the increasingly Islamic fundamentalist political context in which it is articulated and at which time the novel was written and published.[38] In her discussion of gender and spatial boundaries, Fatima Mernissi discusses the traditional Islamic characterization of public space and women's veiling:

> Traditionally, women using public spaces, trespassing on the *umma* universe, are restricted to few occasions and bound by specific rituals, such as the wearing of the veil. . . . The veil means that the woman is present in the men's world, but invisible; she has no right to be in the street. . . . Respectable women were not seen in the street. . . . Women in male spaces are considered both provocative and offensive. (Mernissi 1987, 142–43)

Hajila's self-unveiling is a remarkable act, and we are reminded of just how radical it is under her life circumstances. That she succeeds in remaining unveiled when outdoors is itself a powerful statement. Above all, Hajila's actions are noteworthy because of the type of risk she, a socioeconomically marginalized woman, takes in acting. As Mernissi (1987, 144) points out, for women of the lower middle classes, access to seclusion and the veil signal a separation between them and working-class women obliged to go into the street and earn a living. When Touma and Kenza, Hajila's mother and sister, go to the German's house to cook couscous, they disguise themselves in cheap veils, thus pretending to be servants (i.e., of the working class) and not "themselves" (i.e., of the middle class or, more likely, of the lower middle class). In fact, it is Kenza's old veil that Hajila later dons when she ventures outside the apartment on her walks (1987, 18). Hajila's rejection of seclusion and veiling threatens the stability of her marriage and, therefore, some of the financial security the man offers her family. The boldness of her actions is foregrounded by Djebar's juxtaposition of her situation to Isma's. Unlike the "modern" woman who has her own income, chooses her husband, and is generally unrestricted in her actions, Hajila lives a life that is much more circumscribed. Her move toward emancipation, therefore, is all the more important because through it she defies the man, her family, and traditional Islamic mores—all without support or inspiration from anyone.

Isma frequently claims a female solidarity between herself and Hajila, and the novel echoes the sisterly rhetoric of *One Thousand and One Nights*. The events of *Ombre sultane* nevertheless take place only because of the women's competing interests. At the novel's beginning, again in the first frame, Isma reveals that it is she who has chosen Hajila as the new wife for her former husband, thinking that this will free her from him and their passionate relationship (Djebar 1987, 9; 1993, 1). Because Isma's liberation depends on Hajila's imprisonment, the claim to their sisterhood is always already suspect, as is the attempt to position the man as a marginal third term. He becomes centralized in this configuration, the only motivation for the relationship between the two women. In the paragraph following the expression of the first sororal bond ("Ombre et sultane"), the validity of the bond itself is put into question. Moreover, the subsequent narrative events illustrate that the marriage contract offers the man legal protection under which he can rape and beat Hajila. Isma's ensuing address to Hajila alternates between claims to intimacy and sisterhood and guilt at her suffering:

> Ai-je voulu te donner en offrande à l'homme? . . . Certes, je t'entravais, toi, innocente, depuis que ta mère était devenue mon alliée ou ma complice selon la Tradition." (Djebar 1987, 10)

> Did I intend to offer you up as a sacrifice to the man? . . . To be sure, you were the innocent victim whom I enslaved, from the day when, according to Tradition, your other became my ally or my accomplice. (Djebar 1993, 1)

Although she never denies her own responsibility in Hajila's marital imprisonment, Isma does not hesitate to implicate Touma, referring to her as an accomplice in crime.[39] Highly self-conscious of her power over Hajila, Isma appears to assuage her guilt for consigning the other woman to this marriage: "Je te dis 'tu' pour tuer les relents d'un incertain remords, comme si réaffluait la fascination des femmes d'autrefois (I speak to you as if I had known you intimately, and in so doing suppress the hint of remorse that haunts me)" (Djebar 1987, 10; 1993, 2). The English translation cannot account for the excess of meaning, the word games between *tu* (you), *tue* (feminine participle referring to silence), *tuer* (to kill), and *tutoyer* (to be familiar).

The novel also juxtaposes a highly self-conscious call for women's solidarity against the fact of Hajila's and Isma's grossly disparate access to linguistic and material power. The sororal rhetoric must contend with Isma's all-controlling narrative voice. Isma narrates all of the sections of her own life story in the first person, and she narrates the story of Hajila—who, Scheherazade-like, never corroborates or responds herself—in a second-person familiar, omniscient mode. Isma also narrates the nine embedded fables of other women that make up part II. By using all possible narrative voices (first-, second-, and third-person), Isma controls all of the positions through which narrative discourse may be transmitted.

Isma is also the only source of information about Hajila. There is no proof outside her language to confirm the existence of the other woman. Not only Hajila's emancipatory acts but also her very status as subject might be put in doubt. The text offers the possibility that she might be a discursive fiction, a figment of Isma's literary imagination:

C'est toujours moi qui te parle, Hajila. Comme, si en vérité, je te créais. Une ombre que ma voix lêve. . . . Te dire "tu" désormais, est-ce tuer? Je ne t'invente ni te poursuis. A peine si je témoigne; je me dresse. (Djebar 1987, 91, 167)

Here I am speaking to you again, Hajila. As if, in truth, I were causing you to exist. A phantom whom my voice has brought to life. . . . Shall I destroy you if I continue to address you as an intimate? I neither invent you nor pursue you. I can scarcely even testify; I simply stand here in your presence. (Djebar 1993, 82, 157)

Isma's monologue to Hajila's absent presence (the rhetoric of doubt as well as of her sovereign authority) thus takes on a significance of its own. One might claim that at one level, the text invites us to entertain a solipsistic reading of Hajila, wherein Isma's rhetoric of doubt, combined with her own discursive power, effectively challenges the existence of the silent woman. However, I believe that it is here that Djebar as author makes one of her most powerful narrative statements: she refuses to speak for Hajila, as either author or narrator. Although the text ascribes an important metaphoric space to Hajila, the narrator claims no special authority, imputes little or no motive on the part of the silent woman.[40] Thus, the instrumentality of the narrative is continually problematized, for as it allies itself with Algerian women's emancipation, the text refuses to pretend that its voice offsets the silence and powerlessness of extratextual women. By articulating both sides of ostensibly opposing positions, *Ombre sultane* maintains a dialogic tension that fuels its story.

Textual contradictions do not end there, for even as it establishes a firm difference between the women and refuses to assimilate them under the category of "sisters," it nevertheless suggests a means of ultimately undermining these distinctions. It does so by evoking different permutations of the Arabic word *derra*, one central to both the movement and the meaning (or meanings) of the novel. Translated into French, one of the definitions of *derra* is as flows, *Toute femme s'appelle blessure* (Every woman's name is wound), becomes the title of the novel's first major section. Located at the end of that section is a chapter titled "Derra." In it, the following definitions are suggested:

> **Derra**: en langue arabe, la nouvelle épousée, rivale d'une première femme d'un même homme, se désigne de ce mot, qui signifie "bless-ure": *celle qui fait mal, qui ouvre les chairs, ou celle qui a mal, c'est pareil!* (Djebar 1987, 100; emphasis added)

> **Derra**: the word used in Arabic to denote the new bride of the same man, the first wife's rival; this word means "wound"—*the one who hurts, who cuts open the flesh, or the one who feels hurt, it's the same thing!* (Djebar 1993, 91; emphasis added)

The explication of "derra" as "wound" or pain is obvious. It is also obvious that the pain specifically refers to those women involved in polygynous marriage. However, it is unclear which of the wives—established or new—is the recipient of the hurt, for the definition blurs the difference ("c'est pareil! [it's the same thing!]"). While it is Hajila who is "la nouvelle epousée (the new bride of the same man)," Isma continues to deny that they are rivals. And although the second wife is supposed to inflict pain on the first, in this novel it is the first who has done all the hurting by making the second woman a wife at all.

In addition to the emotional pain or wounding, *Ombre sultane* hammers away at a literal, corporeal sense of wounding, using it as a means of exploring similarities and differences between the two women. When the man finds out that Hajila has been going out unveiled, or "naked," he beats her first with his fist, then with his broken beer bottle, causing physical wounds. The word "naked" reminds him of Isma, since it was the focus of the inscrutable explanation she offered for leaving him, claiming that only she and not he was "naked" in love. Moreover, she added that she had no traditions to teach her how to live naked.[41] The narrative overlaps chronology with subjectivity through language. Isma's use of "naked" triggers Hajila's beating: "Il a frappé au mot 'nue.' Il a continué en répétant ce mot, comme s'il le reconnaissait. Comme si on le lui avait lancé; je le lui avait lancé (He struck at the word 'naked.' He struck blow after blow accompanied by the repetition of this word as if he recognized it. As if someone else had hurled it at him; it was I who had hurled it at him)"

(Djebar 1987, 95; 1993, 86). Though continually aware of the threat of brutality linked to disobedient nakedness, the novel appears more interested in the word's sensual connotations. At one level, the stories of the two women converge around the word "naked" and its very different resonances for each of them. This technique points to how their stories not only begin at different points but move in opposing directions, the novel serving as a meeting point of two discourses. As Hajila progressively claims the right to unveil herself and walk farther and farther outside her house, Isma, through narrative recursion, moves imaginatively more deeply into the cloistered feminine spaces of her childhood.

This narrative progression also foregrounds how each woman regards and constructs sexuality differently and is, in turn, differently constructed by sexuality. Hajila is introduced to sexual intercourse through a rape. Later, she sufferingly acquiesces to sexual relations when the man demands it, a sign of both her "tradition" and, more significant, her social powerlessness. Being unveiled, then, or "naked" in public space is a sensual freedom. Though initially disoriented without her *haik*, Hajila takes increasing pleasure from the new sensual experiences of sun and wind and even men's eyes on her. Here, nakedness signifies sexual pleasure outside the veil. In contrast, the emancipated Isma has had access to "modern" uninhibited sexuality; her early chapters abound with lyrical descriptions of passionate lovemaking with the man. That relationship breaks down, however, when she discovers that romantic love is no more liberating than traditional marriage. The novel's end finds her moving toward spaces where only women gather. Although the text does not say so overtly, it hints that these sites of sequestered women subvert a patriarchal economy of desire and celebrate a homosocial one. As one story moves out, the other moves in. Hajila discovers the outer world as a space of freedom, reclaiming "modernity." Isma, disillusioned with this freedom, recovers the "traditional" community of interior spaces: the hammam and patios.

The following passages, from the last unframed section of the narrative, before the epilogue, practically speak for themselves. They testify to Pierre Macherey's reasoning that, in the act of resolution, texts frequently send up one last set of contradictions, the meaning of which help make visible its allegiances:

*La deuxième épouse refera ce que la première a seulement esquissé:
franchir les mêmes halliers, fair lever, sous l'éclair de diamant de la
lucidite, même folie improvisée.*

La première, guetteuse, furtive, attend; entend. L'étape suivante
nécessite le halo des mêmes projecteurs—soleil ou chandelle d'al-
côve—réallumés. Alors la première femme va disparaître, se dis-
soudre là renaître ailleurs. . . .

La second femme se présente sur le seuil, avaleuse d'espace; *la
première dés lors peut se voiler, ou se dissimuler.* L'homme, quêteur des
mêmes blessures, gesticule dans l'obscurité du jour tombé. Rive du
matin immobile. Au sortir de la longue nuit, l'odalisque est en fuite.
(Djebar 1987, 169; emphasis added)

*The second wife will repeat what the first one only half succeeded in
doing: cutting her way through the same undergrowth, starting the same
impromptu madness, but in the diamond-sharp light of reason.*

The first one keeps secret watch and waits; lending an ear. The
next step requires the same spotlights to be relit—to shed sunlight
or candle glowing in an alcove. Then the first wife will vanish from
the scene, fading away to be reborn elsewhere. . . .

The second wife stands on the threshold, devouring the space:
and now the first one can put on the veil, or go into hiding. The
man, searching for the same wounds, gesticulates in the darkness as
the day ends. The shore of morning is still.

At the end of the long night, the odalisque is still in flight. (Djebar
1993, 159)

Not only do these passages signal a movement away from narrative
confluence as each woman charts her own direction, but Isma clearly
occupies Dinarzade's position here, keeping secret watch, waiting,
and, true to her name, lending an ear. For the first time, Isma's narrative voice privileges Hajila's discourse; she states that the other woman
is on the brink of a greater emancipation. Moreover, she chooses to
journey back to the segregated spaces of cloistered women, thereby
suggesting a refiguration of the notion of "tradition."

Although they do more, as well, both *L'amour, la fantasia* and
Ombre sultane engage in dances of multiple displacement of feminine
national allegory. In *Ombre sultane*, Hajila appears to stand as the

national allegory, as the woman who unveils and rebels, yet Isma's strong narrative voice also gives her claim to that status. Moreover, the novel suggests that allegories are not possible without literary histories, without traditions of reading and interpretation and, especially, without women at the center of such activity. *L' amour, la fantasia* contains even more candidates for women as sign of the nation. The Bildung protagonist is one possibility, though her individual story is interrupted by the making of the modem Algerian state; this sort of undermining suggests that the many women's vignettes have comparable claims to allegorical status, especially when read as a unit. The protagonist's own tale, which ends in marriage, clearly parallels that of the bride of Mazouna, who, as a historical figure, was born in the year of Algeria's conquest and sacrificed during its anticolonial wars; the beautiful Badra stands as counterpoint to the Bildung protagonist, now a young revolutionary working for national independence. And last, but certainly not least, is the pride of place given to Pauline Roland, a historical character about whom important French writers have written; she is not Algerian but French, not nationalist but internationalist. What happens when a French revolutionary becomes mother of an ideal Algeria? Does stretching the feminine figure of the nation in this particular direction or manner lose its allegorical shape?

Conclusion

This book has focused on questions about women's authorship, female characters, and politics in Africa. Perhaps it was inevitable that national independence would form the political frame. Independence itself was less important—for me—than how, or even that, women represented political action or commitment. I found that in their fiction, female writers rarely represented the nation, let alone national struggles. Once I posed the question of what constitutes political commitment, or what it looked like in fiction, the question itself became murkier; even in men's writing, I soon found that it was not always easy to pinpoint what precisely constituted a commitment to national independence. For example, few male writers depicted the union activities that had so much to do with the formation of urban, work-based collectivities in the 1940s and '50s in sub-Saharan Africa. Nevertheless novels by men published from about 1955 to 1965 included stories of boys whose innocent eyes were opened to the unethical behavior of unscrupulous Europeans and Africans (Ferdinand Oyono, Mongo Beti, and later, Ngugi wa Thiong'o); historical fictions about important men who fell from power in their villages (Achebe); and even individual men who urged people to work together to improve the living conditions of the collective (Sembène). Whatever their content, setting, characterological perspective, or ideological position, these literary works allowed Africans educated in European languages to imagine communities and invent traditions. Their authors were writing about the need for sovereignty, self-government, or equal rights—in short, writing for or about the new African nation. Novels by women, in contrast appeared insular, telling stories of the domestic world and of family life, whether set in village, town, or city. Scholars of African literature have not known how to make sense out of the relation of women writers to nationalism, because of the inability to attempt reading practices that included the unsaid. Attending to the ambiguous, potentially ambivalent set of politics of both microdiscursive and macrodiscursive registers was my way of reading a relationship between this domesticity and the national life of politics, which, I suggest, is possible for all readers to do.

Though neither *Efuru* nor *The Joys of Motherhood* represent any explicit rebellion within its pages, I read both novels in relation to women's resistance, to the unnamed Igbo Women's War, and to the challenge that the emergence of women's writing and publishing itself constitutes. I have emphasized that writers who found other, earlier writers with whom to engage, whose stories offered models from which to depart, more easily depicted an explicit relation to public or national politics than did those who did not. I have come to believe that the critiques of local patriarchies produced by these later writers were likely to be sharper, as well. Buchi Emecheta highlights the inequality of indigenous gender relations and the misery of life under colonial rule, a literary intervention that builds on her relation to Flora Nwapa's rhetorical question ("Why did the women worship her?") and fundamental problematic of gender power. Nwapa enables Emecheta, so even the younger writer's critique of the elder—as *The Joys of Motherhood* represents public politics and women's difficulties —reads as a critical revision or an interpretation rather than a violent rejection.

Something slightly different takes place with *Une si longue lettre*. In the set of relations I have traced, *Lettre* stands in genealogical relation to the prescient, powerful, and damning argument put forth by Frantz Fanon in "Pitfalls of National Consciousness." By virtue of the mediation Ousmane Sembène's *Xala* grants her (and because it is Sembène and not Fanon with whom she is in dialogue), Mariama Bâ freely explores a failed national romance, the underside of the Latin American model Doris Sommer charts in *Foundational Fictions* (1991). The great contribution Bâ makes to African belles-lettres lies in her development of characterization. In Ramatoulaye we have a fuller, "rounder," and (despite her choice to remain in a polygynous marriage) more individualist character than had previously been depicted—in short, a character shaped by ambivalence. We might fault Bâ or Ramatoulaye for the novel's liberal feminism, and certainly many early critics did, but the advances and the limits of Bâ's approach are highlighted when contrasted with Aminata Sow Fall's *La grève des bàttu*. Although she is also in dialogue with Sembène and far more sympathetic to Fanon's politics, Sow Fall relies on plot to make her point, which in *Grève* means a satirical mode of unfolding the story rather than the development of a complex character.

Thus far I have been following the developments of complex individuality through influence study. In chapters 3 and 4, I move from a historical approach, the helpfulness of influential predecessors, to a consideration of the development of the female subject and her growth through the genre of the Bildungsroman, a more synchronous approach. The direct influence of one novel on another has no place in my reading of two important Bildungsromane, by Nuruddin Farah and Dangarembga (though I trace briefly later in this conclusion how Dangarembga herself has influenced yet another writer). Within the world of novels, coming to writing is almost like coming into existence, and the making of full characters organizes my reading of novels by Dangarembga and Farah as well as two more by Assia Djebar, *L'amour, la fantasia* and *Ombre sultane*. Dangarembga illustrates Tambu's successful growth but represents the cost of success as the diminishment of another character. Perhaps it is precisely because its author is male—and feminist—that *Maps* does not hesitate to represent the failure of human growth that Bildung represents and, in so doing, illustrates the semiotic overlap between women and nation.

Achieving selfhood is no simple matter, as *Maps, Nervous Conditions*, and the two novels by Djebar illustrate. One sign of Djebar's brilliance as a writer lies in her ability to write two novels that may be

read as one: *L'amour* forms the external, social, and especially national tale; *Ombre sultane* forms the domestic tale of women's emancipation from local patriarchy, including that of other women. It is
completely in line with the argument I have charted thus far that of
the two novels, *L'amour* has generated far more critical attention than
has *Ombre sultane*. I have charted how public politics are more visible
and valued than domestic politics and in that spirit believe that the
greater critical popularity that *L'amour* enjoys fits my claim. It engages the national allegory more openly; it tells the tale of Algeria's
conquest by France, its struggle for independence. And in the character of the Frenchwoman Pauline Roland, it also contains a sign of
hope: a women's movement undeterred by nation or language, motivated instead by revolutionary fellow feeling.

Novels by men evolve out of an understanding of the public political
machinations of the socius; those by women crystallize around the
sphere of the familial as the orchestrating unit that overshadows and
plays out national dramas. This simple formulation captures some
fundamental differences—for instance, in chapter 3 between *Maps*
and *Nervous Conditions*. Both sensitively depict important female
characters, and for both the relations between nations and families
are real and imaginary, historical and symbolic. Nevertheless, Askar
in *Maps*, who is obsessed with the symbolic (whether Misra really is
or can be his mother and how to understand her sexual relationship
with another man), cannot ignore the political machinery of the
state: a residency card when Misra reaches Mogadishu, the shifting
territorial relations between Ethiopia and Somalia (and, as a result,
his hometown), and, of course, his belief that he must choose sides
between nations and between people. In *Nervous Conditions*, by contrast, the struggle for national sovereignty, or Chimurenga, underway
at the time the novel is set, is mentioned but once, and there are only
two other references that have anything to do with national politics.

In the novels by women that I have examined closely, the economic, whether experienced at the level of family, village, or nation,
remains powerful, a character-shaper and determining factor. Examples include Nnu Ego's profound poverty and her children's hunger in
The Joys of Motherhood, although Nwapa's more insular-seeming
world clearly makes financial wealth and self-sufficiency the best sort

of power a woman can have. Wealth is more reliable than men in *Efuru* and offers almost as much pleasure as motherhood. In the middle-class world of *Lettre*, it is not only love that Ramatoulaye misses when her husband abandons her and takes another wife; it is also his financial support of her and their many children. Financial support and men's unwillingness to play by honorable rules of conduct put both families and the nation into jeopardy. In *Nervous Conditions*, Tambu is sharply aware that her father has money for her brother's school fees but none for her, and, above all, she fears becoming a desperately poor, bed-bound woman like her mother. Economic considerations shape her sense of the dynamics of her nuclear family as well as those of her aunt's and uncle's relations to the larger family unit. Finally, in *Ombre sultane*, whatever one might think of the success of cross-class female solidarity, the fact remains that Hajila marries "the man" because her family is impoverished by her father's death, a death that comes about because of his commitment to the new nation-state. Whatever her politics, or even his, she becomes the means by which Isma considers herself liberated—and this liberation can only come about because of Hajila's former impoverishment.

Since the period examined in this book, marked formal changes have taken place in narrative practice. Few African women now write like Nwapa or Ogot—or, if they do, they are not published and read in the same way. Far more write like Dangarembga, and, as I have shown elsewhere, Dangarembga herself has opened up avenues of writing for other writers. No longer can we say that sub-Saharan black women hesitate to represent the nation in conjunction with fully developed female characterization.[1]

Chimananda Adichie, who in some ways continues in the line of Igbo-Nigerian novelists with which this book began, is one of the most popular writers to have come out of Africa in the past ten years. Her first novel, *Purple Hibiscus* (2003), like Dangarembga's, may be said to represent the development of a female character against the backdrop of a new African nation. While the first novel engages the nation-state (it includes the story of a coup, and, indeed the tyrannical father might stand in for any dictator) it is her second novel, *Half of a Yellow Sun* (2006) that best illustrates the argument I have been making here: that women represent the nation in relation to the

family, and that as time progressed, African women began to represent the nation squarely and explicitly, in tandem with gender and the
family. To be sure, Adichie is not the very first woman to do so. Not
only had Emecheta written novels with a national sensibility, as I have
illustrated, her *Destination Biafra* was an earlier part of the Biafran-
genre novel. Nonetheless, one can say that increasingly African
women write about politics, including national politics.[2]

In this book, I have refused to accept the separation of public and
private as spheres and have read actions understood as public or
private as in fact interrelated in practice. By this means, I have made
visible how African women writers took up a political discourse on
their own terms, initially rejecting nationalist symbology (such as
woman as national mother) and telling stories that might be read in
nationalist terms, but only through a different practice of reading. In
particular, I have claimed that greater attentiveness to the workings of
the literary texts themselves makes visible a more complex set of
relations to public and nationalist politics than had previously been
imagined in literary histories of the African novel. Rather than judg-
ing these works to be politically unimportant, one might better perceive public politics by traversing the domestic sphere of the family
and intimate relations. Finally, and now most important, as the gains
of nationalism came into sharper focus and female authors increasingly felt themselves to be on surer ground, they more openly and
explicitly represented macro-political themes.

Selected Chronology
of African Novels

1969   Thérèse Kuoh-Moukoury, *Rencontres essentielles*
       (out of print until 2002)

1970   Flora Nwapa, *Idu*

1973   Ousmane Sembene, *Xala*
       (trans. Clive Wake, 1976)

1975   Nafissatou Diallo, *De Tilène au plateau*

1976   Aminata Sow Fall, *La Grève des bàttu, ou, Les déchets humains*
       (trans. Dorothy Blair as *The Beggars' Strike, or, The Dregs of Society*,
       1981)

1976   Mariama Bâ, *Une si longue lettre*
       (trans. Modupe Bode-Thomas as *So Long a Letter*, 1981)

1977   Ama Ata Aidoo, *Our Sister Killioy*

1977   Buchi Emecheta, *The Slave Girl*

1979   Buchi Emecheta, *The Joys of Motherhood*

1979   Rachid Boujedra, *Les 1001 années de la nostalgie 1988*

1980   Assia Djebar, *Femmes d'Alger dans leur appartement*

1980   Grace Ogot, *The Graduate*

1981   Lauretta Ngcobo, *Cross of Gold*

1981   Wole Soyinka, *Aké: The Years of Childhood*

1985   Assia Djebar, *L'amour, la fantasia*

1986   Nuruddin Farah, *Maps*

1986   Aminata Sow Fall, *L'Ex-père de la nation*

1987   Chinua Achebe, *Anthills of the Savannah*

1987   Calixthe Beyala, *C'est le soleil qui m'a brulée*
       (trans. Marjolijn De Jaeger as *The Sun Hath Looked upon Me*, 1996)

1987   Assia Djebar, *Ombre sultane*
       (trans. Dorothy Blair as *Sister to Scheherazade*, 1993)

1987   Bessie Head, *A Question of Power*

1987   Ngugi wa Thiong'o, *Devil on the Cross*

1988   Tsitsi Dangarembga, *Nervous Conditions*

1988   Chenjerai Hove, *Bones*

1989   Shimmer Chinodya, *Harvest of Thorns*

1991   Assia Djebar, *Loin de Medine*

1991   Ngugi wa Thiong'o, *Petals of Blood*

1992   Obinkaram T. Echewa, *I Saw the Sky Catch Fire*

1993   Yvonne Vera, *Nehanda*

1994   Marlene van Niekerk, *Triompf*
        (trans. Leon de Kock, 1999)

2001   Zoë Wicomb, *David's Story*

2003   Chimananda Adichie, *Purple Hibiscus*

2006   Chimananda Adichie, *Half of a Yellow Sun*

Notes

Introduction

1. Simon Gikandi (2002, 389) says that, despite the emergence of a modern literary tradition of novels in Amharic, Hausa, Swahili, Xhosa, and Zulu, the most influential form of long fiction on the continent, the one that has made Africa central to the study of modern literature, is novels written in the major European languages. Wendy Griswold (2000, 31) puts it more baldly in her sociology of the anglophone Nigerian novel. "While there exists a tradition of poetry and plays in Hausa and Yoruba, full novels in these languages—unlike poetry or plays—are far and few between. . . . Even rarer is a novel in Igbo or in any of the hundreds of minority languages because few Africans can read these languages, most of which lack a standard orthography."

2. Lydie Moudileno offers a useful summary of the conditions that gave rise to Négritude in her dictionary entry, "West African Literature in French," in Gikandi 2002, 567–71. The classic scholarship is Kesteloot 2001; see also Arnold 1981. Lila Azam Zanganeh has quoted Boniface Mongo-Mboussa, a critic from the Congo Republic and the author of *Le désir de l'Afrique,* as calling Négritude the first truly modern African literature: "Before Negritude African literature was a colonial literature that pretended it was African" (Lila Azam Zanganeh, "Out of Africa," *New York Times,* June 12, 2005, 39). My point is not to illustrate the received wisdom that Négritude marks the beginning of authentic, autochthonous, anticolonial African voices in poetic writing. Né-

gritude's importance lies in the excitement it generated in France and among Africans. That is why it deserves its reputation as the first movement of collective response.

3. The national division lived through race produced, especially in South Africa, what David Attwell has called "the unfortunate division between white writers who respond to international currents in modernism and post-modernism, and black writers whose attention has been directed at the more dire project of opposing apartheid, and whose representational range has accordingly, though with some exceptions, been restricted to documentary realism": see David Attwell, "Apartheid and Post-apartheid," in Gikandi 2002, 27. See also Attwell 2005; Chapman 1996; Smit, Van Wyk, and Wade 1996.

4. The show premiered in Düsseldorf and exhibited in London, Paris, and Tokyo between 2004 and 2006. Unfortunately—and this is indeed meaning-ful—it was not scheduled for any showings on the African continent.

5. Feminist critics who have practiced this celebratory mode include Irene d'Almeida (1994), Elleke Boehmer (1990, 1991, and even 2005), Odile Cazenave (1996, 2000), Carole Boyce Davies (1986a), Françoise Lionnet (1989), Juliana Nfah-Abbenyi (1997), Chikwenye Ogunyemi (1996), and Florence Stratton (1994). I do not disparage this scholarship. Not only have I also produced such work, but I could not have written this book without that earlier, often path-breaking body of scholarship. By historicizing this earlier thought and placing it in a larger context, I hope to explore the consequences of not subjecting women's writing to rigorous cross-class and public political scrutiny—as well as to suggest what such a scrutiny might mean.

6. Alain Ricard (2004, 183) substantiates and elaborates: "*Ethiopia Un-bound* (1911) is considered the first fictional text in English by an African writer: J. E. Caseley-Hayford (1866–1930), a Gold Coast lawyer and politician. The anonymous author of *Marita: or the Folly of Love*, published in 1885–88, has yet to be identified, while Liberian writer Joseph J. Walters's *Guyana Pau*, published in Lincoln [Nebraska] in 1891, was discovered only recently."

7. Ricard (2004, 185) is both more elaborate and succinct here: "The beginnings of fictional literature in French are situated between the two world wars. No criticism is leveled at the colonial power; rather, it is naively exalted, as in the novel, *Force-Bonté* (1926) by Bakary Diallo (1892–1979). Indigenous culture is depicted and defended in *L'esclave* (1929) by Félix Couchoro (1900–1968) or placed under the beneficent tutelage of France as in *Karim* (1935) by Ousmane Socé Diop (1922–73) or in *Doguicimi* (1938) by Paul Hazoumé (1890–1980)." For a more complete treatment of Hazoumé, see the chapter on him in Coundouriotis 1999.

8. For more on reception, see Irele 1977. Note also that it is in direct response to the impact of Négritude writing on anglophone African writers

that Soyinka famously uttered his riposte that a tiger does not need to pronounce its tigritude.

9. Irele's essay is an insightful early work, but its breadth does not permit detailed close reading. Ato Quayson's study of Nigerian literature (Quayson 1997) is partly responsible for the popularity of this reading, but the pioneering work of reading Fagunwa as forebear to Tutuola and Soyinka was done by Irele in "Tradition and the Yoruba Writer" (1975), reprinted in Irele 1981.

10. Bernth Lindfors suggests that the rural setting of *Things Fall Apart* allows authors only a few years behind Achebe to locate their novels in the country rather than the city: Innes and Lindfors 1978, introduction.

11. Note that in the first Equiano lecture given at the University of Ibadan in July 1977, Achebe focused precisely on Tutuola. The talk is published in Achebe 1988. I thank Ben Lindfors for calling this to my attention.

12. My "Rewriting History, Motherhood, and Rebellion" (Andrade 1990) helped establish the claims that Efuru was a proto-feminist character and that Nwapa was a "maternal" figure to Buchi Emecheta. The essay forms part of that earlier, historical recovery mode of feminist criticism. Nwapa's importance as a writer has since been thoroughly established. Indeed, the African Literature Association is now home to a Flora Nwapa Society (the only single-author group I know of under the aegis of that organization), whose driving force, Marie Umeh, brings female African intellectuals to the United States to speak to scholars about topics that have to do with gender and Africa.

13. Latin Americanists differ as to which novels actually constitute the beginnings of the Boom, although it is agreed that the preface to *El reino de este mundo* (Carpentier 1949), a novel about the Haitian Revolution by the Cuban writer, Alejo Carpentier, constitutes the first nonfiction formulation of what would become "*el real maravilloso.*" Amos Tutuola's *The Palm-Wine Drinkard* (1952) was published three years later, well before Carpentier's preface was translated into English, for it took forty years for that essay to be published in English. Curiously, Tutuola's remarkable style of writing— neither pidgin nor standard English—was celebrated by Dylan Thomas, V. S. Pritchett, and other famous European writers but rejected by many anglophone Africans who were uncomfortable with what the author himself called its "broken English."

Although magical realism has adherents among those with African ancestry, it is not particularly "African" in mode. However, one might wish to extend the claim of race value further by exploring the relation between the Cuban novel about the Haitian Revolution and the fact that the Haitians who revolted and established the first independent state of former slaves were made up primarily of Africans who had not been in the New World for long.

14. I do not claim that Tutuola was unimportant when he began to publish, only that in the early years of what we now consider to be the

African literary canon, he lagged behind other, less remarkable writers. Nor do I claim that realism itself is a regressive or backward form (in fact, far from it), although I do assert that it is currently out of fashion. For an important statement that both names and advocates the historical swing away from reading for realism to reading for antirealism, see Harrow 1994.

15. Important milestones in this respect were the publication of Davies and Graves 1994 and of the special issue on women of *Research in African Literatures* in 1988 edited by Rhonda Cobham and Chikwenye Ogunyemi.

16. Cheryl Toman claims in her introduction to Thérèse Kuoh-Moukory's *Rencontres essentielles* (2002 [1969], x) that it is a critically important work of women's authorship in an African novelistic tradition. "First published in 1969 but written about a decade earlier, *Rencontres essentielles* is the first novel by a woman of sub-Saharan francophone Africa" (x). The novel was republished by L'Harmattan in 1995 and by the Modern Language Association (MLA) in French and in English translation in 2002. Toman links the novel with a half-dozen later Camerounian novels by women and names common themes, but she does little to substantiate her assertion that Kuoh-Moukoury is the reason these authors share literary concerns. Toman offers neither a history of reception (who bought and read); nor does she engage in close reading of more than a phrase per novel. I am convinced by her claim that the novel was written much earlier, and it may well be that Kuoh-Moukoury is a literary forebear to other writers, but there is no evidence offered to prove the claim of influence. Like other anglophone and francophone works of literature, this novel is recounted in a feminine narrative voice precariously balanced between the modernity that secondary education brings and romantic love signifies, on the one hand, and on the other, the tradition that makes her a failure unless she bears a child

17. Bâ's remarks were part of an interview with Jan Kees van dem Werk and accompanied the Dutch translation of her first and most famous novel, *Une si longue lettre*. The interview was conducted months before Bâ's death in 1981, and this often cited extract of it is usually attributed to Schipper's article, a highly mediated text that presumably was translated from French into Dutch and then into English. I have been unable to find a French version of the interview.

18. Edward Said (1994) makes a very similar point.

19. All over the continent, women of differing ethnic, religious, and cultural groups either worked as traders or supplemented their farming income with money from trading. The Church of Scotland, which helped promote the notion that men ought to be uplifted into education, albeit at the expense of women, was most influential in eastern and southern Africa.

20. Anne McClintock (1995) and others have written very well about this relation, but Stratton (1994) offers the most literary-specific readings of African fiction.

21. The term "sex-gender system" comes from Gayle Rubin, whose title to the classic "The Traffic in Women" (1975) is taken directly from the Marxist feminist writing of Rosa Luxemburg.

22. "It is exactly when we do not conflate the linguistic with the social, representation with what it purports to represent; when, that is, we insist on a fundamental conceptual demarcation of these two realms, that we are most incisively placed to appreciate the challenge of the real world" (George 2003, 189).

23. I thank David Attwell and Tejumola Olaniyan for helping me see the Boy Scout.

24. I thank Terri Smith for pointing the woman out to me.

25. See especially Lukács (1964, 1971, 1974, 1977).

26. For more here, see Gikandi 1991.

27. Todorov and Asad quoted in Clifford 1986, 99.

28. I thank Madhu Dubey for this formulation. For more on Jameson and realism, see Jameson 1985. See also his concluding remarks in Bloch, Lukács, Brecht, Benjamin, and Adorno (1977, 196–213).

29. Note that in the last footnote in "Third World Literature in the Era of Multinational Capitalism" (1986), Jameson specifically links the project of cognitive mapping, which he then developed more fully in his book on postmodernism, to the national allegory in the Third World. Had he not been vigorously criticized by those who objected to his inadequate fellow-traveling, I believe he might have gone on to develop this idea more fully.

30. Significantly, Jameson deploys and metaphorizes Marx's examples of the most important non-capitalist—that is, non-Western economic systems. The tribal groups of Africa and other "primitive" models are visible in Sembène; the imperial bureaucracy of Asia is visible through Lu Xun.

31. Indeed, Ahmad acknowledges that nationalism forms part of the cultural consciousness, but his pointed critique permits no more than a rhetorical nod in this direction. For literary scholarship on colonial and postcolonial nationalism that gives affirmative attention to the national allegory, see Tim Brennan (1989), Simon Gikandi (1991), Neil Larsen (1995), Neil Lazarus (1990), and Doris Sommer (1991).

32. Not until Yvonne Vera's *Nehanda* (1993) do we have in the African context so explicit an example of the relation between woman, anticolonialism, and women's power in a text produced by a *woman*. One might claim that Miriam Tlali's *Muriel at Metropolitan* (1975) functions in a similar way, and it certainly renders the daily life of a working-class black woman in apartheid Johannesburg. However, *Muriel* does not easily represent itself as part of a national(ist) conversation in the same authoritative way as does *Nehanda*.

33. See Jameson 1979, which Jameson published later but that was clearly conceived as part of the same project as *The Political Unconscious*.

34. Irele suggests that decolonization is a result of nationalism, an effect arising from a reluctant acceptance by the colonizer of the claims of nationalism.

35. I thank Irene d'Almeida for bringing this novel to my attention.

36. Aidoo's first play, *The Dilemma of a Ghost*, first performed in 1964 when she was only twenty-two, tells the story of the struggle of an African American woman who marries a Ghanaian man and finds that moving to Africa is not, after all, a "homecoming." Aidoo couples cultural conflict with marital conflict.

37. *Nervous Conditions* has gone through three editions since its initial publication with Seal and is helping to launch a relatively new press, Ayebia-Clarke, which has also brought out Dangarembga's second novel, *The Book of Not* (2006). Heather Zwicker and I are the first two critics to have attributed specifically nationalist sensibilities to the first novel.

38. It is precisely this sort of character fullness that Jameson speaks to when he asserts, in the interests of a strongly represented politics, that the Third World novel "does not offer the satisfactions" of the First. Jameson neglects to note (of novels written by men and by women) that later novels do in fact become more psychologically complex.

39. See my essay, "Adichie's Genealogies: National and Feminine Novels" in *Research in African Literatures* (May 2011) for an elaboration of this argument about literary historical thinking.

40. This argument is made boldly because it is one of the first in its class. I do not believe that one can discern the sex or gender of a writer by the way she or he represents female characters or the collective of the family rather than that of the nation. Nor do I wish to be normative (à la Stratton) in claiming that men ought to write in this way or women in that. Rather, I hope to lay out a rough historical reading of the ways by which female writers negotiated the complexities of character individuation (formerly called subject construction but usually in a context reserved for psychological analysis) and their imagined relation to collectivities, whether those collectivities are nations or families.

41. One of the most cited novels in this regard is Camara Laye's Bildungs-roman *L'enfant noir* 1953. The fact that Laye's authorship of both this novel and *Le regard du roi* (1954) has been powerfully challenged does not diminish the force of my argument that *L'enfant noir* serves as a nationalist novel that was needed at the time and for that purpose, so whether it was Laye or someone else who wrote it is largely irrelevant. Of course, for literary scholarship as such, whether Laye did or did not write his novels is extremely important. For the most detailed discussion of the controversy, see King (2002), who has made these allegations most strongly. Irele 2006 is a direct and thoughtful response to King on behalf of Laye.

42. Spivak's reading practices have taught me for years. As she makes

clear in many of her writings, the national allegory as such is not of interest to her. However, she is quick to point to its invocation, as in her translation of Mahasweta Devi's caustic tale "The Breast Giver."

43. The novels I study and the history I chart draw a picture of African women's exclusion from a novelistic tradition in part because women entered the writing and publishing scene later and in smaller numbers than men, and in part because when they did arrive, their work looked so different from the men's that it was written off as apolitical. I hope to change this interpretive tradition by illustrating that one convention of reading on behalf of decolonizing nationalism assumes that the reading position is a masculine one. So strongly naturalized is this position that for years we have read women's novels about the domestic world of family life as treating not merely the micro-political but the insignificant. Women's focus on the realm of intimacy has been read as a narrow vision, as the failure of women to have a national imagination

44. Elechi Amadi, Nkem Nwankwo, Uzodinma, John Munyoye, and Clement Agunwa, otherwise known as the Achebe School.

45. One exception is Mba 1988, an excellent work of historical scholarship.

46. Rhonda Cobham suggests that *Things Fall Apart* be read as participating in a direct, historical response to the anthropologists who went to Igboland, and particularly to the town of Aba, after the uprising. I have extended her work and elaborated it particularly by asking about the literary history this provides for feminists working on African materials: see Cobham, "Making Men and History: Achebe and the Politics of Revisionism in *Things Fall Apart*."

1 The Joys of Daughterhood

1. The degree of timidity is still more sharply visible since the publication of *Purple Hibiscus* (2003) and *Half of a Yellow Sun* (2006) by Chimananda Adichie, both of which involve strong female characterization and increasingly present the characters in each novel in relation to Nigerian national situations.

2. He said, "What we properly understand by Africa is the Unhistorical, Undeveloped Spirit, still involved in the conditions of mere nature, and which had to be presented here only as on the threshold of the World's History."

3. See also Van Allen 1972, as well as a somewhat different feminist interpretation in Ifeka-Moller 1985. For British records of the events, see Leith-Ross 1965 (1939). And for a recent feminist, anticolonial, and explicitly native reading of women's organizations and access to power in Igbo societies, see Amadiume 1997.

4. One of the most interesting literary responses to the Women's War is *I Saw the Sky Catch Fire* (Echewa 1992), a novel written by a man and explicitly feminist in its perspective.

5. Carole Boyce Davies (1986b) has put forth an important reading suggesting that there are traces of a larger feminine narrative in the story of Chielo and Ezinma. I would add that the contradiction this narrative interpretation suggests (i.e., the development of women's subjectivity that is not dependent on men) must be relegated to the margins of the text for the novel to produce the illusion of coherence. Other feminist readings include Cobham 1991; Nnaemeka 1997.

6. Okonkwo's third wife, Ojiugo, is named primarily so that a discrete subject identity can be attributed to the woman he beats during the sacred Week of Peace, thereby causing him to be censured. Okonkwo's second wife, Ekwefi, who leaves her first husband for him, is distinctly characterized: they have a love romance (Cobham 1991). Okonkwo's favorite daughter, Ezinma, is so smart and spirited—in many ways so much like him—that he often wishes that she were a boy.

7. I am influenced partly in my thinking by a critique by Abiola Irele (2000) of the earlier reading, although I am sure I have not modified as much of my original argument as he would like.

8. Nwabara (1978, 201) offers some details: "Dr C. K. Meek was temporarily transferred from the anthropological department in the northern provinces to help with the study. Margaret Green and Sylvia Leith-Ross were also members of the study group, while Ida Ward concentrated on the Ibo language. These studies were published as books. In addition administrative officers were busy gathering information about the people (known as intelligence reports) which, by the end of 1934, had amounted to about two hundred."

9. For different perspectives on contradiction in the novel, see Maugham-Brown 1991, ten Kortenaar 1993, and Erritouni 2006; for those with specific attention to gender politics, see Alden 1991 and Boehmer 1990.

10. Amadiume recounts the story this way: "When news reached the women, they demonstrated their anger by bypassing the local court, controlled by equally fanatical Christians, and marching half-naked to the provincial headquarters, Onitsha, to besiege the resident's office. He pleaded for calm and patience and asked the women to go home, saying that he would look into the case. The women considered this a feeble response, so they returned to Nnobi, went straight to the man's house and razed it to the ground. This was the indigenous Igbo female custom of dealing with offending men. . . . Two weeks after the incident, the man is said to have died" (1987, 122).

11. This statement was less true in 1996 than when the first version of this chapter was published (see Andrade 1990). See also the chapters on Nwapa

in Ogunyemi 1996, Stratton 1994, and Wilentz 1992. Nevertheless, compared with the attention given to Mariama Bâ, Bessie Head, Ama Ata Aidoo, and Emecheta, Nwapa is usually addressed only in broad comparative studies of African women's literature.

12. See the introductory chapter in Brown 1981. Even Emmanuel Obie-china argues that "Jagua's personality shines through the vicissitudes and corruption of the city" (1975, 104).

13. That Brown (1981, 7) reads Jagua's "redemption" at the end of the narrative as corresponding to her pregnancy and in her new interest in "rural living" only supports my point here.

14. Uzoma Esonwanne, personal correspondence, 1995.

15. I have corrected two minor errors, one in recounting this story, from my earlier article after reading Florence Stratton's criticism, for which I thank her. Stratton bases much of the premise of *Contemporary African Literature and the Politics of Gender* (1994), including her readings of *Efuru* and *The Joys of Motherhood*, on the notion of an African woman's intertextual tradition—a premise introduced four years earlier in my article.

16. He illustrates, citing from the novel: "For example, a pregnant woman should 'not go out alone at night. If she must go out, then somebody must go with her and she must carry a small knife. When she is sitting down, nobody must cross her leg.' . . . If at birth the child does not cry at once, you 'took hold of its two legs, lifted it in the air and shook it until it cried.' . . . The mother should put her legs together or else she will not be able to walk properly in the future. Breastfeeding should go on for a year or more" (Taiwo 1984, 54).

17. In addition to *Efuru*, Nwapa had published *Idu* (1970); and Buchi Emecheta had already published *The Slave Girl* (1977), which contains specific references to the Igbo Women's War. The year 1979 is also the one in which Mariama Bâ published her Noma Award–winning *Une si longue lettre*.

18. Amadiume relates how separate gender space in the village could engender autonomy for women and hinder marital rape: "Sex was not forced upon a woman; she was constantly surrounded by children and other people. Men did not enter the women's quarters freely or casually. Avenues were open for 'politicking.' . . . Indigenous architecture and male/female polygyny made these choices possible" (1987, 114).

19. Amadiume (1987, 114) points out that it was historically acceptable for women to refuse to give their husbands food if they "did not contribute meat or yam for the meal." Van Allen explains the manner in which cooking strikes were traditionally used by women: "All the women refused to cook for their husbands until the request was carried out. For this boycott to be effective, *all* women had to cooperate so that men could not go and eat with their brothers" (1972, 170).

20. So understated is the text's treatment of prostitution that some critics

refuse to acknowledge it. Eustace Palmer denies that Adaku becomes a prostitute, without offering any textual evidence to the contrary. Palmer's attempt to read sympathetically feminist texts coupled with a certain morality makes his approach similar to that of Ernest Emenyonu (1970); see Palmer 1983.

21. Stratton (1994, 92) mistakenly attributes Emecheta's ideological perspective—that *Efuru* "elides indigenous patriarchy and the colonial oppression of Igbo women"—to me personally and claims that I use this as evidence that Nwapa privileges tradition over modernity. Nwapa *does* privilege tradition, not via an elision of patriarchy, but by celebrating Uhamiri, a signifier of women's traditional power. (Puzzlingly, Stratton identifies Uhamiri with modernity.) Stratton also claims that I construct Igbo culture as patriarchal and that the discourse of tradition is therefore patriarchal discourse. It is—in part. That it has patriarchal elements does not mean that Igbo culture does not also have proto-feminist ones; the assumption that tradition equates with patriarchy and excludes feminism is inaccurate.

2 The Loved and the Left

1. See Zell 1980. The article quotes favorable reviews by Abiola Irele in *West Africa* and Dorothy Blair in the *Guardian*.

2. Miller (1990, 285) lists information on the printing and sale of books from which one might gauge patterns of novelistic consumption and, thereby, canon formation: "Whereas an average printing of a novel for [Nouvelle Éditions Africaines, an organization dedicated to the promotion of African literature published in Africa] runs to three thousand copies, Heinemann estimates that there are perhaps about twenty thousand copies of *So Long a Letter* in print." Quoting one of Bernth Lindfors's studies on the teaching of African literature on the continent, Miller notes that, while there are only six francophones out of a total of about thirty-five authors, Bâ is the lone francophone woman. She is also one of only three women in the group as a whole.

A recent search of the databases of the Modern Language Association revealed about one hundred fifty entries on this novel published thirty years ago; the entries comprise dissertations, articles in journals, and essays in edited collections, all of which treat the novel in substantial fashion. Miller finds these surveys questionable. Whatever their exact level of accuracy, it seems fair to claim, as does Nicki Hitchcott (2000), that Bâ is the most commonly taught female francophone novelist from Africa and, now that there are many more younger writers, the earliest who is commonly taught. Writing out of a theoretically informed North American context that seeks to introduce multiculturalism into an English-language context, John Champagne

(1996, 26) says of the novel that "its accessibility and brevity make it ideal for an introductory class in postcolonial literature—particularly one that attempts to achieve some kind of 'balance' between male and female writers."

3. See the chapters on Bâ in Julien 2007; Hitchcott 2000; Nfah-Abbenyi 1997; and Stringer 1996; as well as in Hitchcott 1996.

4. For more on Bâ, Sow Fall, and especially Diallo, see Stringer 1996. For a more extensive discussion of francophone writing by female authors, see Hitchcott 2000 (chaps. 2–4) and Mortimer 2007.

5. As Miller takes some pains to illustrate, *La parole aux negresses* (Thiam 1978), a collection of oral interviews, is thoroughly women-centered and feminist. However, it is not a work of fiction. Miller claims Bâ as foremother, and while I do not emphasize that reading, I believe she might be so read because she advances character development in the francophone tradition.

6. According to some early commentators, Ramatoulaye is so traditional a Muslim woman that she has essentially no choice other than to remain married, a state that she is presumed to prefer over the ignominy of divorce. For example, Pierette Herzenberger-Fofana (1987, 193) states: "La ferveur religieuse de Ramatoulaye ... est le ferment de son action et ciment sa force de caractère. Sa foi religieuse l'aide à subir le calvaire d'épouse délaissée au profit d'une plus jeune rivale. C'est dans la priére qu'elle puise son courage." Dorothy Blair (1984, 138) says that Ramatoulaye "retains a strong sense of the traditional role of Muslim women and the old moral values," and Cyril Mokwenyé (1983, 92) praises her "stoicism" and "psychological revolt" over Aissatou's "impetuousness." In one of the few essays on the subject that departs from a simple binarism, Uzo Esonwanne (1997) reads tradition and modernity as discursive terms.

7. In her discussion of the novel, *Destiny*, Stephanie Newell implies that author Hauwa Ali gives voice to some of the same concerns about female right to choose and feminine independence of employment as Bâ (2006, 140–46).

8. Mariama Bâ was not Wolof but Fulbe / Peul. As a Dakaroise, however, she partook of a Wolofized Dakar culture and so might be included in the national-ethnic rubric. I am indebted to Eileen Julien for clarification about Bâ as well as insight into Dakar's ethnic culture. For a more extended discussion of the Wolofization of residents of Dakar, see the work of Fiona McLaughlin (2001).

9. David Murphy (2000, 98–99) claims that in Senegal *Xala* was an immensely popular film, finishing second in the ratings for 1975 only behind a kung-fu film starring Bruce Lee.

10. In this manner, it gives proof of Mariama Bâ's French and francophone education, as well as to the sentimental tradition in French belles-lettres.

11. There is one moment in which Ramatoulaye does speak directly to

national politics. It comes when she is in the process of being wooed by Daouda Dieng. In refusing Dieng, she dwells more on the relatively few women in Parliament, giving little expression to how she does not really love him; one might claim that this is yet another example of the displacement of public and private realms, erotics and politics, each standing in for the other. Thanks to Abiola Irele for calling my attention to this.

12. Mildred Mortimer offers some background information about Germaine Le Goff, who taught Bâ and is the prototype for Ramatoulaye's teacher: "A dynamic and ambitious educator in her time, Le Goff was quick to take advantage of the fact that her pedagogical objectives coincided with the political objectives of the French colonial administration who considered the education of women to be crucial to its success. . . . [T]he Ecole Normale d'institutrices opened in Rufisque, Senegal, in 1938 with Germaine Le Goff as headmistress. . . . Mariama Bâ would profit from this educational opportunity; admitted to the school in 1943, she graduated in 1947" (86).

13. Anderson (1990, 124) continues: "The interchangeability of French West African boys on the benches of William Ponty was not paralleled by their later bureaucratic substitutability in the French West African colonial administration. Hence, the school's Old Boys went home to become, eventually, Guinean or Malian nationalist leaders, while retaining a 'West African' camaraderie and solidarity intimacy lost to succeeding generations." Ramatoulaye nostalgically looks back at this moment for what, from her perspective, is a form of pan-Africanism.

14. The following quote from Kumari Jayawardena (1985, 12–13) is rooted in the specifics of Asia and the Mediterranean "Middle East," but for this purpose it also translates easily to the new African context that Ramatoulaye eagerly entered: "The new consciousness demanded an 'enlightened' woman. The new bourgeois man, himself a product of Western education or missionary influence, needed as his partner a 'new woman,' educated in the relevant foreign language, dressed in the new styles and attuned to Western ways—a woman who was 'presentable' in colonial society yet whose role was primarily in the home. These women had to show that they were the negation of everything that was considered 'backward' in the old society: that they were no longer secluded, veiled and illiterate, with bound feet and minds, threatened with death on the husband's funeral pyre. The concept and terminology of the 'new woman,' so fashionable in Europe in the 19th century, was eagerly adopted by both men and women of the educated class."

15. While I disagree with the thrust of Esonwanne's argument, I do fundamentally uphold his point: Ramatoulaye's feminism is bourgeois above all, and, as I will show, its price is a patent refusal to name the class critique Sembène puts forth. However, there is nothing wrong with wishing for an excellent education, and when your husband abandons you and your many children, it is far better to have money than not to have it.

16. After quoting the same passage in a more recent reading, Newell (2006) seems unable to put forth an interpretation. Though she references the book in which Esonwanne's argument is published, Newell does not mention Esonwanne's essay which is pointedly clear about its argument. Instead she speculates about the "pro-colonial framework" in which *Une si longue lettre* has positioned itself, then wonders whether the passage might be "an ambivalent statement containing both a parody of colonial attitudes and a promotion of the colonial education system?" (146). She claims that Bâ and other female authors require "a combination of close reading with other interpretational tools," a point with which it would be difficult to disagree, but seems unable to position herself in relation to a reading of the novel.

17. The two secondary definitions of *dépouillement* in the Petit Robert are (1) [a] action de priver qqn de ses biens; état d'une personne dépouillée, privée de tout; [b] fait d'être débarasser de superflu des omements; (2) Examen minutieux (de documents). However, *dépouiller* has as its primary meaning "enlever la peau de (un animal); ... Dégamir qqn de ce qui couvre."

18. The famous verse from the chapter on women in the Qur'an is "Marry of the women who seem good to you, two, three or four, and if ye fear that ye cannot do justice [to so many] then one [only]" (quoted in Mernissi 1987, 46).

19. Newell claims that Onitsha market literatures and their use of plots about a woman's wish or right to choose her marriage partner traveled north to Muslim areas and so influenced the plots of anglophone Hausa narratives. *Destiny* by Hauwa Ali (1988) comes in for particular attention; the protagonist does not wish to marry the older, wealthy man her parents want for her: "Romantic love is inseparable from women's formal education in Ali's novel, and it is disconnected from the Islamic faith which conditions the attitudes of the other characters in the heroine's community. . . . The teacher training college where the heroine completes her education is presented as a non-Islamic space in which her romantic fantasies and desires can be freely enacted and indulged. It is here that the figure of her ideal husband, Farouk, materializes like a fairy-tale prince, remaining at the forefront of her mind for the duration of the novel" (Newell 2006, 142). Based only on the quotation, it would appear that there are similarities between this plot structure and that of *Une si longue lettre*. While Ali might well have been influenced by Onitsha writing, she seems just as likely to have been influenced by Bâ's famous and more conventionally literary novel. A close reading of Ali against Bâ might well illustrate the sort of influence I am suggesting.

20. "Aujourd'hui elle s'exprime ostensiblement en billets de banque et personne ne veut donner moins que l'autre. Troublante exteriorization du sentiment intérieur inévaluable, évalué en francs! Et je pense encore: combine de morts auraient pu survivre si, avant de'organiser ses funérailles en festin, le parent ou l'ami avait acheté o'ordonnance salvatrice ou payé l'hospitalisation" (1979, 14).

Today it is made conspiciously in banknotes, and no one wants to give less than the other. A disturbing display of inner feeling that cannot be evaluated now measured in francs! And again I think how many of the dead would have survived if, before organizing these festive funeral ceremonies, the relative or friend had bought the life-saving prescription or paid for hospitalization (Bâ 1981, 6).

21. This may be why only ("traditional") Ramatoulaye retains her voice in the novel while ("modem") Aissatou is silent: Bâ cannot allow Ramatoulaye to seem anything but traditional while she advances a modem critique based on romantic love and women's education. This also suggests one reason for Aissatou's elision from the novel, except as a presence constructed by Ramatoulaye. Her divorce, a powerful marker of the dangers of modernity, means departure not only from Senegal but also from the narrative.

22. For my purposes in this chapter, there is no difference between the film and the novella, and I will refer to both as parts of the same text. For a thorough discussion of the differences between the two, as well as of the different audiences intended and possible, see Gugler and Diop 1998; see also Harrow 1980.

23. My reading of *Xala* (film and novella) is somewhat schematic, as I am primarily interested in "thickening a description" of *Lettre*. There are, however, many fine, more complex readings of the film, in particular Mulvey 1991.

24. In this respect, Sow Fall's novella advances Sembène's agenda. Her beggars not only act, they also think, they "organize," and they go on strike.

25. In the novel, she cries out "no, no" early on, when it is discovered that El Hadji has the "xala," but that is the extent of her articulation and agency.

26. "As they marched through the streets of Myanmar's cities last week leading the biggest antigovernment protests in two decades, some barefoot monks held their begging bowls before them. But instead of asking for their daily donations of food, they held the bowls upside down, the black lacquer surfaces reflecting the light. It was a shocking image in the devoutly Buddhist nation. The monks were refusing to receive alms from the military rulers and their families—effectively excommunicating them from the religion that is at the core of Burmese culture. . . . The country—the former Burma—has roughly as many monks as soldiers. The military rules by force, but the monks retain ultimate moral authority. The lowliest soldier depends on them for spiritual approval, and even the highest generals have felt a need to honor the clerical establishment. They claim to rule in its name. Begging is a ritual that expresses a profound bond between the ordinary Buddhist and the monk. 'The people are feeding the monks and the monks are helping the people make merit,' said Josef Silverstein, an expert on Myanmar at Rutgers University. 'When you refuse to accept, you have broken the bond that has tied them for centuries together.' Instead, the monks drew on a

different and more fundamental bond with Myanmar's population, leading huge demonstrations after the government tried to repress protests that began a month ago over a rise in fuel prices" (Seth Mydans, "What Makes a Monk Mad," *New York Times*, September 30, 2007).

27. To be sure, one has to accept the notion that the rich benefit from the poor, a notion that is both perfectly Marxist and, within a religious context, harmonious with Islam. The poor have the ability to pray, to bless, to make visible the luxuries of the rich. By illustrating the dependence of the rich on the poor, as well as the way in which the poor are vulnerable to extraction, *Grève* illustrates one of the substrates of the economy, the equivalent of "surplus value" that keeps the rich in power. This, then, is the reason for the strike.

3 Bildung in Formation and Deformation

1. I thank Patricia Alden for this formulation (see Alden 1988). My thinking throughout this chapter has been deeply stimulated by Moretti 1987. For an argument about the interrelation between the genre and the ideological implications of human rights legal discourse, especially in the Global South, see Joseph Slaughter (2007).

2. Germany, we know, was a nation without a state until 1871.

3. Alden and Tremaine (1999, 15) claim of *Maps* that it extends into the future of the time of writing. I believe I have found the place in the novel that grounds this claim, although I do not agree with their reading.

4. Some have suggested that the structure of doubled protagonists reflects a feminist sensibility. Rita Felski (1989) claims that the women's Bildungsroman often involves more than one protagonist, as one might claim, does *Nervous Conditions*. My knowledge of African Bildungsromane written by men (e.g., Laye's *L'enfant noir* [1953], Cheik Hamidou Kane's *L'aventure ambiguë* [1962], Wole Soyinka's *Aké*, [1981]) does not lead me to believe that doubling is a particularly African response.

5. Recent interpretive readings of the novel by distinguished Africanist critics, even those strongly sympathetic to the condition of African women, illustrate that my general point about the novel remains correct. Eustace Palmer (2008, 192), for example, admires the novel greatly, calling Nyasha "a triumph of characterization," with which I am wholly in agreement. He does not see a relation between the private politics of the family, including the overbearing father, and the complications of Nyasha's psychic development.

6. Moretti does have a fourth important aspect of Bildungsroman characterization: a classic Bildungsroman must have marriage as its act of closure. From the perspective of both of the novels I examine here—indeed, from that of *L'enfant noir*, *L'aventure ambiguë*, or *Aké*—this point is not germane.

7. I thank Joey Slaughter for referring me to this essay.

8. The second essay is less boldly sketched, although it is also recent enough to show signs of some defensive response.

9. "Subjectivity," he continues, "indeed, is a mythic concept if there ever was one; but that emergence of a certain kind of storytelling documents the existence of the kind of social life in which those stories can be found—that, as a tautology, is surely an irrefutable position" (Jameson 1996, 173).

10. A recent story in the *New York Times* called the Ogaden "a spindle-legged corner of Ethiopia that urbane officials in Addis Ababa, the capital, would rather outsiders never see" (Jeffrey Gettleman, "In Ethiopia, Fear and Cries of Army Brutality," *New York Times*, June 18, 2007, 1). The article pays particular attention to the practice of Ethiopian soldiers' raping women in the Ogaden region, which Ethiopia now controls.

11. In its representation of an individual standing for the nation, and especially in its overturning of that simple form of allegory, *Maps* greatly resembles *Xala*, although each narrative is recounted in a very different mode: modernist versus realist, for example.

12. I am not claiming that Farah himself believes that only men are national citizens, but certainly his characterization of Askar suggests such a world.

13. Gopal Balakrishnan (1996, 204) points out that an important caveat is that Anderson asserts the metaphoric value of kin groups early on but does not adhere to its logic throughout.

14. True to Andersonian dictates, *Maps* juxtaposes a sacred and written language, Arabic, with one used daily, Somali. The Andersonian argument would have the transition from Arabic to Somali serve as a unifying force. Arabic remains a language limited to a few (boys with some money), and it serves to distract from the complex relation Askar has to Somali.

15. English, the language in which Farah has written all of his novels, is his third or fourth language, suggesting at the very least that he does not support Hilaal's position, which would attribute to Farah, the author, a position of fundamental alienation.

16. Of Misra, we know only that she is understood to be Oromo and that she had been married to a Somali. " 'The problem is, who are "my people"?' she said. 'For me, my people are Askar's people; my people are my former husband's people, the people I am most attached to' " (Farah 1986, 184).

17. Because of the French tradition of the *nouveau roman*, I will argue that the second-person narration Djebar employs in *Ombre sultane* does not feel as alienated or alienating in the original French as does this one in its original English.

18. Significantly, this model of nation versus family is quite different from the one I claim female novelists work out.

19. "Thus the critical task is not simple; it necessarily implies the super-

position of two questions, not in a choice between them, but in the point from which they appear to become differentiated. The complexity of the critical problem will be the articulation between the two questions. To grasp this articulation is to accept a discontinuity, to establish discontinuity: the questions are not spontaneously given in their specificity. Initially, the questions must be asked—asked simultaneously, in a way that amounts to allowing them an equal status" (Macherey 1978, 90).

20. It is important to bear in mind that the enormous sum of ten pounds that guarantees Tambu's education for at least two school terms, comes directly from a benevolently racist white woman in Umtali. Doris, believing Tambu to be an exploited native child, first excoriates her teacher, Mr. Matimba, then, when she hears his explanation of the girl's situation, guiltily offers him the money. Dangarembga's choice of narrative strategy here reflects a brutal honesty about neocolonial economies and global markets. She does not pretend to depict a level playing field on which developing nations and their citizenry are able to advance without help from external sources of funding. I thank Charles Sugnet for this idea.

21. "Thus began the period of my reincarnation. I liked to think of my transfer to the mission as my reincarnation. With the egotistical faith of fourteen short years, during which my life had progressed very much according to plan, I expected this era to be significantly profound and broadening in terms of adding wisdom to my nature, clarity to my vision, glamour to my person. In short, I expected my sojourn to fulfil all my fourteen-year-old fantasies, and on the whole I was not disappointed" (Dangarembga 1988, 93).

22. Penny Boumhela (1988, 326), writing about Eliot's *Mill on the Floss*, links sexuality and marriage succinctly: "Realism, bounded more or less by its project of representing in some typical form the real conditions of social existence, has tended to reduce the options for its female protagonists to either marriage or death. Of course, the virtual interchangeability of the two is itself telling."

23. Carole Vance (1984, 4) convincingly argues that the feminine virtues of self-control and watchfulness are signifiers of having been dominated: "Sexual constriction, invisibility, timidity, and uncuriosity are less the signs of an intrinsic and specific female sexual nature and more the signs of thoroughgoing damage."

24. It does comes in for criticism from Tambu's mother (Dangarembga 1988, 120 and *passim*). However, Chido's desire for individual space is never interpreted by his parents as signs of selfishness or promiscuity. Moreover, by spending weekends with the Baker family, Chido escapes the otherwise obligatory visits to the homestead, where the Siguake girls provide most of the labor.

25. The dominant theoretical thrust of much feminist criticism in the late

1970s and early 1980s was to integrate a gender-based analysis into the male-dominated canon without much attention to gender's relation to other modes of analysis. Although two of the editors of *The Voyage In* (Abel, Hirsch, and Langland 1983), Elizabeth Abel and Marianne Hirsch, have gone on to write and edit important books that pay significant feminist attention to race, this early collection exemplifies exactly those limitations of the early 1970s.

26. In an article delineating the contours of the Latin American testimonio against the Bildungsroman, with the latter's investment in the ascendance of the bourgeois subject, Beverley (1992, 106) declares: "If the novel had a special relationship with humanism and the rise of the European bourgeoisie, testimonio is by contrast a new form of narrative literature in which we can at the same time witness and be part of the emerging culture of an international proletarian/popular-democratic subject in its period of ascendancy."

27. "It was good to be validated in this way. Most of it didn't come from the lessons they taught at school but from Nyasha's various and extensive library. I read everything from Enid Blyton to the Brontë sisters, and responded to them all. Plunging into these books I knew I was being educated and I was filled with gratitude to the authors for introducing me to places where reason and inclination were not at odds. It was a centripetal time, with me at the centre, everything gravitating towards me. It was a time of sublimation with me as the sublimate" (Dangarembga 1988, 93).

28. " 'This business of womanhood is a heavy burden,' she said. . . . 'When it is like that you can't just decided [*sic*] today I want to do this, tomorrow I want to do that, the next day I want to be educated!. . . . And these days it is worse, with the poverty of blackness on one side and the weight of womanhood on the other' " (Dangarembga 1988, 16).

29. In this manner, Lucia offers a very different perspective on reproduction from the one we have seen thus far, such as in Efuru's greatest flaw or even Emecheta's ironic comment on it. For what it is worth, Lucia does get pregnant later and "settles down," and she seeks steady employment and an education via Babamukuru's sponsorship.

30. Note that *Purple Hibiscus* by Chimananda Adichie, published subsequent to *Nervous Conditions*, also represents the family as violent in its patriarchy. See my reading (2011a) of how Adichie departs from narrative structures she learns from Dangarembga: the violence exhibited between father and daughter is reworked in the Nigerian novel (the father becomes harsher, the daughter far more passive) in order to produce a yet-sharper critique of the passivity of Tambudzai, the character whose narrative of development we read.

31. Exceptions include Sembène's *Xala*, Emecheta's *The Joys of Motherhood*, and Calixthe Beyala's *C'est le soleil qui m'a brulée*.

32. See Grace Ogot's *The Graduate* (1980) for an example of one of few novels written by women that explicitly thematizes nationalism and feminism. The precocious Nyokabi matter-of-factly links the ascendance to ministerial power of her mother, Mrs. Karungaru, to the death of the man who previously occupied the position.

33. Sue Thomas (1992, 31) suggests that Nyasha's "refusal of food at the family table or here self-induced vomiting after having to eat there is a response to the sexual and cultural politics enacted at it: the ritualized subservience, baby-talk, fussiness of the mother; the father's assertions of domestic authority."

34. Toward the novel's end, after Nyasha's instability has become full-blown, Mainini has this to say: " 'It's the Englishness,' she said. 'It'll kill them all if they aren't careful,' and she snorted. 'Look at them. That boy Chido can hardly speak a word of his own mother's tongue, and you'll see, his children will be worse.' . . . She went on like this for quite a while, going about how you couldn't expect the ancestors to stomach so much Englishness." (Dangarembga 1988, 202–3)

35. In Zimbabwe, as in much of Africa, the majority of individual farm-plant cultivation is done by women. Men are responsible for contributing in the form of either meat or money.

36. Throughout the African continent, boys were given—and continue to be given—advantage over girls in access to education; they were more likely to receive formal schooling and were less likely to have it interrupted when family fortunes were diminished, as the examples of Nhamo and Tambu illustrate.

37. At this point in the text, Tambu cannot articulate her anger and humiliation about Babamukuru's imposition of the farcical ceremony, although she recognizes the anger before the wedding itself and refuses to participate. However, she cannot bring herself to oppose Babamukuru and instead becomes physically incapacitated; she is unable to get out of bed on the morning of the wedding and therefore cannot act as her mother's bridesmaid. Tambu's response to her uncle's authority is a conventionally feminine one, resembling the passive refusal of the Victorian "angel of the house," and, of course, it differs radically from that of Nyasha.

38. Only in a few essays, such as "Algeria Unveiled" (Fanon, 1965b), does Fanon make gender a constituent—and progressive—part of his analysis. For an essay that reclaims Fanon for a feminist politics, see Dubey 1988.

39. Palmer (2008) highlights the cultural differences in the likely reception of Babamukuru's punishment of his daughter: "Babamukuru might be harsh, dictatorial, even chauvinistic, but he also appears . . . as the concerned African parent trying to protect the reputation of his fourteen-year-old daughter. This is how most Africans, male and female, would interpret the situation, although Western feminists would probably see it in a different

light. To them, as to Nyasha, Babamukuru appears as the brutal African male trying to impose his will on the female" (194).

40. Bringing the decolonized state into existence is not the sum total of Fanon's hopes, as we know from "The Pitfalls of National Consciousness," wherein he expresses a prescient warning against the avarice and co-optation of the national bourgeoisie. See chapter 2 in this volume, in which I trace a genealogical relationship between Fanon, Sembène, and Bâ.

4 Bildung at Its Boundaries

1. For other examinations of the literary relations between gender politics and national politics, see Sommer 1991. See also Armstrong 1987 on the rise of the eighteenth-century novelistic tradition in England and Dubey 1998 on the relation between twentieth-century African American novels by women and black cultural nationalism.

2. As I hope is clear by now, I understand my book to form part of a much-needed, historically oriented, though not comprehensive, approach to African women's writing. In the absence of such a literary history focused on gender, there are good political reasons within the sub-Saharan context that one might consider Nwapa and Ogot as "firsts" and temporarily bracket the work of progressive southern African writers such as Olive Schreiner, Doris Lessing, and Nadine Gordimer, as well as North African writers such as Malika Mokkedem. This is a political intervention in literary history based in part on the fact that Schreiner and Lessing have received much attention by scholars of colonialism. It is worth noting that two African writers, each from one of the continent's most populous countries, won the Nobel Prize in the 1980s. The Nigerian Wole Soyinka won in 1986, and the Egyptian Naguib Mahfouz in 1988, but only one is regularly characterized as African.

3. Whether the novel adequately reflects the social events of that moment is not my real concern, although it might be noted that during the Algerian struggle for independence, Djebar worked for an FLN newspaper in Tunis while completing her doctorate in history.

4. Unlike many other Maghrebi writers, Djebar understands herself not only as Algerian but also as African. The first time I heard her claim her Africanness was in 1988 at a meeting of the African Literature Association at Cornell University.

5. Djebar has said of these two novels that they are preparatory to an autobiography. Indeed, the third novel, *Vaste est la prison* (1995), the most explicitly autobiographical, is somewhat different in tone.

6. The third novel is *Vaste est la prison*. The books published subsequently—*Loin de Medine* (1991), *Le blanc de l'Algerie* (1996), and *La disparition de la langue françoise* (2003)—constitute interruptions in the cycle. (*La*

disparition de la langue françoise is Djebar's first novel with a male protagonist.) She is currently at work on the final volume of the quartet.

7. Mildred Mortimer (1990) was one of the very first. Gayatri Spivak has
also done so in her references to Djebar's work: see Spivak 1993. Donadey
(2001, 84–85) discusses this conflation along with the similarities of a car
accident experienced by the Westernized character in *L'amour* and Hajila of
Ombre sultane. In a book broadly about francophone Maghrebi literature,
Jarrod Hayes (2000) devotes a chapter to each novel, noting structural
similarities. Hamid Gafaiti (1996, 164) is the only one who hints at an
intertextual reading: "Ces livres [*L'amour* and *Ombre sultane*] constituent,
d'une part, une continuation et, d'une autre part, une sorte de rupture."

8. "Il y eut un cri déchirant—je l'entends encore au moment ou je
t'écris—puis, des clameurs, puis un tumulte. . . . *Une année dans le Sahel*"
(Djebar 1985a, np); "Un grand cri s'éleva (je l'entends encore au moment ou
je t'écris) puis une clameur, puis un tumulte" (Djebar 1987, 168). The phrase
in italics is from Fromentin 1859, 172.

9. For a more complete statement on autobiography, see the work of
Philippe Lejeune (1975 and others).

10. The most important are Amable Matterer, first officer of the ship *Ville
de Marseille*, and Baron Barchou, often sharply racist, who pens his observa-
tions from a quarantine station in Marseille. Djebar finds Barchou insightful,
especially when he writes graphically about the "terrible poetry" of the
female victims of warfare. The last French chronicler, J. T. Merle, is a theater
manager who conveys the drama, excitement, and spectacle of the events
and who variously reveals himself to be cowardly.

11. The Petit Larousse defines "fantasia" as both a musical event and a
military tactic or spectacle.

12. In their characterization of the difference between Western and non-
Western autobiography, Sidonie Smith and Julia Watson (1992, xvii) declare:
"This Enlightenment 'self' ontologically identical to other 'I's, sees its destiny in
a teleological narrative enshrining the 'individual' and 'his' uniqueness. Autobiography also entwines the definition of the human being in a web of privileged characteristics. Despite their myriad differences, of place, of time, histories, economies, cultural identifications, all 'I's are rational, agentive, unitary."

13. Examples of character complexity include Isma's often expressed doubt
about whether she ought to have put Hajila in this marital situation. Another
example is that, while it is clear that Isma has no ambivalence about having
ended her marriage, in the wake of some of the scenes of youthful sexuality
and intimacy it is entirely unclear what the reason was for ending it.

14. Jarrod Hayes (2000) has suggested that Djebar might be in dialogue
with Kateb Yacine's classic nationalist novel *Nedjma* (1956), wherein the
eponymous heroine, allegory of the nation and character with no voice of
her own, is talked about by four men, each of whom desires her.

15. In the register of the audible or aural (rather than the written), I note in passing something much commented on by others and noted by the novel itself—that *s'écrit* is homophonic with *ses cris* (suggesting that love is not only written but cried out): "L'amour, ses cris (s'écrit): ma main qui écrit etabli le jeu de mots francoise sur les amours qui s'exhale" (Djebar 1985a, 240).

16. Having resisted French taxation for years, the Kabyles retreated in 1845 to a network of caves, followed closely by Pélissier. He found all of the entrances, blocked them up, then saturated the caves and tunnels with smoke from the fires he had lit at all of the entrances, creating what Djebar has called an *enfumade*.

17. It was Cavaignac who returned to France, having practiced on the Kabyles what he would then do to the French working classes in 1848.

18. Djebar is proposing an imaginative engagement with the archive and so cannot or should not be held to the same standards of historical methodology as someone writing as a historian would be. Many literary critics forget and treat Djebar's representation as unmediated fact: see Hayes 2000; Steedman 2003.

19. The narrator forcefully expresses the state of that secret, referring to witnesses' accounts by later historians, the originals of which have since been lost. In my general reading of Algerian history, I have found no mention of this particular massacre, although I have not searched extensively.

20. In some ways, Arnaud serves as villain in the entire quartet and certainly of *L'amour* and *Vaste est la prison*. As one comes to learn in the third autobiographical novel, the ancestral family of the narrating "I" engages in war with him during the Kabyle uprisings of the 1870s.

21. The reference here are to Hayes 2000 and Steedman 2003 among others.

22. Djebar is careful in almost all respects but this one: she neglects to mention that Algeria was not a sovereign territory before French colonialism. It was under Ottoman Turkish rule.

23. Bou Maza (or Bou Maaza, as spelled by the historian Charles-Robert Agérnon) is glimpsed in the chapter on the Sbeah massacre because one of his lieutenants, involved with a Sbeah women, was an eyewitness to the massacre, the record of which has disappeared and is known now only by indirect reference and novelistic conjuring. According to Charles-Robert Agéron, the incitement to rebellion among the Kabyles by Bou Maaza (Goat Man) led to swift and severe repression, one expression of which was the asphyxiation of the Ouled Riah. It is of some significance that Agéron's mortality statistics differ greatly from Djebar's. Djebar says in her novel, published in 1985, that fifteen hundred died. Agéron, a liberal-left French historian who wrote in 1964, put the number at about half that, or eight hundred (see Agéron 1964 [1991], 19–20).

24. Mazouna (or Mazuma) is near Djebar's hometown, Cherchell.

25. Recall that marriage is the fourth condition named by Moretti (1987) for a successful conclusion to the classic Bildungsroman. In the discussion of *Nervous Conditions* in the previous chapter, the dangers of the romance plot are unambiguous. Nyasha's transgressive behavior, which is strongly oriented toward public politics, is reflected back to her by her father as sexually inappropriate. Tambu channels all of her libidinal energy into her drive for educational and financial success. *Maps* tells the story of a subject whose failure to cohere results from difficulty in recognizing differences between himself and an "unperson." In both of Djebar's novels, however, marriage is part of the plot, although it is also marginally important to each.

26. Elizabeth Abel and colleagues continue this line of thought. "The protagonists of novels of development grow significantly only after fulfilling the fairy tale expectation that they will marry and live 'happily ever after.' Because it frequently portrays a break not from parental but from marital authority, the novel of awakening is often a novel of adultery. . . . Development may be compressed into brief, epiphanic moments. Since the significant changes are internal, flashes of recognition often replace the continuous unfolding of an action": Abel et al. 1983, 12.

27. In French the term is *fantasie,* and it has stylistic affiliations with the oral. Although these women's stories are made available in French, the narrator indicates that they were originally spoken in Arabic.

28. Djebar has said publically that she interviewed in Arabic female resistance fighters. She transcribed their responses and re-transcribed them in the act of incorporation of oral fragments into *La Nouba, L'amour,* and *Ombre sultane.*

29. Even more than *fantasia,* which has a French meaning apart from (in addition to) its Maghrebi one, *nouba* entered French as an Arabic word. It refers to martial music of the "tirailleurs d'Afrique du Nord": Larousse.

30. Significantly, she is not mistreated by the French. It is Bou Maaza who most threatens her, and even he does not harm her, the narrative suggests.

31. Victor Hugo wrote "Pauline Roland" in 1852, the year of Roland's death:

Elle ne connaissait ni l'orgueil ni la haine;
Elle aimait; elle était pauvre, simple et sereine;
Souvent le pain qui manque abrégeait son repas.
Elle avait trois enfants, ce qui n'empêchait pas
Qu'elle ne se sentit mère de ceux qui souffrent.
Les noirs événements qui dans la nuit s'engouffrent,
Les flux et les reflux, les abîmes béants,
Les nains, sapant sans bruit l'ouvrage des géants,
Et tous nos malfaiteurs inconnus ou célèbres,
Ne l'épouvantaient point; derrière ces ténèbres,

Elle apercevait Dieu construisant l'avenir.
Elle sentait sa foi sans cesse rajeunir;
De la liberté sainte elle attisait les flammes,
Elle s'inquiétait des enfants et des femmes,
Elle disait, tendant la main aux travailleurs:
La vie est dure ici, mais sera bonne ailleurs.
Avançons!—Elle allait, portant de l'un à l'autre
L'espérance; c'était une espèce d'apôtre
Que Dieu, sur cette terre où nous gémissons tous,
Avait fait mère et femme, afin qu'il fût plus doux.
L'esprit le plus farouche aimait sa voix sincère.
Tendre, elle visitait, sous leur toit de misère,
Tous ceux que la famine ou la douleur abat,
Les malades pensifs, gisant sur leur grabat,
La mansarde où languit l'indigence morose;
Quand, par hasard moins pauvre, elle avait quelque chose,
Elle le partageait à tous comme une sœur;
Quand elle n'avait rien, elle donnait son cœur.
Calme et grande, elle aimait comme le soleil brille.
Le genre humain pour elle était une famille.
Comme ses trois enfants étaient l'humanité.
Elle criait: progrès! amour! fraternité!
Elle ouvrait aux souffrants des horizons sublimes.
Quand Pauline Roland eut commis tous ces crimes,
Le sauveur de l'église et de l'ordre la prit
Et la mit en prison. (Hugo 1853,11. 1–36)

32. The revolutionary uprisings in 1848 were pan-European, affecting what today are as many as thirteen nation-states. It was the most radical political change France had experienced since 1789.

33. Gayatri Spivak says that Djebar makes of Roland "the true ancestress of the mujahidat [*mujāhidät*]" (Spivak 1993).

34. Both Farah and Djebar make into allegories characters whose relation to the nation at hand is the opposite of national. In fact, they are what the nation—Ethiopia or France—defines itself against. However, while Farah's novel stands as a strong indictment of nationalism as a whole, one might well read Djebar's as one that hopes for a better nationalism.

35. See also Alain Robbe-Grillet's *La jalousie* (1959).

36. Richard Burton's translation—itself not fully reliable, of course—says of scholarly opinion about when *One Thousand and One Nights* was written down that it may have been between the tenth century and the sixteenth century: Burton 1885 (1962). Though there are forms of prose narrative in Latin that were written before *One Thousand and One Nights*, it is certainly

possible to claim in a cultural nationalist fashion that this was the first novel in Arabic and that it preceded the rise of the European novel.

37. In both instances, the infidelity is heightened, or made more shocking, because it is with someone beneath the sultana, an unattractive black slave or servant.

38. For background information on women's rights and Algerian fundamentalism, see Abdelkdrim-Chikh 1989; Hélie-Lucas 1986.

39. Later she adds, "Les matrons emmaillotent leurs fillettes pas encore pubères de leur angoisse insideuse. Mère et fille, ô harem renouvelé! (The matriarchs swaddle their little girls in their own insidious anguish, before they even reach puberty. Mother and daughter, oh, harem restored)": Djebar 1987, 155; 1993, 145.

40. It is worth recalling here especially that Mortimer (1990, 159) points out that Isma's name means "listen" in Arabic.

41. "J'avais ricané bien plus tard: 'les homes son tils jamais nus? Hélas! Peurs de la tribu, angoisses que les mères frustrées vous transmettent, obsessions d'un ailleurs informulé, tout vois est lien, bandelettes et carcan! . . . Montre-moi un homme vraiment nu sur cette terre, alors jet e quitterai pour cet home.' . . . J'ai fait mieux, je l'ai quitté pour moi-meme": Djebar 1987, 95.

Conclusion

1. Having thickly outlined a model for producing a feminine national literary history in various parts of Africa, I suggest a reading beyond literature alone to the interrelations between literature and history, between the public social sphere and the domestic social one. For a fuller treatment of the relation between women's writing, women's uprisings, and the development of a public sphere in nationally independent Africa, see my essay, "Rioting Women, Writing Women: Gender, Class and the Public Sphere in Africa" in *Africa After Gender?*, ed. Stephan Miescher, Takyiwah Manuh, and Catherine Cole.

2. For a fuller discussion of predecessors to Adichie's two novels, including Chinua Achebe and Tsitsi Dangarembga, as well as greater elaboration of the relation of her more explicitly nationalist work to the work of earlier writers, such as Nwapa, see my "Adichie's Genealogies: National and Feminine Novels."

References

Abdelkrim-Chikh, Rabia. 1989. "Les enjeux politiques et symboliques de la lutte des femmes pour l'egalité entre les sexes en Algerie." *Peuples Mediterraneens* 48–49 (July–December), 257–78.

Abel, Elizabeth, Marianne Hirsch, and Elizabeth Langland, eds. 1983. *The Voyage In: Fictions of Female Development*. Boston: University Press of New England.

Abrams, M. H. 1981. *A Glossary of Literary Terms*, 4th ed. New York: Holt, Rinehart, and Winston.

Accad, Evelyne. 1996. "Assia Djebar's Contribution to Arab Women's Literature: Rebellion, Maturity, Vision." *World Literature Today* 70, no. 4 (Autumn), 801–12.

Achebe, Chinua. 1958 [1996]. *Things Fall Apart*. London: Heinemann.

——. 1975. "Colonialist Criticism." In *Morning Yet on Creation Day: Essays*, 3–18. London: Heinemann.

——. 1978. "An Image of Africa." *Research in African Literatures* 9, no. 1 (Spring), 1–15.

——. 1987. *Anthills of the Savannah*. New York: Anchor.

——. 1988. *Hopes and Impediments: Selected Essays, 1965–1987*. London: Heinemann.

Adichie, Chimananda. 2006. *Half of a Yellow Sun*. New York: Anchor.

Agéron, Charles-Robert. 1991 (1964). *Modem Algeria: A History from 1830 to the Present*, trans. Michael Brett. Trenton, N.J.: Africa World Press.

Ahmad, Aijaz. 1999. "*The Communist Manifesto*: In Its Own Time and in Ours." *A World to Win: Essays on* The Communist Manifesto, ed. Prakash Karat, 14–47. Delhi: LeftWord.

Aidoo, Ama Ata. 1971. *The Dilemma of a Ghost*. New York: Collier.

———. 1977. *Our Sister Killjoy*. Essex: Longman.

Alden, Patricia. 1988. *Social Mobility in the English Bildungsroman: Gissing, Hardy, Bennett, and Lawrence*. Ann Arbor: University of Michigan Press.

———. 1991. "New Women and Old Myths: Chinua Achebe's *Anthills of the Savannah* and Nuruddin Farah's *Sardines*." *Critical Approaches to* Anthills of the Savannah, ed. Holger Ehling. Special issue of *Matatu*.

Alden, Patricia, and Louis Tremaine. 1999. *Nuruddin Farah*. New York: Twayne Publishers.

Amadiume, Ifi. 1987. *Male Daughters, Female Husbands: Sex and Gender in an African Society*. London: Zed.

Anderson, Benedict. 1990. *Imagined Communities: Reflections on the Origin and Spread of Nationalism*, rev. ed. New York: Verso.

Andrade, Susan Z. 1990. "Rewriting History, Motherhood, and Rebellion: Naming an African Women's Literary Tradition." *Research in African Literatures* 21, no. 1 (Winter), 91–110.

———. 1996. "The Joys of Daughterhood: Gender, Nationalism, and the Making of Literary Tradition(s)." *Cultural Institutions of the Novel*, ed. Deidre Lynch and William B. Warner, 249–75. Durham: Duke University Press.

———. 2007. "Rioting Women, Writing Women: Gender, Nationalism, and the Public Sphere in Africa." *Africa After Gender*, ed. Catherine Cole, Takyiwaa Manuh, and Stephan Miescher, 85–107. Bloomington: Indiana University Press.

———. 2011. "Adichie's Genealogies: National and Feminine Novels." *Research in African Literatures* 42 no. 2 (Summer), 91–101.

Armah, Ayi Kwei. 1968. *The Beautyful Ones Are Not Yet Born*. Oxford: Heinemann.

Armstrong, Nancy. 1987. *Desire and Domestic Fiction: A Political History of the Novel*. New York: Oxford University Press.

Arnold, James. 1981. *Modernism and Negritude: The Poetry and Poetics of Aimé Césaire*. Cambridge: Harvard University Press.

Attwell, David. 2005. *Rewriting Modernity: Studies in Black South African Literary History*. Johannesburg: Thorold's Africana Books.

Bâ, Mariama. 1979. *Une si longue lettre*. Dakar: Les Nouvelles Editions Africaines.

———. 1981a. *So Long a Letter*, trans. Modupe Bode-Thomas. London: Heinemann.

———. 1981b. *Un chant écarlate*. Dakar: Nouvelles Editions Africaines.

Bahri, Deepika. 1994. "Disembodying the Corpus: Postcolonial Pathology in Tsitsi Dangarembga's *Nervous Conditions*." *Journal of Postmodern Culture* 5, no. 1. http://muse.jhu.edu/journals/postmodern_culture.

Balakrishnan, Gopal. 1996. "The National Imagination." In *Mapping the Nation*, ed. Balakrishnan, 198–213. London: Verso.

Banyiwa-Home, Naana. "African Womanhood: The Contrasting Perspectives of Flora Nwapa's *Efuru* and Elechi Amadi's *The Concubine*." In *Ngambika: Studies of Women in African Literature*, ed. Carole Boyce Davies and Anne Adams Graves, 119–29. Trenton, N.J.: Africa World Press, 1986.

Barker-Benfield, G. J. *The Horrors of the Half-Known Life: Male Attitudes Toward Women and Sexuality in Nineteenth-Century America*. New York: Harper, 1976.

Barrett, Michèle. *Women's Oppression Today*. London: Verso, 1980.

Barrett, Michèle and Mary McIntosh. *The Anti-social Family*. London: Verso, 1982.

Bayart, Jean-Francois. 1989. *The State in Africa: The Politics of the Belly*, trans. Mary Harper, Christopher Harrison, and Elizabeth Harrison. London: Longman.

Beverley, John. 1992. "The Margin at the Center: On Testimonio (Testimonial Narrative)." *De/Colonizing the Subject*, ed. Sidonie Smith and Julia Watson, 91–114. Minneapolis: University of Minnesota Press.

Beyala, Calixthe. 1987. *C'est le soleil qui m'a brulée*. Paris: Stock.

———. 1996. *The Sun Hath Looked upon Me*, trans. Marjolijn De Jaeger. Oxford: Heinemann.

Bhabha, Homi. 1984. "Of Mimicry and Man: The Ambivalence of Colonial Discourse." *October* 28, 317–25.

Blair, Dorothy. 1984. *Senegalese Literature: A Critical History*. Boston: Twayne.

Bloch, Ernst, Georg Lukács, Bertolt Brecht, Walter Benjamin, Theodor Adorno. 1977. *Aesthetics and Politics*. London: Verso Press.

Boehmer, Elleke. 1990. "Of Goddesses and Stories: Gender and a New Politics in Achebe's *Anthills of the Savannah*." *Chinua Achebe: A Celebration*, ed. Kirsten Holst Petersen and Anna Rutherford, 102–12. Sydney: Dangaroo.

———. 1991. "Stories of Women and Mothers: Gender and Nationalism in the Early Fiction of Flora Nwapa." *Motherlands: Black Women's Writing from Africa, the Caribbean, and South Asia*, ed. Susheila Nasta, 3–23. New Brunswick: Rutgers University Press.

———. 2005. *Stories of Women: Gender and Narrative in the Postcolonial Nation*. Manchester: Manchester University Press.

Boujedra, Rachid. 1979 [1988]. *Les 1001 années de la nostalgie*. Paris: Gallimard.

Boumhela, Penny. 1988 [1992]. "Realisms and the Ends of Feminisms." In *Realism*, ed. Lilian R Furst. London: Longman.

Brennan, Timothy. 1989. *Salman Rushdie and the Third World*. New York: St. Martin's Press.

Brown, Lloyd W. 1981. *Women Writers in Black Africa*. Westport, Conn.: Greenwood.

Bryce, Jane. "West Africa." *The Bloomsbury Guide to Women's Literature*, ed. Claire Buck. New York: Prentice Hall, 1992.

Bunn, David. "A Reply to Meghan Vaughn." *Social Dynamics* 20.2 (1994): 24–32.

Burton, Richard F., trans. 1885 [1962]. *The Book of the Thousand Nights and a Night*. New York: The Heritage Press.

Butler, Judith. 1990. *Gender Trouble: Feminism and the Subversion of Identity*. New York: Routledge.

Butor, Michel. 1957. *La modification*. Paris: Minuit.

Cabral, Amílcar. 1973. "Identity and Dignity in the Context of the National Liberation Struggle." *Return to the Source: Selected Speeches by Amílcar Cabral*, 9–25. New York: Africa Information Service and Monthly Review Press.

Carpentier, Alejo. 1949. *El reino de este mundo*. Mexico City: Ibero Americana de Publicaciones.

Caseley-Hayford, Joseph. 1911 [1969]. *Ethiopia Unbound: Studies in Race Emancipation*. London: Cass.

Cazenave, Odile. *Femmes Rebelles: Naissance d'un nouveau roman africain au feminin*. Paris: L'Harmattan, 1996. Trans. 2000, *Rebellious Women: The New Generation of African Female Novelists*. Boulder: Lynne Rienner.

Chabal, Patrick. *Power in Africa: An Essay in Political Interpretation*. New York: St. Martin's, 1992.

Cham, Mbye. 1987. "Contemporary Society and the Female Imagination: A Study of the Novels of Mariama Bâ." *Women in African Literature Today* 15, 89–101.

Champagne, John. 1996. "A Feminist Just Like Us?: Teaching Mariama Bâ's *So Long a Letter*." *College English* 58, no. 1, 22–42.

Chapman, Michael. 1996. *Southern African Literatures*. London: Longman.

Chatterjee, Partha. 1993. *The Nation and Its Fragments: Colonial and Postcolonial Histories*. Princeton: Princeton University Press.

Chinodya, Shimmer. 1989. *Harvest of Thorns*. Harare: Baobab Books.

Clifford, James. 1986. "On Ethnographic Allegory." *Writing Culture: The Poetics and Politics of Ethnography*, ed. Clifford and George Marcus. Berkeley: University of California Press.

Cobham, Rhonda. 1988. "Introduction." *Research in African Literatures* 19, no. 2 (Summer), 137–42.

——. 1991. "Making Men and History: Achebe and the Politics of Revisionism in *Things Fall Apart*." In *Approaches to Teaching Things Fall Apart*, ed. Bernth Lindfors, 91–100. New York: MLA Publications.

——. 1992. "Misgendering the Nation: African Nationalist Fictions and Nuruddin Farah's *Maps*." *Nationalisms and Sexualities*, ed. Andrew Parker,

Mary Russo, Doris Sommer, and Patricia Yaeger, 42–59. New York: Routledge.

Condé, Maryse. 1972. "Three Female Writers in Modern Africa: Flora Nwapa, Ama Ata Aidoo, Grace Ogot." *Presence Africaine* 82, 136–39.

Coundouriotis, Eleni. 1999. *Claiming History: Colonialism, Ethnography, and the Novel*. New York: Columbia University Press.

Coward, Rosalind. 1985. *Female Desires: How They Are Sought, Bought, and Packaged*. New York: Grove.

Creamer, Heidi. 1994. "An Apple for the Teacher?: Femininity, Coloniality, and Food in *Nervous Conditions*." *Kunapipi* 16, no. 1, 349–60.

Dangarembga, Tsitsi. 1988. *Nervous Conditions*. Seattle: Seal.

——. 2006. *The Book of Not: A Novel*. Banbury: Ayebia Clarke.

Davies, Carole Boyce. 1986a. "Introduction: Feminist Consciousness and African Literary Criticism." *Ngambika: Studies of Women in African Literature*, ed. Carol Boyce Davies and Anne Adams Graves, 1–23. Trenton, N.J.: Africa World Press.

——. 1986b. "Motherhood in the Works of Male and Female Igbo Writers." *Ngambika: Studies of Women in African Literature*, ed. Carol Boyce Davies and Anne Adams Graves, 241–57. Trenton, N.J.: Africa World Press.

Davies, Carole Boyce, and Anne Adams Graves, eds. 1986. *Ngambika: Studies of Women in African Literature*. Trenton, N.J.: Africa World Press.

de Beauvoir, Simone. 1953. *The Second Sex*, trans. H. M. Parshley. New York: Knopf.

Diallo, Nafissatou. 1975. *De Tilène au plateau*. Dakar, Senegal: Les Nouvelles Editions Africaines.

Dib, Mohammed. 1962. *Qui se souvient de la mer*. Paris: Seuil.

Djebar, Assia. 1957. *La soif*. Paris: R. Julliard.

——. 1980. *Femmes d'Alger dans leur appartement*. Paris: Editions des femmes.

——. 1985a. *L'amour, la fantasia*. Paris: Jean-Claude Lattes.

——. 1985b. *Fantasia, an Algerian Cavalcade*, trans. Dorothy S. Blair. London: Quartet.

——. 1987. *Ombre sultane*. Paris: Jean-Claude Lattes.

——. 1991. *Loin de Medine*. Paris: Albin Michel.

——. 1993. *Sister to Scheherazade*, trans. Dorothy Blair. London: Quartet.

——. 1995a. *Le blanc de l'Algerie*. Paris: Albin Michel.

——. 1995b. *Vaste est la prison*. Paris: Albin Michel.

——. 2003. *La disparition de la langue françoise*. Paris: Albin Michel.

Donadey, Anne. 2001. *Recasting Postcolonialism: Women Writing between Words*. Portsmouth, N.H.: Heinemann.

Driver, Dorothy. "Southern Africa." *The Bloomsbury Guide to Women's Literature*, ed. Claire Buck. New York: Prentice Hall, 1992.

Dubey, Madhu. 1998. "The 'True Lie' of the Nation." *differences* 10, no. 2, 1–29.

Du Plessis, Rachel Blau. 1985. *Writing beyond the Ending: Narrative Strategies of Twentieth-Century Women Writers*. Bloomington: Indiana University Press.

Echewa, T. Obinkaram. 1992. *I Saw the Sky Catch Fire*. New York: Penguin.

Ekwensi, Cyprian. 1954. *People of the City*. London: Dakers.

——. 1961. *Jagua Nana*. London: Heinemann.

Eliot, George. 1880 [1979]. *The Mill on the Floss*. New York: Penguin.

Emecheta, Buchi. 1977. *The Slave Girl*. London: George Braziller.

——. 1979. *The Joys of Motherhood*. London: George Braziller.

Emenyonu, Ernest. 1970. "Review of *Efuru*." *Ba Shiru* 1, no. 1, 58–61.

Erritouni, Ali 2006. "Contradictions and Alternatives in Chinua Achebe's *Anthills of the Savannah*." *Journal of Modern Literature* 29, no. 2, 50–74.

Esonwanne, Uzoma. 1990. "The Madness of African(s): Or, Anthropology's Reason." *Cultural Critique* (Winter), 107–26.

——. 1997. "Enlightenment Epistemology and 'Aesthetic Condition': Mariama Bâ's *So Long a Letter*." In *The Politics of (M)Othering: Womanhood: Identity and Resistance in African Literature*, ed. Obioma Nnaemeka, 33–49. London: Routledge.

Fagunwa, Daniel O. 1968. *The Forest of a Thousand Daemons*, trans. Wole Soyinka. London: Thomas Nelson and Sons Ltd.

——. 1973 (1938). *Ogboju ode ninu igbo irunmale*. Apapa, Nigeria: Nelson.

Fanon, Frantz. 1952. *Peau noire, masques blancs*. Paris: Seuil.

——. 1961. *Les damnés de la terre*. Paris: F. Maspero.

——. 1965a. *A Dying Colonialism*, trans. Haakon Chevalier. New York: Grove.

——. 1965b. "Algeria Unveiled." In *A Dying Colonialism*, trans. Haakon Chevalier, 34–67. New York: Grove.

——. 1968. *The Wretched of the Earth*, trans. Constance Farrington. New York: Grove.

——. 1982. *Black Skin, White Masks*, trans. Charles Lam Markham. New York: Grove.

Farah, Nuruddin. 1986. *Maps*. New York: Pantheon.

——. *Sardines*. 1981 [1992]. St. Paul, Minn.: Graywolf Press.

Felski, Rita. 1989. *Beyond Feminist Aesthetics: Feminist Literature and Social Change*. Cambridge: Harvard University Press.

Fleissner, Jennifer L. 2002. "Is Feminism a Historicism?" *Tulsa Studies in Women's Literature* 21, no. 1, 45–66.

Franco, Jean. 1989. *Plotting Women: Gender and Representation in Mexico*. New York: Columbia University Press.

Fromentin, Eugéne. 1859 [1881]. *Une année dans le Sahel*. Paris: Plon.

Fuss, Diana. *Essentially Speaking: Feminism, Nature and Difference*. New York: Routledge, 1989.

Gafaiti, Hafid. 1996a. "The Blood of Writing: Assia Djebar's Unveiling of Women in History." *World Literature Today* 70, no. 1, 813–22.

———. 1996b. *Les femmes dans le roman Algérien*. Paris: L'Harmattan.

Gaidzanwa, Rudo. 1985. *Images of Women in Zimbabwean Literature*. Harare: The College Press.

George, Olakunle. 2003. *Relocating Agency: Modernity and African Letters*. Albany: State University of New York Press.

Ghali, Noureddine. 1987. "Interview with Sembene Ousmane." *Film and Politics in the Third World*, ed. John G. H. Downing, 41–54. New York: Autonomedia.

Gikandi, Simon. 1991. *Reading Chinua Achebe: Language and Ideology in Fiction*. London: James Currey.

———. 1996. *Maps of Englishness*. New York: Columbia University Press.

———. 2001. "Chinua Achebe and the Invention of African Culture." In *Research in African Literatures* 32, no. 3, 3–8.

———, ed. 2002. *Encyclopedia of African Literature*. London: Routledge.

Griswold, Wendy. 2000. *Bearing Witness: Readers, Writers, and the Novel in Nigeria*. Princeton: Princeton University Press.

Gugler, Joseph, and Oumar Cherif Diop. 1998. "Ousmane Sembene's *Xala*: The Novel, the Film, and Their Audiences." *Research in African Literatures* 29, no. 2 (Summer), 147–58.

Harrow, Kenneth. 1980. "Sembene's 'Xala': The Use of Film and Novel as a Revolutionary Weapon" in *Studies in Twentieth Century Literature*, 4 no. 2, 177–88.

———. 1994. *Thresholds of Change in African Literature: The Emergence of a Tradition*. Portsmouth, N.H.: Heinemann.

Hayes, Jarrod. 2000. *Queer Nations: Marginal Sexualities in the Maghreb*. Chicago: University of Chicago Press.

Head, Bessie. 1987. *A Question of Power*. Portsmouth, N.H.: Heinemann.

Hegel, G. W. 1821 [1956]. *The Philosophy of History*, trans. J. Sibree. New York: Dover.

Hélie-Lucas, Marie-Aimée. 1987. "Bound and Gagged by the Family Code." In *Third World, Second Sex*, vol. 2, ed. Miranda Davies, 3–15. London: Zed.

Herzenberger-Fofana, Pierette. 1987. "Les influences religieuses dans la litterature feminine francophone d'Afrique noire." *Nouvelles du Sud* 7, 191–99.

Hitchcott, Nicki. 1996. "'Confidently Feminine'?: Sexual Role-Play in the Novels of Mariama Bâ." In *African Francophone Writing: A Critical Introduction*, ed. Laïla Ibnlfassi and Nicki Hitchcott, 139–52. Oxford: Berg.

———. 2000. *Women Writers in Francophone Africa*. Oxford: Berg.

Hove, Chenjerai. 1988. *Bones*. Oxford: Heinemann.

Hugo, Victor. 1853. "Pauline Roland." *Les Châtiments, Livre V: L'autorité est sacrée*. Paris: J. Girard & Cie., Editeurs.

Ifeka-Moller, Caroline. 1985. "Female Militancy and Colonial Revolt: The

Women's War of 1929, Eastern Nigeria." *Perceiving Women*, ed. Shirley Ardener, 127–57. London: Malaby.

Innes, C. L. 1992. *Chinua Achebe*. Cambridge: Cambridge University Press.

Innes, C. L., and Bernth Lindfors, eds. 1978. *Critical Perspectives on Chinua Achebe*. Washington: Three Continents.

Irele, Abiola F., ed. 1977. *Selected Poems of Léopold Sédar Senghor*. Cambridge: Cambridge University Press.

——. 1981. *African Experience in Literature and Ideology*. London: Heinemann.

——. 1992. "In Praise of Alienation." *The Surreptitious Speech*: Presence Africaine *and the Politics of Otherness, 1947–1987*, ed. V. Y. Mudimbe. Chicago: University of Chicago Press.

——. 2000. "The Crisis of Cultural Memory in Chinua Achebe's *Things Fall Apart*." *African Studies Quarterly* 4, no. 3, 1–40.

——. 2001. *The African Imagination*. New York: Oxford University Press.

——. 2006. "In Search of Camara Laye." *Research in African Literatures* 37, no. 1 (Spring), 110–27.

Isichei, Elizabeth. 1973. *The Ibo People and the Europeans*. New York: St. Martin's.

——. 1976. *A History of the Igbo People*. New York: St. Martin's.

Jameson, Fredric. 1979. *Fables of Aggression: Wyndham Lewis, the Modernist as Fascist*. Berkeley: University of California Press.

——. 1981. *The Political Unconscious*. Ithaca: Cornell University Press.

——. 1985. "The Realist Floor-Plan." *On Signs*, ed. Marshall Blonsky. Baltimore: Johns Hopkins University Press.

——. 1986. "Third World Literature in the Era of Multinational Capitalism." *Social Text* 15 (Fall), 65–88.

——. 1996. "On Literary and Cultural Import-Substitution in the Third World: The Case of the Testimonio (1992/93)." *The Real Thing: Testimonial Discourse and Latin America*, ed. Georg M. Gugelberger, 172–91. Durham: Duke University Press.

Jayawardena, Kumari. 1985. *Feminism and Nationalism in the Third World*. London: Zed.

Jeyifo, Biodun. 1993. "Okonkwo and His Mother: *Things Fall Apart* and Issues of Gender in the Constitution of African Postcolonial Discourse." *Callaloo* 16, no. 4, 847–58.

Johnson, Barbara. 1988. "Apostrophe, Animation, Abortion." *A World of Difference*. Baltimore: Johns Hopkins University Press.

Johnson, Cheryl [Odim]. 1982. "Grass Roots Organizing: Women in Anticolonial Activity in Southwestern Nigeria." *African Studies Review* 25, nos. 2/3, 137–57.

Johnson-Odim, Cheryl, and Nina Mba. 1997. *For Women and the Nation: Funmilayo Ransome-Kuti of Nigeria*. Chicago: University of Illinois Press.

Julien, Eileen. 1992. *African Literature and the Question of Orality*. Bloomington: Indiana University Press.

———. 1995. "African Literatures in Comparative Perspective." *Yearbook of Comparative and General Literature* 43, 15–24.

———. 2007. "When a Man Loves a Woman: Gender and National Identity in Wole Soyinka's *Death and the King's Horseman* and Mariama Bâ's *Scarlet Song*." *Africa after Gender?*, ed. Catherine M. Cole, Takyiwaa Manuh, and Stephan F. Miescher, 205–22. Bloomington: Indiana University Press.

July, Robert. 1987. *An African Voice: The Role of the Humanities in African Independence*. Durham: Duke University Press.

Jusdanis, Gregory. 1995. "Beyond National Culture?" *boundary 2* 22, no. 1 (Spring), 23–60.

Kabbani, Rama. 1986. *Europe's Myths of the Orient: Devise and Rule*. London: Macmillan.

Kandiyoti, Deniz. 1988. "Bargaining with Patriarchy." *Gender and Society* 2 no. 3, 274–90.

———. 1991. "Identity and its Discontents: Women and the Nation." *Millennium: Journal of International Studies* 20 no. 1, 429–43.

Kane, Cheikh Hamidou. 1961. *L'aventure ambiguë*. Paris: Julliard.

Kanogo, Tabitha. 1987. *Squatters and the roots of Mau Mau, 1905–1963*. London: James Currey.

Kaplan, Cora. 1983. "Wild Nights: Pleasure/Sexuality/Feminism." In *Formations of Pleasure*, ed. Fredric Jameson, Terry Eagleton, Cora Kaplan, and Laura Mulvey, 15–35. London: Routledge.

Kazan, Francesca. 1993. "Recalling the Other Third World: Nuruddin Farah's *Maps*." *Novel* (Spring), 309–19.

Kelly, Hilarie. 1988. "A Somali Tragedy of Political and Sexual Confusion: A Critical Analysis of Nuruddin Farah's *Maps*." *Ufahamu* 16 no. 2, 21–37.

Kenyatta, Jomo. 1962 [1965]. *Facing Mt. Kenya*. New York: Vintage.

Kesteloot, Lilyan. 2001. *Histoire de la literature négro-africaine*. Paris: Karthala.

King, Adèle. 2002. *Rereading Camara Laye*. Lincoln: University of Nebraska Press.

Kuoh-Moukory, Thérèse. 1969 [2002]. *Rencontres essentielles*, ed. Cheryl Toman. New York: MLA Publications.

Larsen, Neil. 1995. *Reading North by South*. Minneapolis: University of Minnesota Press.

Laye, Camara. 1953. *L'enfant noir*. Paris: Plon.

———. 1954. *Le regard du roi*. Paris: Plon.

Lazarus, Neil. 1990. *Resistance in Postcolonial African Fiction*. New Haven: Yale University Press.

———. 1994. "National Consciousness and the Specificity of (Post)Colonial Intellectualism." *Colonial Discourse/Postcolonial Theory*, ed. Francis Barker, Peter Hulme, and Margaret Iversen. Manchester: Manchester University Press.

Lazreg, Marnia. 1994. *The Eloquence of Silence: Algerian Women in Question.* New York: Routledge.

Leith-Ross, Sylvia. 1939 [1965]. *African Women: A Study of the Ibo of Nigeria.* London: Routledge and Kegan Paul.

Lejeune, Philippe. 1975. *Le pacte autobiographique.* Paris: Seuil.

Lionnet, Françoise. 1989. *Autobiographical Voices: Race, Gender, and Self-Portraiture.* Ithaca: Cornell University Press.

Lukács, Georg. 1964. "The Ideology of Modernism." In *Realism in Our Time,* trans. John Mander and Necke Mander, 17–46. New York: Harper Torch Books.

———. 1971. "Narrate or Describe?" In *Writer and Critic and Other Essays,* trans. Arthur Kahn, 110–48. New York: Grosset.

———. 1977. "Realism in the Balance." In *Aesthetics and Politics,* ed. and trans. Ronald Taylor, 28–59. London: Verso

———. 1974 [1916]. *The Theory of the Novel* trans. Anna Bostock. Cambridge: MIT Press.

Macherey, Pierre. 1978. *A Theory of Literary Production,* trans. Geoffrey Wall. London: Routledge.

Malti-Douglas, Fedwa. 1991. *Woman's Body, Woman's Word: Gender and Discourse in Arabo-Islamic Writing.* Princeton: Princeton University Press.

Maugham-Brown, David. 1991. "*Anthills of the Savannah*: Achebe's solutions to 'The Trouble with Nigeria.'" In *Critical Approaches to* Anthills of the Savannah, ed. Holger G. Ehling, 3–22. Amsterdam: Rodopi.

Mba, Nina E. 1988. "Kaba and Khaki: Women and the Militarized State in Nigeria." Office of Women in International Development Working Paper no. 159, Michigan State University, East Lansing, February.

McClintock, Anne. 1995. *Imperial Leather: Race, Gender, and Sexuality in the Colonial Contest.* New York: Routledge.

McLaughlin, Fiona. 2001. "Dakar Wolof and the Configuration of an Urban Identity." *Journal of African Cultural Studies* 14, no. 3, 153–72.

Mernissi, Fatima. 1987. *Beyond the Veil: Male–Female Dynamics in Modem Muslim Society,* rev. ed. Bloomington: Indiana University Press.

Miller, Christopher. 1990. *Theories of Africans: Francophone Literature and Anthropology in Africa.* Chicago: University of Chicago Press.

Mohanty, Chandra Talpade. 1987. "Feminist Encounters: Locating the Politics of Experience." *Copyright* 1, 30–44.

———. 1991. "Under Western Eyes: Feminist Scholarship and Colonial Discourses." *Third World Women and the Politics of Feminism,* ed. Chandra Talpade Mohanty, Ann Russo, and Lourdes Torres. Bloomington: Indiana University Press.

Mokwenyé, Cyril. 1983. "La polygamie et la révolte de la femme africaine moderne: Une lecture d'*Une si longue lettre* de Mariama Bâ." *Peuples Noirs/Peuples Africains* 31 (January–February), 87–94.

Moore, Gerald. 1962. *Seven African Writers*. Oxford: Oxford University Press.

——. 1980. *Twelve African Writers*. Bloomington: Indiana University Press.

Moretti, Franco. 1987. *The Way of the World: The Bildungsroman in European Culture*. London: Verso.

——. 2000. "Conjectures on World Literature." *New Left Review* 1, 54–68.

Mortimer, Mildred. 1990. *Journeys through the French African Novel*. Portsmouth, N.H.: Heinemann.

——. 2007. *Writing from the Hearth*. Lanham, Md.: Lexington Press.

Mulvey, Laura. 1991. "*Xala*, Ousmane Sembéne 1976: The Carapace That Failed." *Third Text* 16–17 (Fall–Winter), 19–37.

Murphy, David. 2000. *Sembene: Imagining Alternatives in Film and Fiction*. Oxford: James Currey.

Newell, Stephanie. 2006. *West African Literatures: Ways of Reading*. New York: Oxford University Press.

Nfah-Abbenyi, Juliana Makuchi. 1997. *Gender in African Women's Writing*. Bloomington: Indiana University Press.

Ngaboh-Smart, Francis. 2001. "Nationalism and the Aporia of National Idenity in Farah's *Maps*." *Research in African Literatures* 32, no. 3, 86–102.

Ngcobo, Lauretta. 1981. *Cross of Gold*. London: Longman.

Ngugi wa Thiong'o. 1987. *Devil on the Cross*. London: Heinemann.

——. 1991. *Petals of Blood*. New York: E. P. Dutton.

Njami, Simon. 2005. "Chaos et Metamorphoses." *Africa Re-Mix: L'art contemporain d'un continent*, 14–25. Paris: Centre George Pompidou.

——. 2006. "Chaos and Metamorphosis." *Africa Re-Mix: Contemporary Art of a Continent* (abbreviated), trans. Gail de Courcy-Ireland, 13–21. London: Tate Gallery.

Nnaemeka, Obioma, ed. 1997. *The Politics of (M)Othering: Womanhood, Identity, and Resistance in African Literature*. London: Routledge.

Nwabara, S. N. 1978. *Iboland: A Century of Contact with Britain, 1860–1960*. Atlantic Highlands, N.J.: Humanities.

Nwapa, Flora. 1966. *Efuru*. London: Heinemann.

——. 1970. *Idu*. London: Heinemann.

Obiechina, Emmanuel N. 1975. *Culture, Tradition, and Society in the West African Novel*. Cambridge: Cambridge University Press.

O'Brien, Donal. 1975. *Saints and Politicians*. Cambridge: Cambridge University Press.

O'Connell, Michael. 1990. "Allegory." In *The Spenser Encyclopedia*, ed. A. C. Hamilton, 16–25. Toronto: University of Toronto Press.

Ogot, Grace. 1966. *The Promised Land*. Nairobi: East Africa Publishing.

——. 1980. *The Graduate*. Nairobi: Uzima.

Ogunyemi, Chikwenye Okonjo. 1985. "Womanism: The Dynamics of the Contemporary Black Female Novel in English." *Signs* 11, no. 1, 63–80.

———. 1996. *Africa Wo/Man Palava: The Nigerian Novel by Women*. Chicago: University of Chicago Press.

Oyono, Ferdinand. 1956. *Une vie de boy*. Paris: Julliard.

Palmer, Eustace. 1983. "The Feminine Point of View: Buchi Emecheta's *The Joys of Motherhood*." *African Literature Today* 13, 38–57.

———. 2008 *Of War and Women, Oppression and Optimism*. Trenton, N.J.: Africa World Press.

Parker, Andrew, Mary Russo, Doris Sommer, and Patricia Yaeger. 1992. "Introduction." *Nationalisms and Sexualities*, ed. Andrew Parker, Mary Russo, Doris Sommer, and Patricia Yaeger. New York: Routledge.

Petersen, Kirsten Holst. 1994. "Between Gender, Race, and History: Kirsten Holst Petersen Interviews Tsitsi Dangarembga." *Kunapipi* 16, no. 1, 344–48.

Plaatje, Sol T. 1930. *Mhudi*. Lovedale, South Africa: Lovedale Press.

Quayson, Ato. 1997. *Strategic Transformations in Nigerian Writing*. Bloomington: Indiana University Press.

Radhakrishnan, R. 1992. "Nationalism, Gender, and the Narrative of Identity." *Nationalisms and Sexualities*, ed. Andrew Parker, Mary Russo, Doris Sommer, and Patricia Yaeger, 77–95. New York: Routledge.

Ricard, Alain. 2004. *The Languages and Literatures of Africa*. Trenton, N.J.: Africa World Press.

Rubin, Gayle. 1975. "The Traffic in Women: Notes toward a Political Economy of Sex." *Toward an Anthropology of Women*, ed. Rayna Reiter, 157–210. New York: Monthly Review Press.

Sagan, Françoise. 1954. *Bonjour tristesse*. Paris: Julliard.

Said, Edward W. 1994. *Representations of the Intellectual*. New York: Pantheon.

Sangari, Kumkum, and Sudesh Vaid, eds. 1990. *Recasting Women: Essays in Indian Colonial History*. New Brunswick: Rutgers University Press.

Scheub, Harold. 1970. "When a Man Fails Alone." *Présence Africaine* 74, no. 2, 61–89.

Schipper, Mineke. 1987. "Mother Africa on a Pedestal: The Male Heritage in African Literature and Criticism." *Women in African Literature Today* 15, 35–54.

Sembène, Ousmane. 1973. *Xala*. Paris: Présence Africaine.

———. 1976. *Xala*, trans. Clive Wake. Chicago: Lawrence Hill.

Senghor, Léopold Sédar, ed. 1948. *Anthologie de la nouvelle poésie nègre et malgache de langue française*. Paris: Presses Universitaires de France.

Slaughter, Joseph R. 2007. *Human Rights, Inc.* New York: Fordham University Press.

Smit, Johannes A., Johan Van Wyk, and Jean-Philippe Wade, eds. 1996. *Rethinking South African Literary History*. Durban: Y-Press.

Smith, Sidonie, and Julia Watson, eds. 1992. *De/Colonizing the Subject*. Minneapolis: University of Minnesota Press.

Socé, Ousmane. 1835 [1948]. *Karim: Roman sénégalais*. Paris: Nouvelles Editions Latines.

Sommer, Doris. 1991. *Foundational Fictions: The National Romances of Latin America*. Berkeley: University of California Press.

Sow Fall, Aminata. 1976. *Le Revenant*. Dakar, Senegal: Les Nouvelles Editions Africaines.

——. 1987. *L'ex-père de la nation*. Paris: L'Harmattan.

——. 1979 [2001]. *La grève des bàttu, ou, Les déchets humains*. Paris: Le Serpent a Plumes.

——. 1981. *The Beggars' Strike, or, The Dregs of Society*, trans. Dorothy S. Blair. Harlow, Essex: Longman.

Soyinka, Wole. 1981. *Aké: The Years of Childhood*. New York: Vintage.

Spivak, Gayatri Chakravorty. 1985a. "Can the Subaltern Speak?" *Wedge* 7–8, 120–30.

——. 1985b. "The Rani of Sirmur: An Essay in Reading the Archives." *History and Theory* 24, no. 3, 247–72.

——. 1987. "Explanation and Culture: Marginalia." In *In Other Worlds: Essays in Cultural Politics*, 103–17. New York: Methuen.

——. 1990. *The Post-Colonial Critic: Interviews, Strategies, Dialogues*, ed. Sarah Harasym. New York: Routledge.

——. 2003. *Death of a Discipline*. New York: Columbia University Press.

——. 1993. "Echo." *New Literary History* 24, no.1 (Winter), 17–27.

Steedman, Jennifer Bernhardt. 2003. "A Global Feminist Travels: Assia Djebar and Fantasia." *Meridians* 4, no. 1, 173–99.

Stratton, Florence. 1988. "The Shallow Grave: Archetypes of Female Experience in African Fiction." *Research in African Literatures* 19, no. 2 (Summer), 143–69.

——. 1994. *Contemporary African Literature and the Politics of Gender*. New York: Routledge.

Stringer, Susan. 1996. *The Senegalese Novel by Women: Through Their Own Eyes*. New York: Peter Lang.

Sugnet, Charles. 1997. "*Nervous Conditions*: Dangarembga's Feminist Reinvention of Fanon." *The Politics of (M)Othering: Womanhood, Identity, and Resistance in African Literature*, ed. Obioma Nnaemeka, 83–101. London: Routledge.

Tagore, Rabindranath. 1915. *The Home and the World*, trans. Sundranath Tagore. London: Macmillan.

Taiwo, Oladele. 1984. *Female Novelists in Modern Africa*. New York: St. Martin's.

ten Kortenaar, Neil. 1993. " 'Only Connect': *Anthills of the Savannah* and Achebe's 'The Trouble with Nigeria.' " *Research in African Literatures* 24, no. 3, 59–72.

Thiam, Awa. 1978. *La parole aux negresses*. Paris: Denoel / Gonthier.

Thomas, Sue. 1992. "Killing the Hysteric in the Colonized's House." *Journal of Commonwealth Literature* 27, no. 1, 26–36.

Tlali, Miriam. 1979 [1987]. *Muriel at Metropolitan*. Essex: Longman Group.

Tutuola, Amos. 1952. *The Palm-Wine Drinkard and His Dead Palm-Wine Tapster in the Dead's Town*. London: Faber and Faber.

Van Allen, Judith. 1972. " 'Sitting on a Man': Colonialism and the Lost Political Institutions of Igbo Women." *Canadian Journal of African Studies* 4, no. 2, 165–81.

——. 1976. " 'Aba Riots' or Igbo 'Women's War'? Ideology, Stratification, and the Invisibility of Women." In *Women in Africa*, ed. Nancy J. Hatkin and Edna G. Bay. Stanford: Stanford University Press.

Vance, Carole S., ed. 1984. *Pleasure and Danger: Exploring Female Sexuality*. Boston: Routledge and Kegan Paul.

van Niekerk, Marlene. 1994 [1999]. *Triompf*, trans. Leon de Kock. Johannesburg: Jonathan Ball Publishers.

Vera, Yvonne. 1994. *Nehanda*. Toronto: TSAR Publications.

Wicomb, Zoë. 2001. *David's Story*. New York: The Feminist Press.

Wilentz, Gay. 1992. *Binding Cultures*. Bloomington: Indiana University Press.

Woodhull, Winifred. 1992. "Unveiling Algeria." *Genders* 10 (Spring), 112–31.

——. 1993. *Transfigurations of the Maghreb: Feminism, Decolonization and Literatures*. Minneapolis: University of Minnesota Press.

Woolf, Virginia. 1929 [1989]. *A Room of One's Own*. San Diego: Harcourt Brace.

Yacine, Kateb. 1956. *Nedjma*. Paris: Seuil.

Yadov, Alok. 1994. "Nationalism and Contemporaeity: Political Economy of a Discourse." *Cultural Critique* (Winter), 191–229.

Young, Robert. 1990. *White Mythologies: Writing History and the West*. London: Routledge.

——. 2001. *Postcolonialism: An Historical Introduction* London: Blackwell.

Yousaf, Nahem. 1995. "The 'Public' versus the 'Private' in Mariama Ba's novels." *Journal of Commonwealth Literature* 30, no. 2, 85–98.

Zell, Hans M. 1980. "The First Noma Award for Publishing in Africa." *African Book Publishing Record* 6, nos. 3–4, 199–201.

Index

sexuality: in *L'amour, la fantasia*, 182, 185, 188, 191, 196, 199; in *Efuru*, 61; in *Maps*, 119, 127, 129, 137; in *Nervous Conditions*, 141–42, 144, 148, 229 n23, 230 n29; in *Ombre sultane*, 185, 188, 191, 199; rape in Nigerian-Igbo context and, 221 n18; romance genre and, 27; in *Une si longue lettre*, 81, 89–90, 96, 108. *See also* desire; marriage; motherhood and mothering; rape; reproduction; romance as love plot

Une si longue lettre (Bâ), 71–100, 112–13

Somalia: education and schooling in, 124, 129–32, 234–35 n25; national political history of, 116, 124–25

Sommer, Doris, *Foundational Fictions*, 27–28, 41, 99–100, 113, 204, 217, 231 n1

Sow Fall, Aminata, 30, 32, 39, 41; *L'ex-père de la nation*, 30, 39; *La grève des báttu*, 72–75, 108–13, 165, 168, 204; Marxism and, 226 n4, 226–27 n27. *See also* reading strategies for gender and women in relation to nation

Soyinka, Wole, 7, 8, 15, 214–15 n8, 215 n9, 227 n4, 232 n2

Spivak, Gayatri C., 37, 218–19 n42, 232–33 n7, 236 n33

state: colonial, 49, 52–53, 57, 104, 122; decolonization and, 186, 206, 231 n40; neocolonial, 41, 74–76, 97, 101; violence and, 28, 30, 33, 49, 132, 205; women and, 30, 150, 168, 190, 201, 205–6. *See also* nationalism, cultural; national political history

Stratton, Florence: female figures of the nation and, 13–15, 56, 91, 93, 95, 216 n20, 218 n40, 220–21 n11, 221 n15, 222 n22; on *Une si longue lettre* and *Xala*, 85, 91, 96

strikes, 35; in *La grève des báttu*, 109–11, 226 n26, 226–27 n27; hunger strike in *Nervous Conditions*, 150–52, 231 n33; in *The Joys of Motherhood*, 67, 221 n19,

226 n24; in *Une si longue lettre*, 97. *See also* Women's War of 1929

Sugnet, Charles, 149, 156, 159

Things Fall Apart (Achebe), 7–9, 14, 21, 40, 44–46, 49–55

transgression: female guerilla fighters and, 180–83, 235n28; in *The Joys of Motherhood*, 67; in *Nervous Conditions*, 150–52, 154–55, 159, 162; in *Ombre sultane*; 185–88, 194, 198. *See also* prostitution; public sphere; veil and unveiling; Women's War of 1929

Tutuola, Amos, *The Palm-Wine Drinkard*, 6, 8–9, 215 n9, 215 n11, 215 n13, 215–16 n14

unveiling. *See* veil and unveiling

Van Allen, Judith, 46–48, 219 n3, 221 n19. *See also* Women's War of 1929

veil and unveiling, 43; Jayawardena on, 224 n14; Mernissi on, 194; in *Ombre sultane*, 171, 174, 185–88, 194–95, 198–99, 200–201

Women's War of 1929 (Ogu Umunwanyi): as historical event, 40, 45–49, 53–54, 220 n4, 221 n17; as metaphor for Nigerian women's novelistic history, 40, 46, 52, 69–70, 203

Woodhull, Winifred, 87–88. *See also* Algeria: literary history of

The Wretched of the Earth (Fanon), 4–5, 32, 41–42, 77–78, 97, 184, 203–4, 231 n38, 231–32 n40

Xala (Sembène), 71, 74–78, 100–102, 104–13, 161, 203–4, 210

Zimbabwe (Rhodesia): cultural nationalism of, 137–64; education and schooling in, 115–16, 119, 123, 139–40, 149–60; literary history of, 115–16, 123; national political history of, 117, 122–23, 156–57

SUSAN Z. ANDRADE was born in Dar-es-Salaam, Tanzania,
and raised there and in Los Angeles. She is associate professor of English
at the University of Pittsburgh and the co-editor of *Atlantic Cross-Currents/
Transatlantiques* (2001). She was guest editor of "The Form of Postcolonial
African Fiction," a special issue (Spring/Summer 2008)
of the journal *NOVEL*.

Library of Congress Cataloging-in-Publication Data
Andrade, Susan Z.
The nation writ small : African fictions and feminisms, 1958–1988 /
Susan Z. Andrade.
p. cm.
Includes bibliographical references and index.
ISBN 978-0-8223-4897-9 (cloth : alk. paper)
ISBN 978-0-8223-4921-1 (pbk. : alk. paper)
1. African literature—Women authors—History and criticism.
2. African literature—20th century—History and criticism.
3. Africa—In literature. I. Title.
PN849.A35A53 2011
809'.89287096—dc23
2011021904